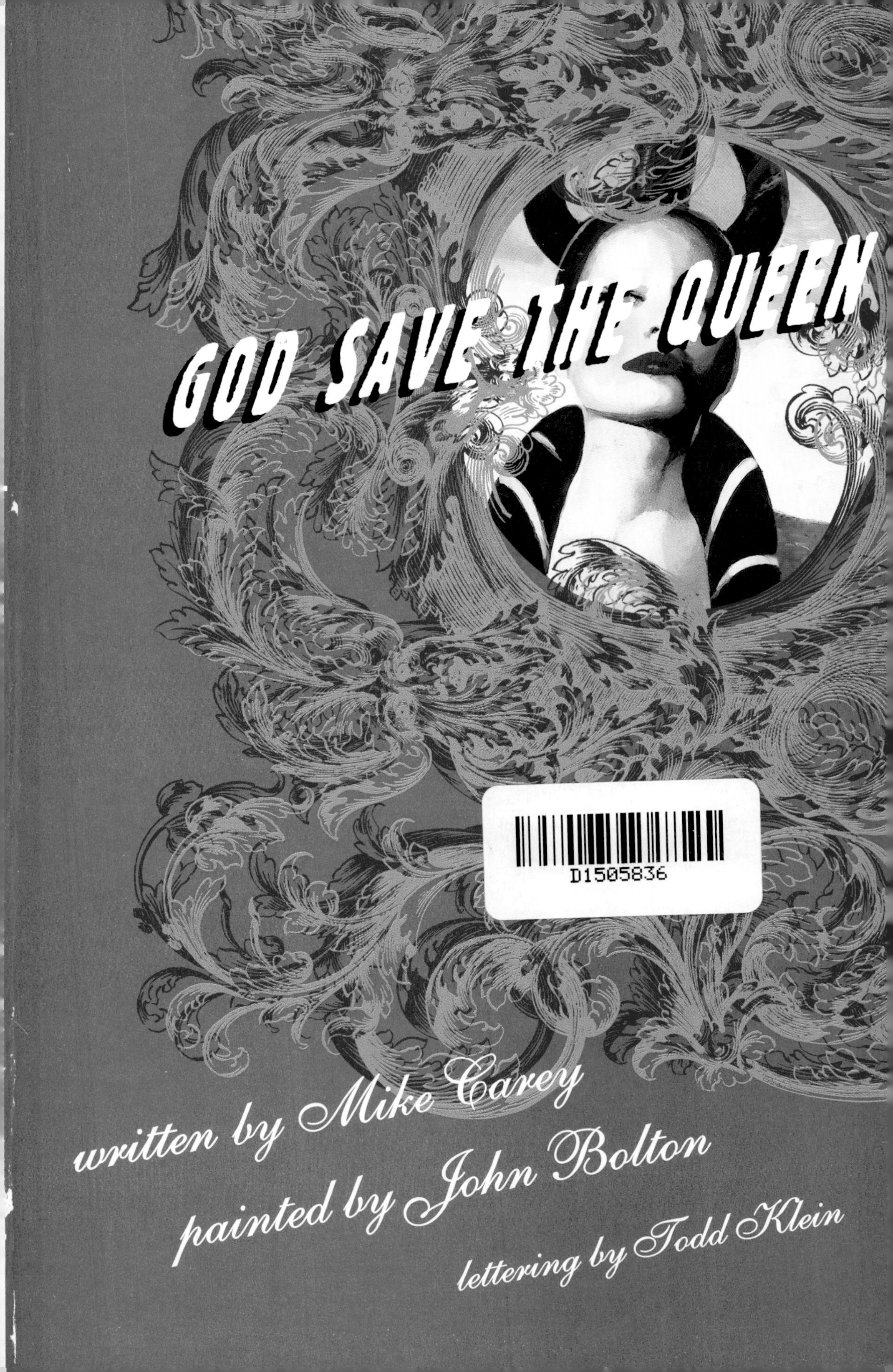
GOD SAVE THE QUEEN
written by Mike Carey
painted by John Bolton
lettering by Todd Klein

Karen Berger, Sr. VP-Executive Editor

Shelly Bond, Editor

Angela Rufino, Assistant Editor

Robbin Brosterman, Senior Art Director

Paul Levitz, President & Publisher

Georg Brewer, VP-Design & DC Direct Creative

Richard Bruning, Sr. VP-Creative Director

Patrick Caldon, Exec. VP-Finance & Operations

Chris Caramalis, VP-Finance

John Cunningham, VP-Marketing

Terri Cunningham, VP-Managing Editor

Stephanie Fierman, Sr. VP-Sales & Marketing

Alison Gill, VP-Manufacturing

Hank Kanalz, VP-General Manager, WildStorm

Jim Lee, Editorial Director-WildStorm

Paula Lowitt, Sr. VP-Business & Legal Affairs

MaryEllen McLaughlin, VP-Advertising & Custom Publishing

John Nee, VP-Business Development

Gregory Noveck, Sr. VP-Creative Affairs

Cheryl Rubin, Sr. VP-Brand Management

Jeff Trojan, VP-Business Development, DC Direct

Bob Wayne, VP-Sales

GOD SAVE THE QUEEN

Published by DC Comics, 1700 Broadway, New York, NY 10019. Copyright © 2007 DC Comics. All rights reserved.
All characters featured in this book, the distinctive likenesses thereof and related elements are trademarks of DC Comics.
Vertigo is a trademark of DC Comics. The stories, characters and incidents mentioned in this book are entirely fictional.
Printed in Canada.
DC Comics, a Warner Bros. Entertainment Company.

HC ISBN: 1-4012-0303-5 HC ISBN 13: 978-1-4012-0303-0
SC ISBN: 1-4012-0304-3 SC ISBN: 13: 978-1-4012-0304-7

COVER BY JOHN BOLTON

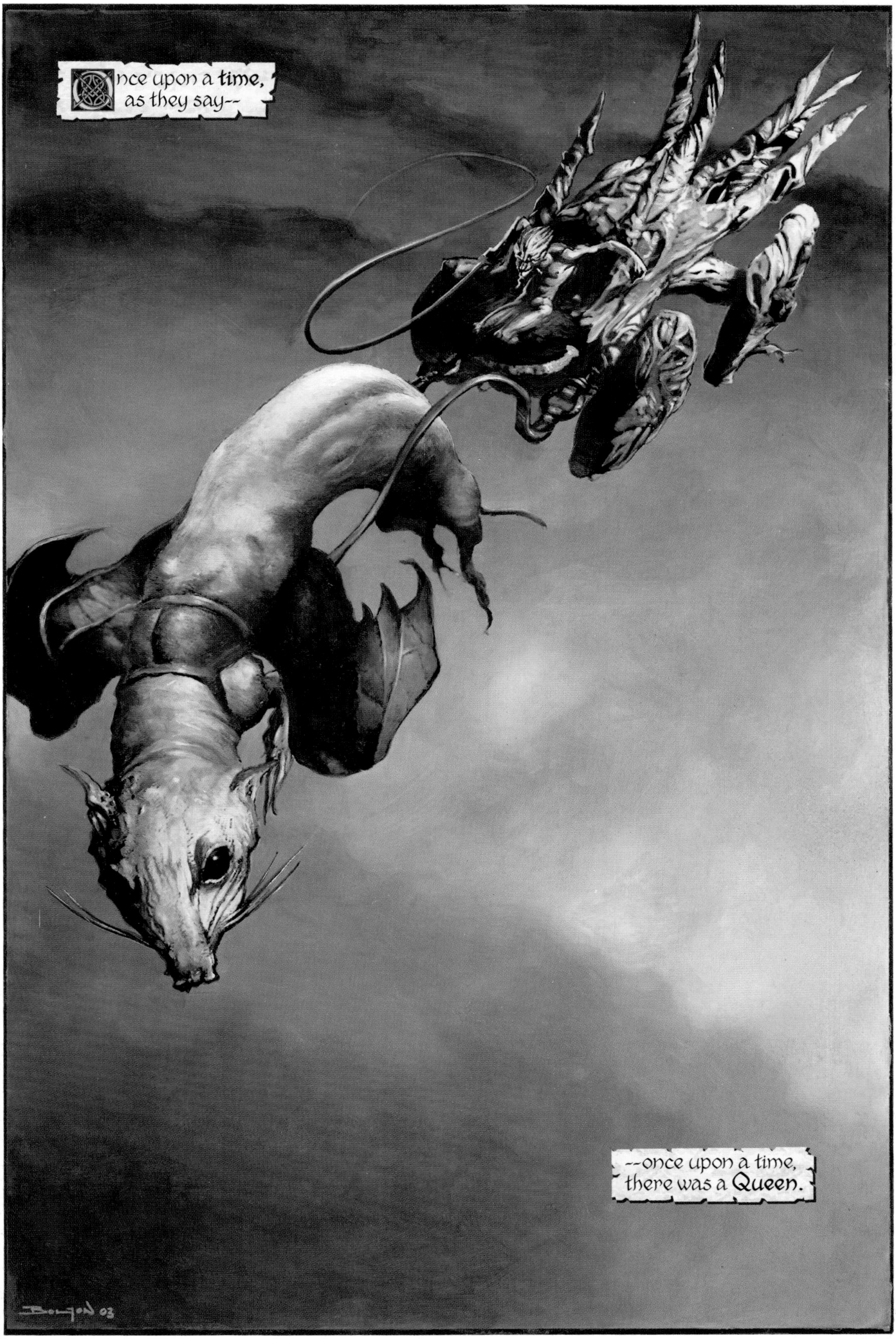
Once upon a time, as they say--
--once upon a time, there was a Queen.
Bolton 03

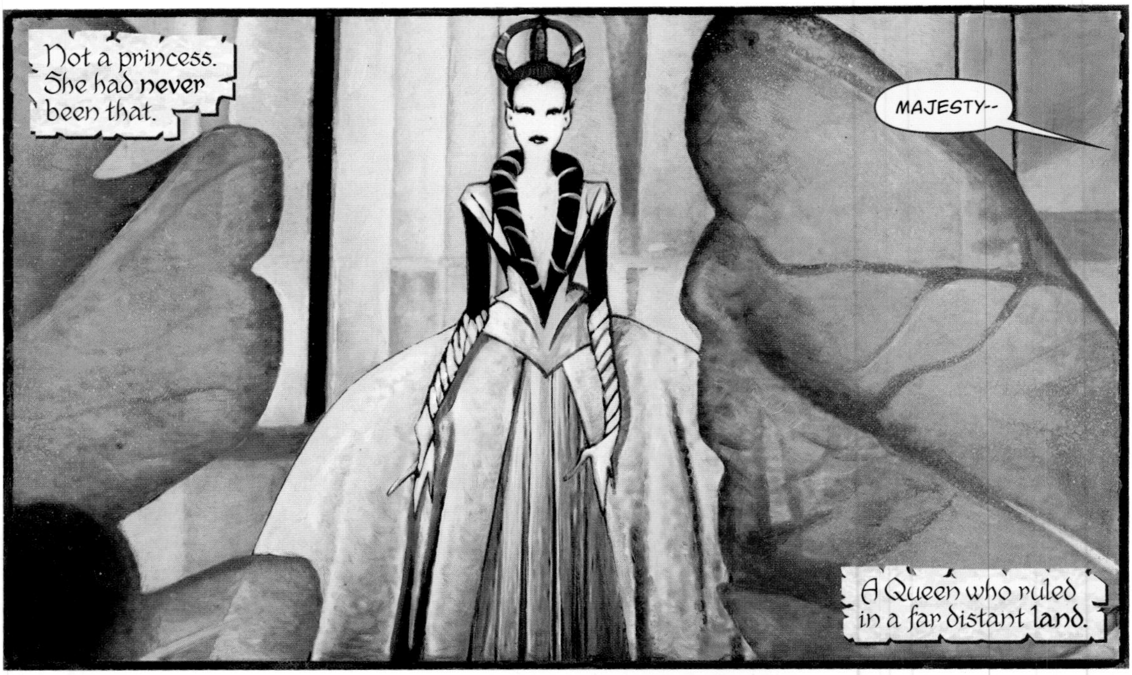
Not a princess. She had never been that.
MAJESTY--
A Queen who ruled in a far distant land.

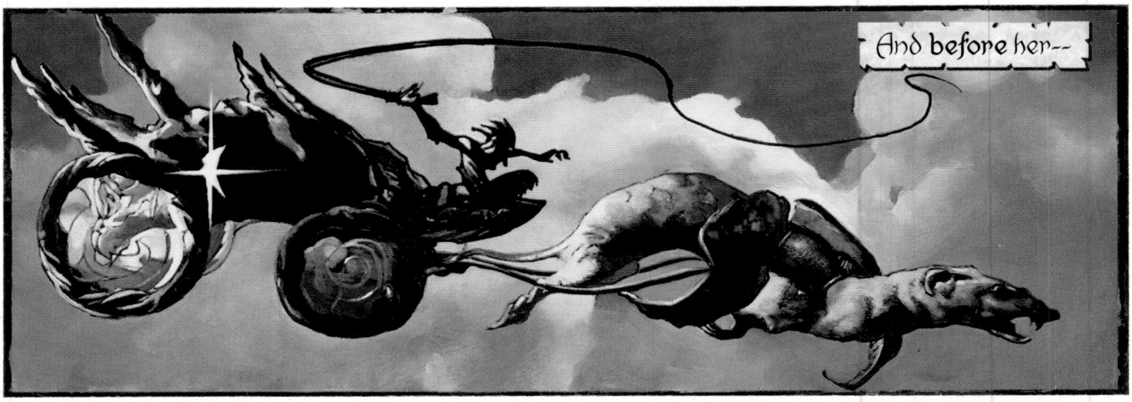
And before her--

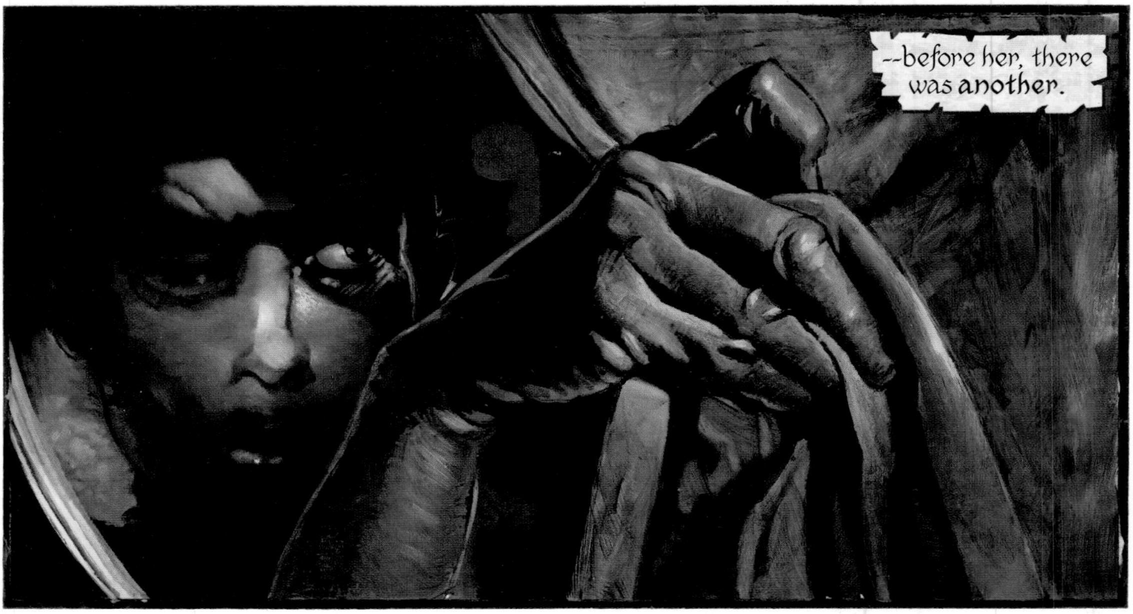
--before her, there was another.

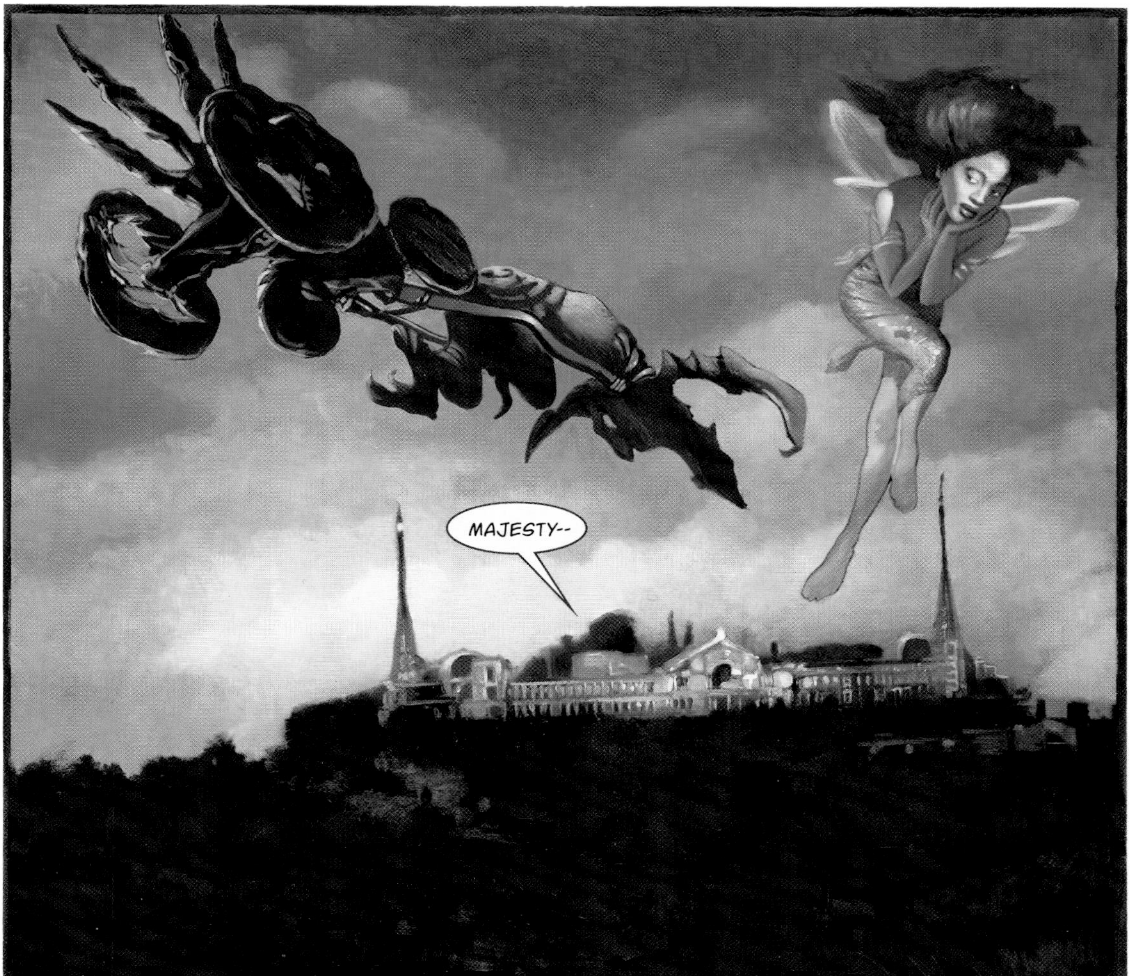
MAJESTY--

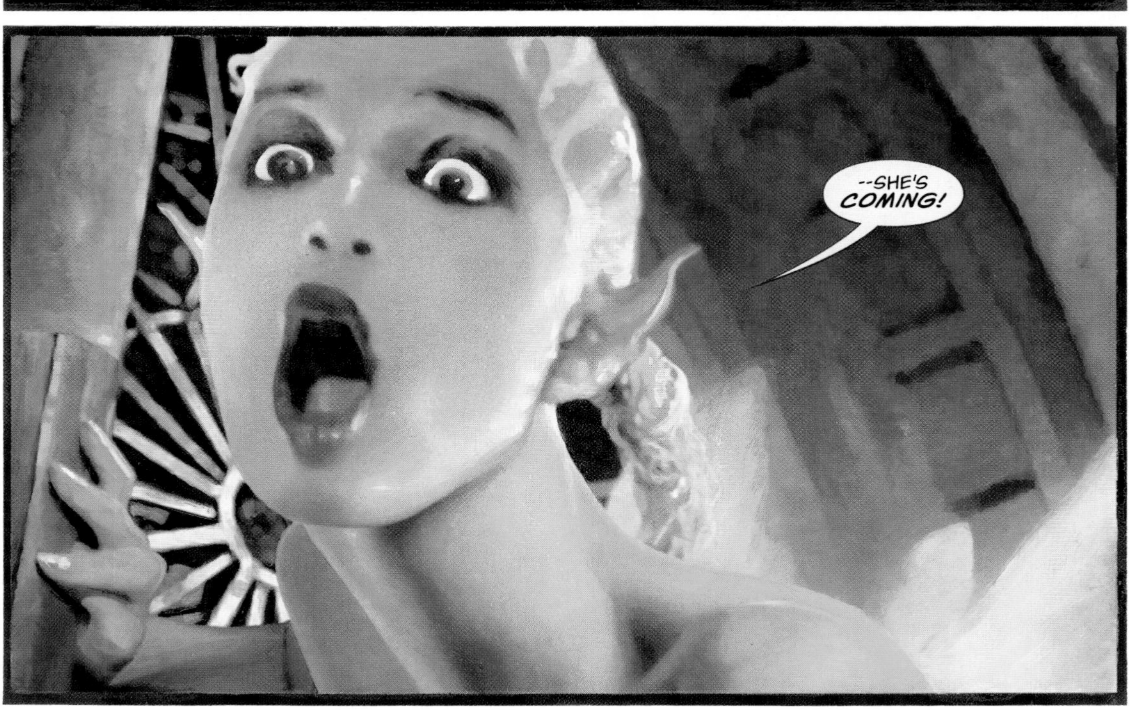
--SHE'S COMING!

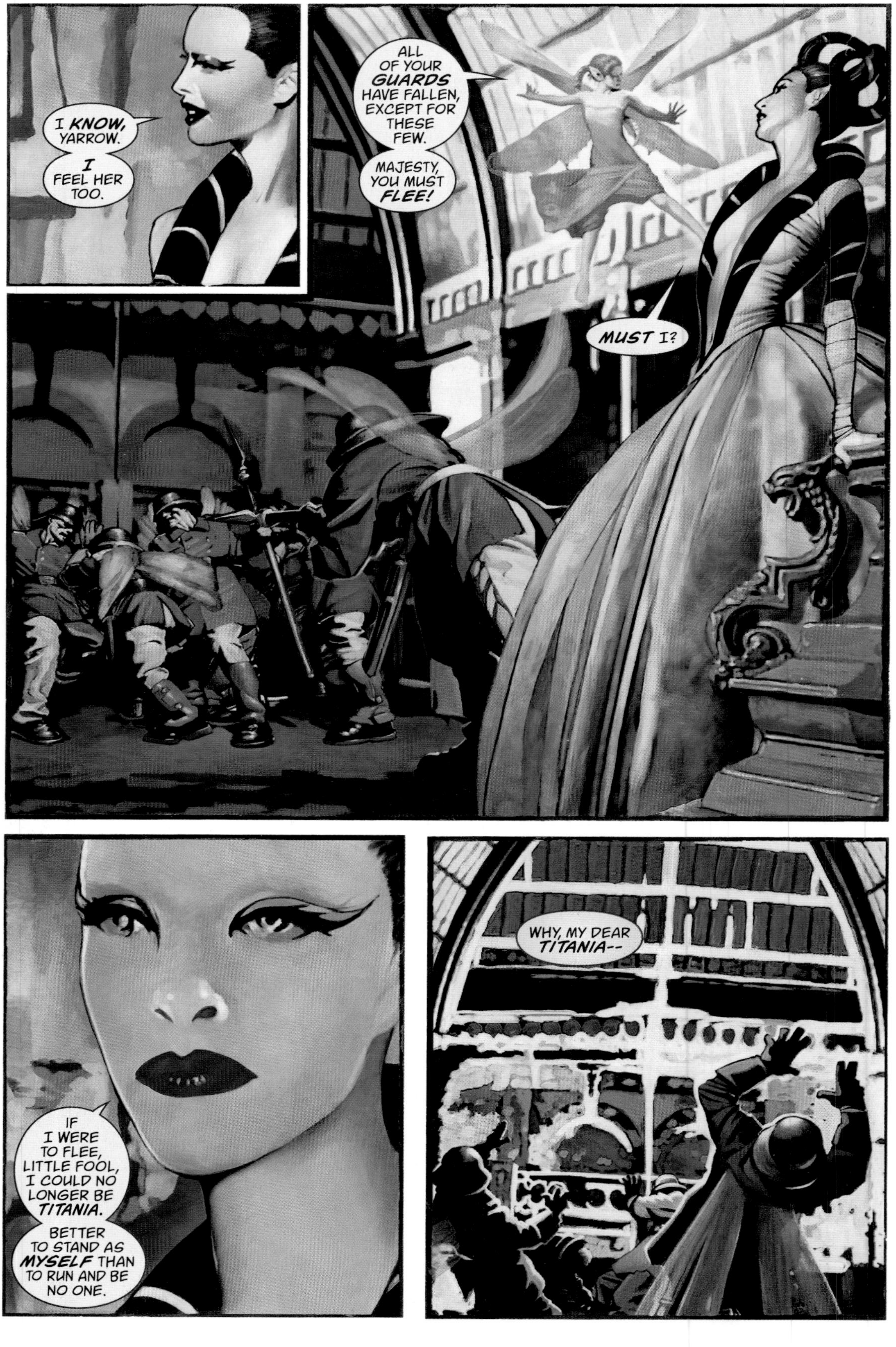
I KNOW, YARROW.
I FEEL HER TOO.
ALL OF YOUR GUARDS HAVE FALLEN, EXCEPT FOR THESE FEW.
MAJESTY, YOU MUST FLEE!
MUST I?
IF I WERE TO FLEE, LITTLE FOOL, I COULD NO LONGER BE TITANIA.
BETTER TO STAND AS MYSELF THAN TO RUN AND BE NO ONE.
WHY, MY DEAR TITANIA--

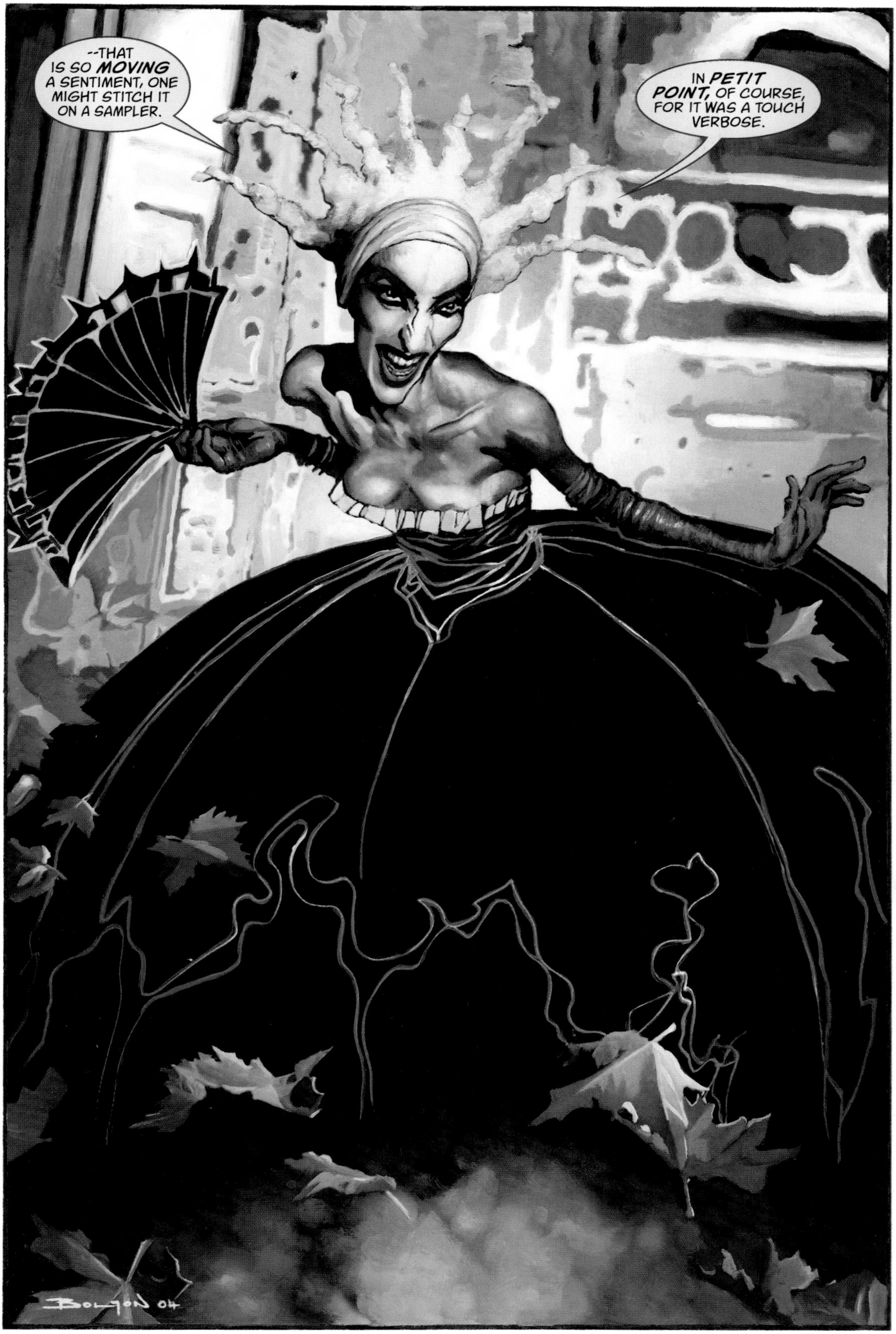
--THAT IS SO **MOVING** A SENTIMENT, ONE MIGHT STITCH IT ON A SAMPLER.
IN **PETIT POINT,** OF COURSE, FOR IT WAS A TOUCH VERBOSE.
BOLTON 04

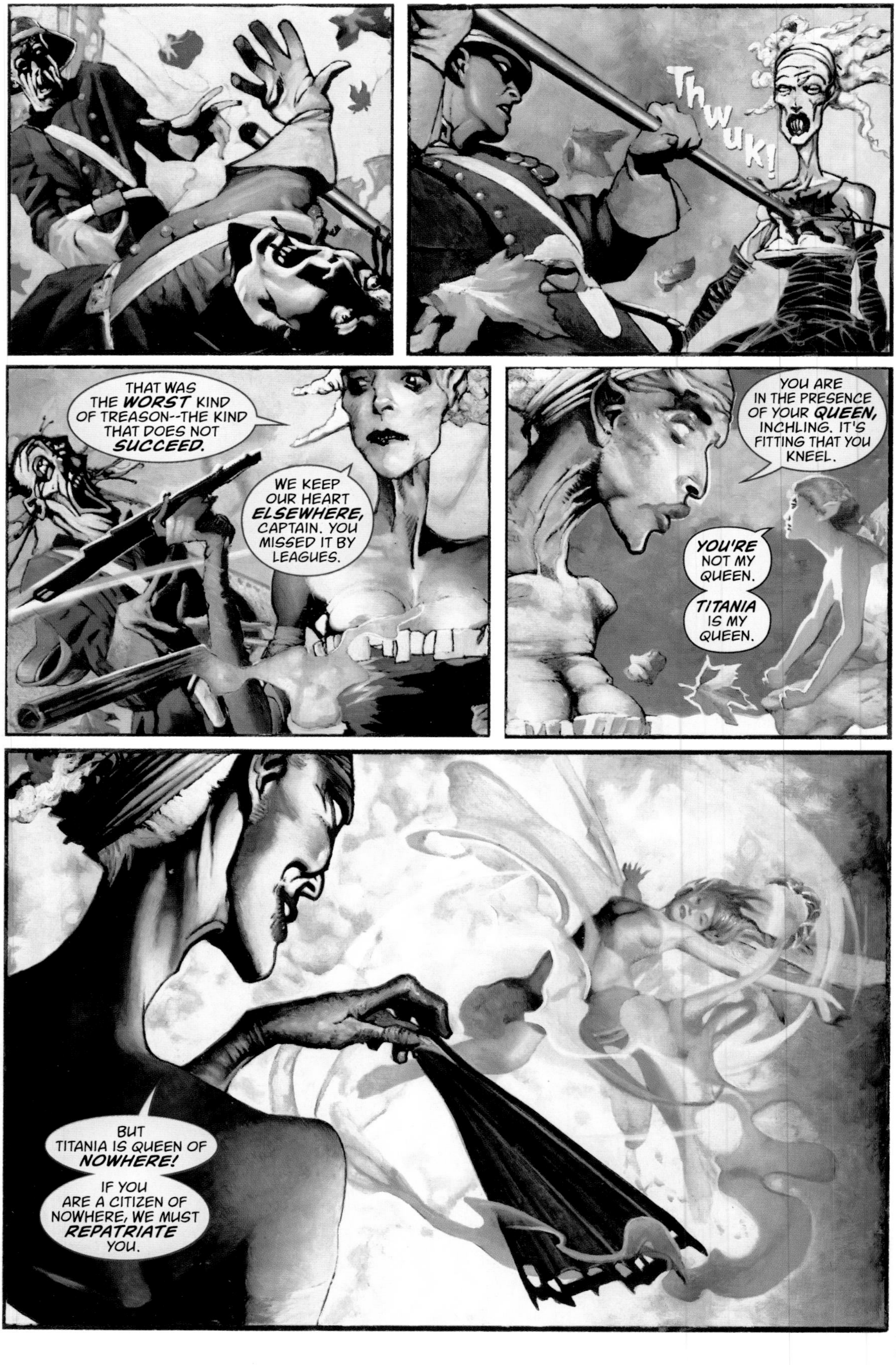
THWUK!
THAT WAS THE WORST KIND OF TREASON--THE KIND THAT DOES NOT SUCCEED.
WE KEEP OUR HEART ELSEWHERE, CAPTAIN. YOU MISSED IT BY LEAGUES.
YOU ARE IN THE PRESENCE OF YOUR QUEEN, INCHLING. IT'S FITTING THAT YOU KNEEL.
YOU'RE NOT MY QUEEN.
TITANIA IS MY QUEEN.
BUT TITANIA IS QUEEN OF NOWHERE!
IF YOU ARE A CITIZEN OF NOWHERE, WE MUST REPATRIATE YOU.

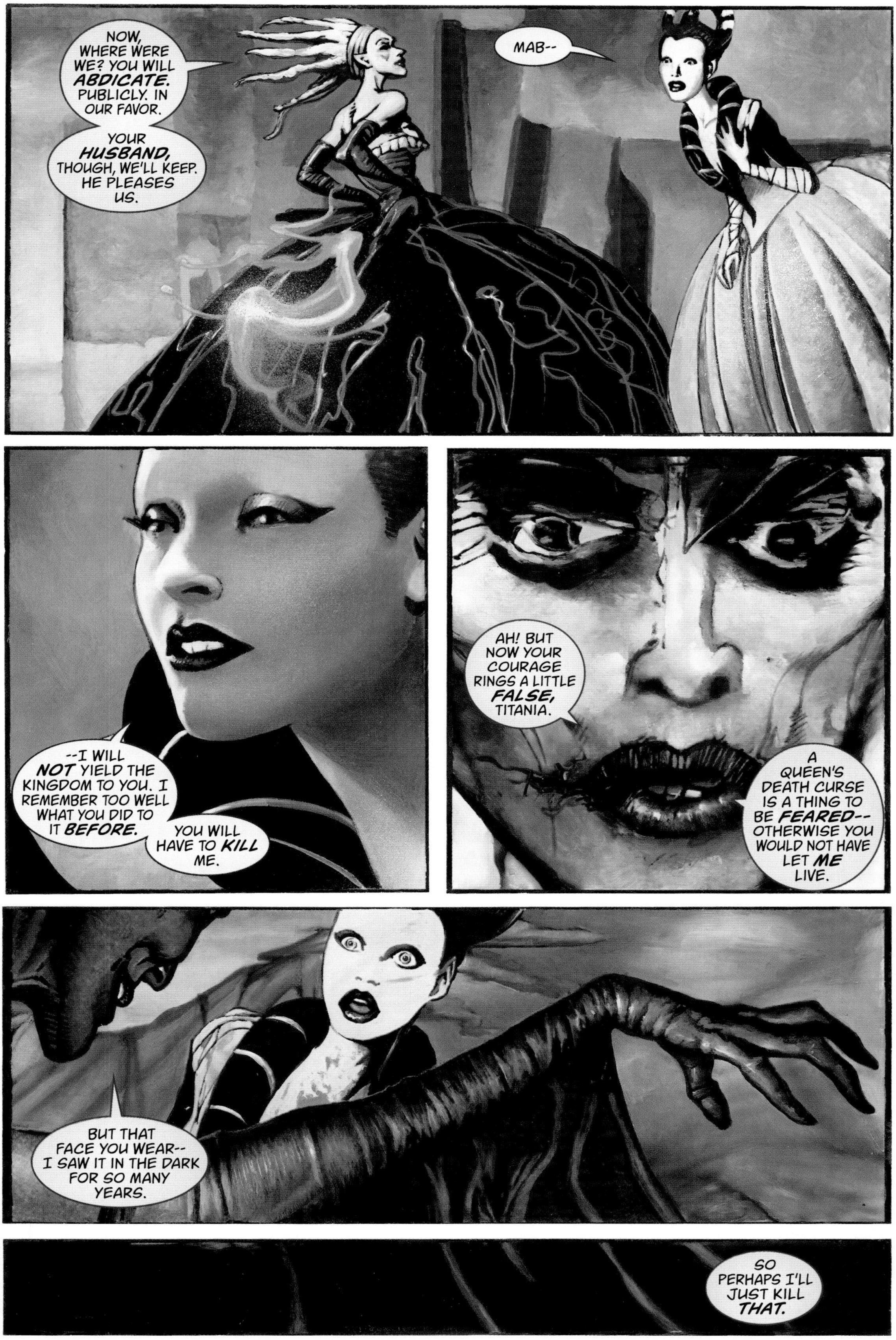
NOW, WHERE WERE WE? YOU WILL ABDICATE. PUBLICLY. IN OUR FAVOR.
YOUR HUSBAND, THOUGH, WE'LL KEEP. HE PLEASES US.
MAB--
--I WILL NOT YIELD THE KINGDOM TO YOU. I REMEMBER TOO WELL WHAT YOU DID TO IT BEFORE.
YOU WILL HAVE TO KILL ME.
AH! BUT NOW YOUR COURAGE RINGS A LITTLE FALSE, TITANIA.
A QUEEN'S DEATH CURSE IS A THING TO BE FEARED-- OTHERWISE YOU WOULD NOT HAVE LET ME LIVE.
BUT THAT FACE YOU WEAR-- I SAW IT IN THE DARK FOR SO MANY YEARS.
SO PERHAPS I'LL JUST KILL THAT.

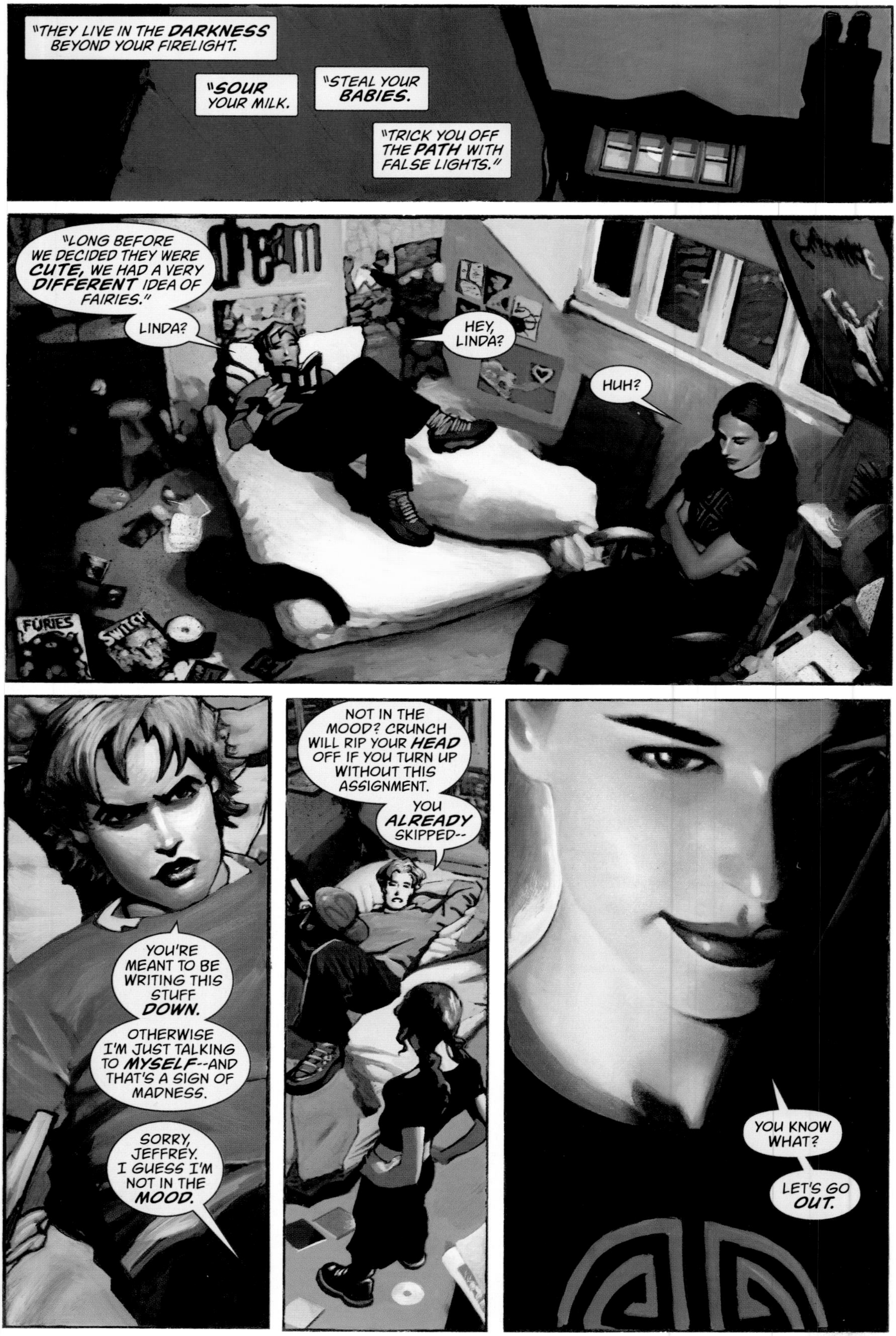
"THEY LIVE IN THE DARKNESS BEYOND YOUR FIRELIGHT.
"SOUR YOUR MILK.
"STEAL YOUR BABIES.
"TRICK YOU OFF THE PATH WITH FALSE LIGHTS."
"LONG BEFORE WE DECIDED THEY WERE CUTE, WE HAD A VERY DIFFERENT IDEA OF FAIRIES."
LINDA?
HEY, LINDA?
HUH?
FURIES
SWITCH
YOU'RE MEANT TO BE WRITING THIS STUFF DOWN.
OTHERWISE I'M JUST TALKING TO MYSELF--AND THAT'S A SIGN OF MADNESS.
SORRY, JEFFREY. I GUESS I'M NOT IN THE MOOD.
NOT IN THE MOOD? CRUNCH WILL RIP YOUR HEAD OFF IF YOU TURN UP WITHOUT THIS ASSIGNMENT.
YOU ALREADY SKIPPED--
YOU KNOW WHAT?
LET'S GO OUT.

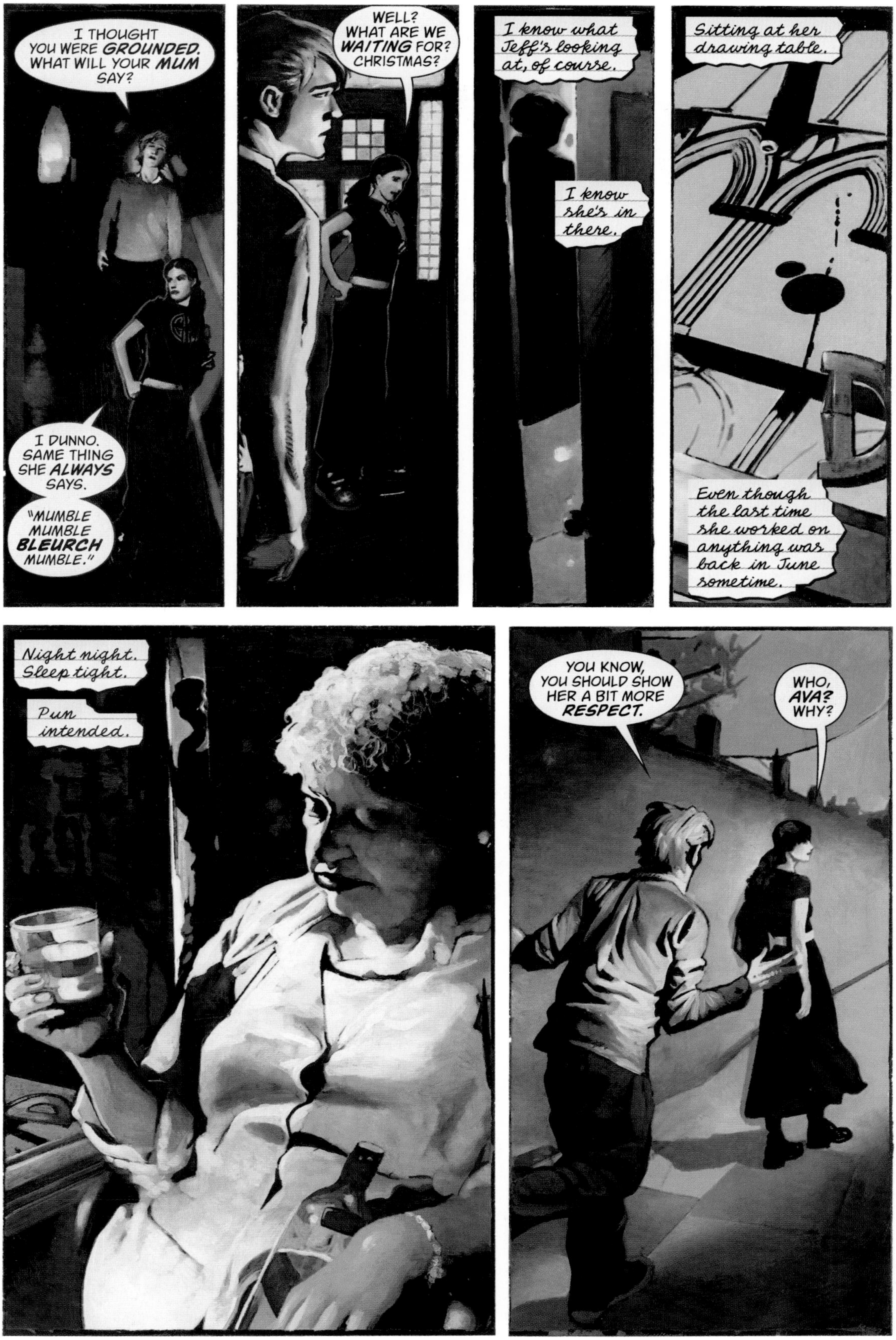
I THOUGHT YOU WERE GROUNDED. WHAT WILL YOUR MUM SAY?
I DUNNO. SAME THING SHE ALWAYS SAYS.
"MUMBLE MUMBLE BLEURCH MUMBLE."
WELL? WHAT ARE WE WAITING FOR? CHRISTMAS?
I know what Jeff's looking at, of course.
I know she's in there.
Sitting at her drawing table.
Even though the last time she worked on anything was back in June sometime.
Night night. Sleep tight.
Pun intended.
YOU KNOW, YOU SHOULD SHOW HER A BIT MORE RESPECT.
WHO, AVA? WHY?

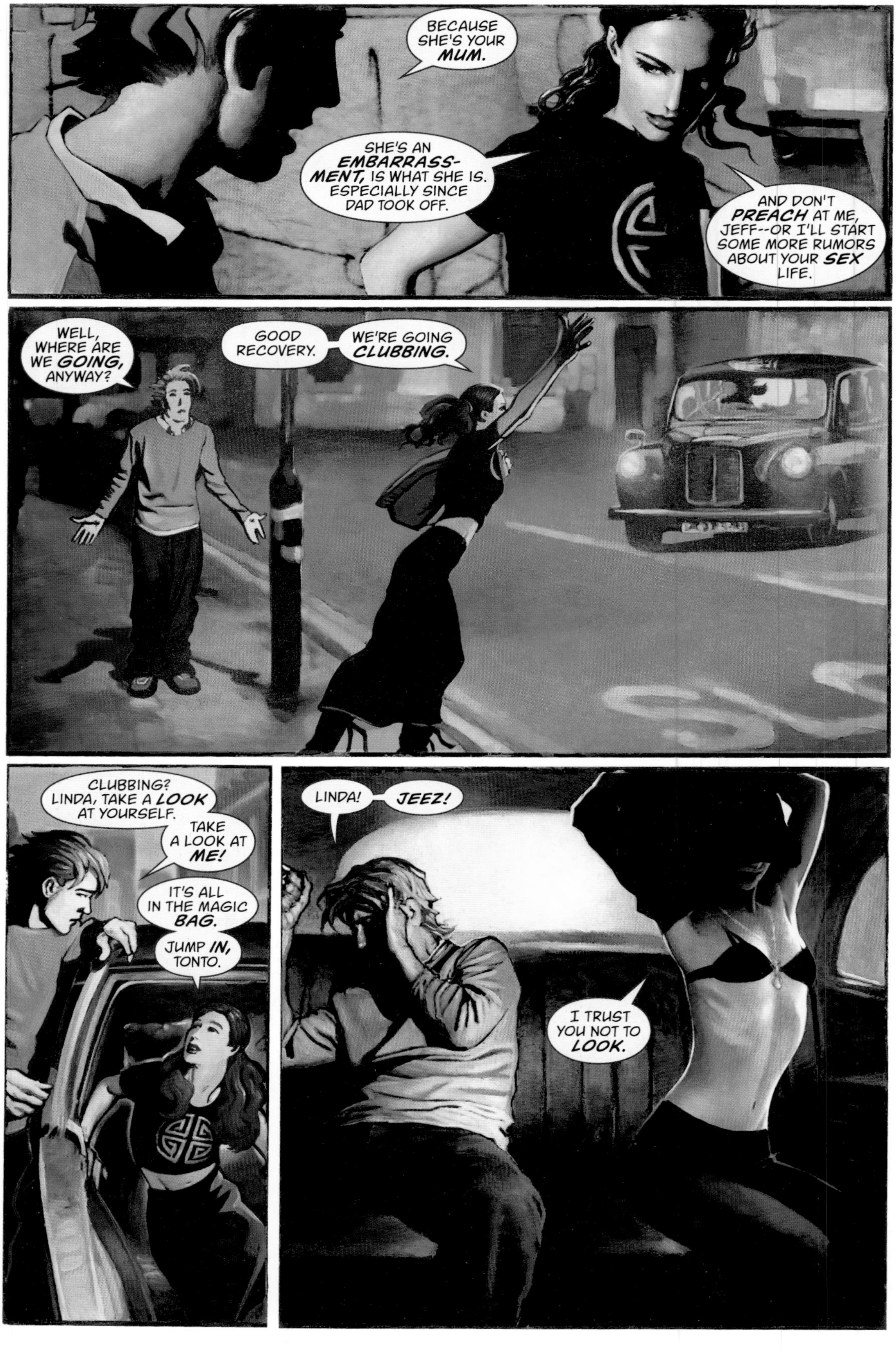
BECAUSE SHE'S YOUR MUM.
SHE'S AN EMBARRASS-MENT, IS WHAT SHE IS. ESPECIALLY SINCE DAD TOOK OFF.
AND DON'T PREACH AT ME, JEFF--OR I'LL START SOME MORE RUMORS ABOUT YOUR SEX LIFE.
WELL, WHERE ARE WE GOING, ANYWAY?
GOOD RECOVERY.
WE'RE GOING CLUBBING.
CLUBBING? LINDA, TAKE A LOOK AT YOURSELF.
TAKE A LOOK AT ME!
IT'S ALL IN THE MAGIC BAG.
JUMP IN, TONTO.
LINDA!
JEEZ!
I TRUST YOU NOT TO LOOK.

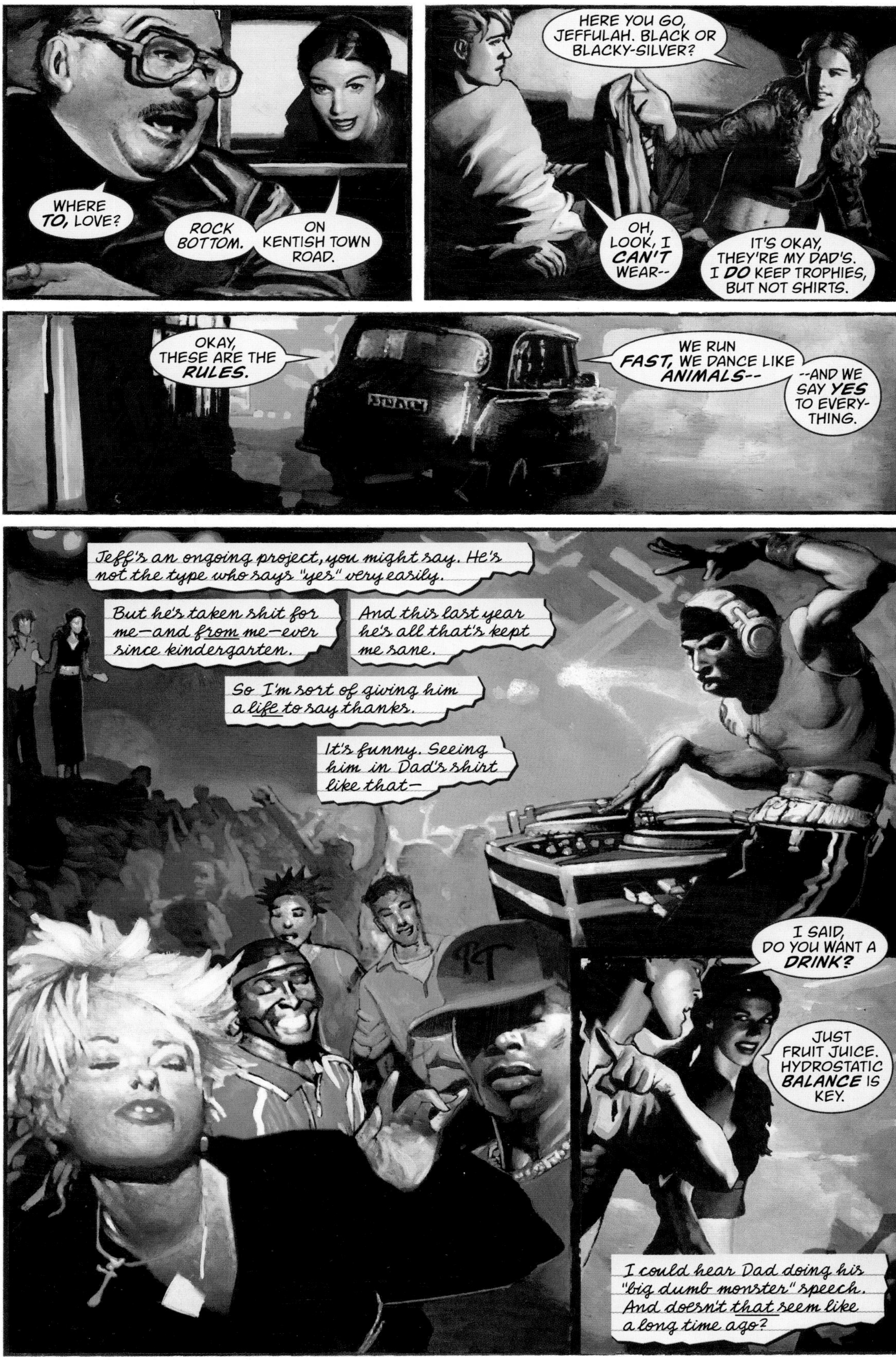
WHERE TO, LOVE?
ROCK BOTTOM.
ON KENTISH TOWN ROAD.
HERE YOU GO, JEFFULAH. BLACK OR BLACKY-SILVER?
OH, LOOK, I CAN'T WEAR--
IT'S OKAY, THEY'RE MY DAD'S. I DO KEEP TROPHIES, BUT NOT SHIRTS.
OKAY, THESE ARE THE RULES.
WE RUN FAST, WE DANCE LIKE ANIMALS--
--AND WE SAY YES TO EVERY-THING.
Jeff's an ongoing project, you might say. He's not the type who says "yes" very easily.
But he's taken shit for me—and from me—ever since kindergarten.
And this last year he's all that's kept me sane.
So I'm sort of giving him a life to say thanks.
It's funny. Seeing him in Dad's shirt like that—
I SAID, DO YOU WANT A DRINK?
JUST FRUIT JUICE. HYDROSTATIC BALANCE IS KEY.
I could hear Dad doing his "big dumb monster" speech. And doesn't that seem like a long time ago?

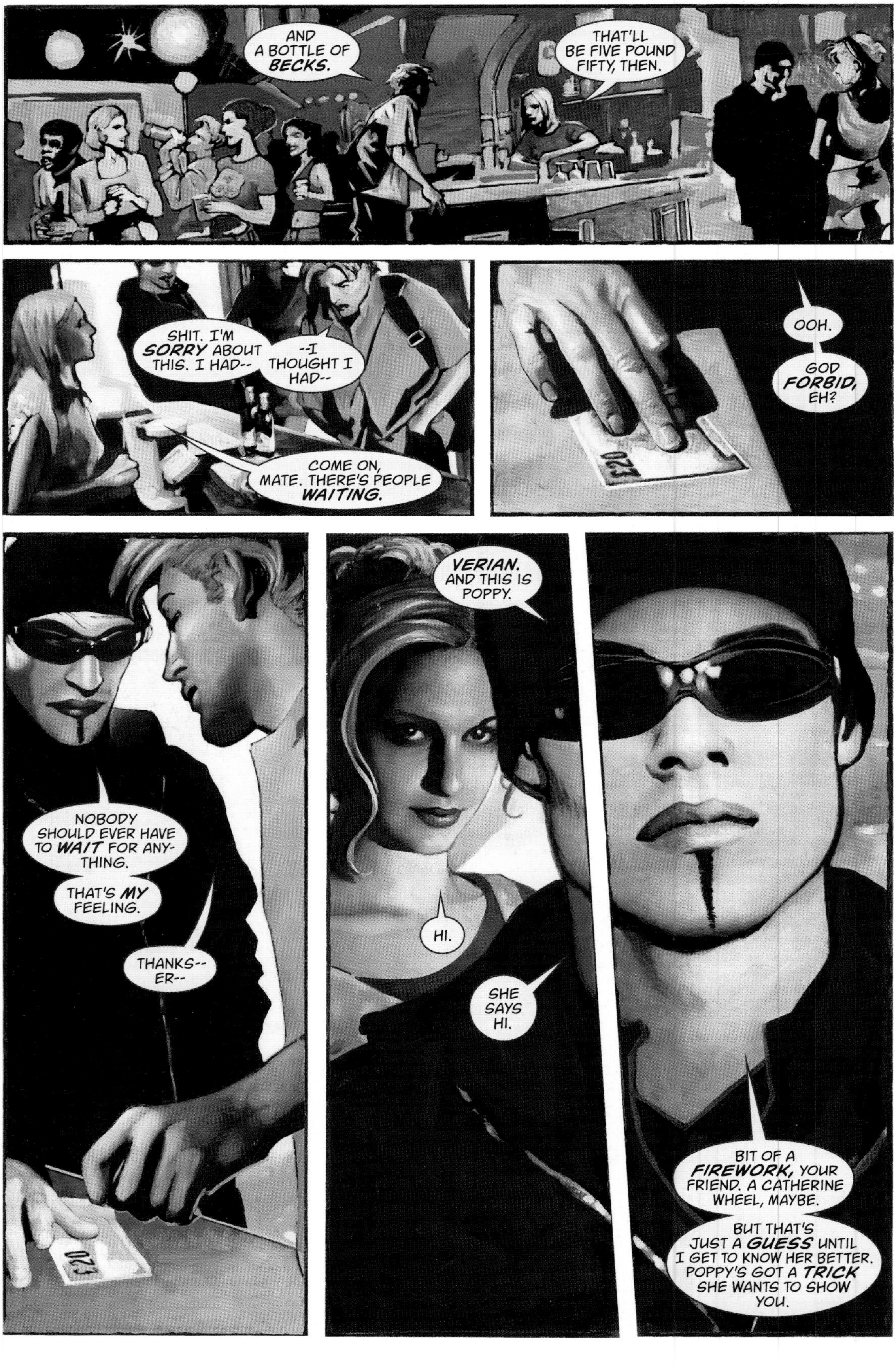
AND A BOTTLE OF BECKS.
THAT'LL BE FIVE POUND FIFTY, THEN.
SHIT. I'M SORRY ABOUT THIS. I HAD--
--I THOUGHT I HAD--
COME ON, MATE. THERE'S PEOPLE WAITING.
OOH.
GOD FORBID, EH?
£20
NOBODY SHOULD EVER HAVE TO WAIT FOR ANYTHING.
THAT'S MY FEELING.
THANKS-- ER--
£20
VERIAN. AND THIS IS POPPY.
HI.
SHE SAYS HI.
BIT OF A FIREWORK, YOUR FRIEND. A CATHERINE WHEEL, MAYBE.
BUT THAT'S JUST A GUESS UNTIL I GET TO KNOW HER BETTER. POPPY'S GOT A TRICK SHE WANTS TO SHOW YOU.

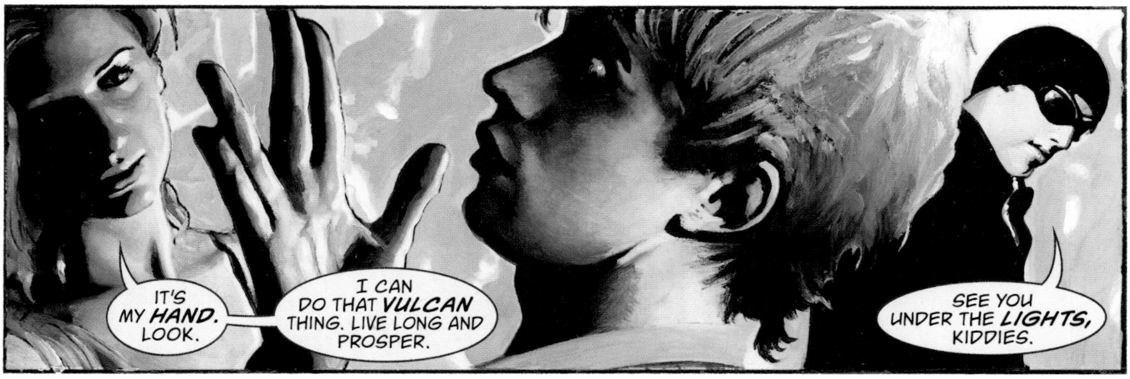
IT'S MY HAND. LOOK.
I CAN DO THAT VULCAN THING. LIVE LONG AND PROSPER.
SEE YOU UNDER THE LIGHTS, KIDDIES.

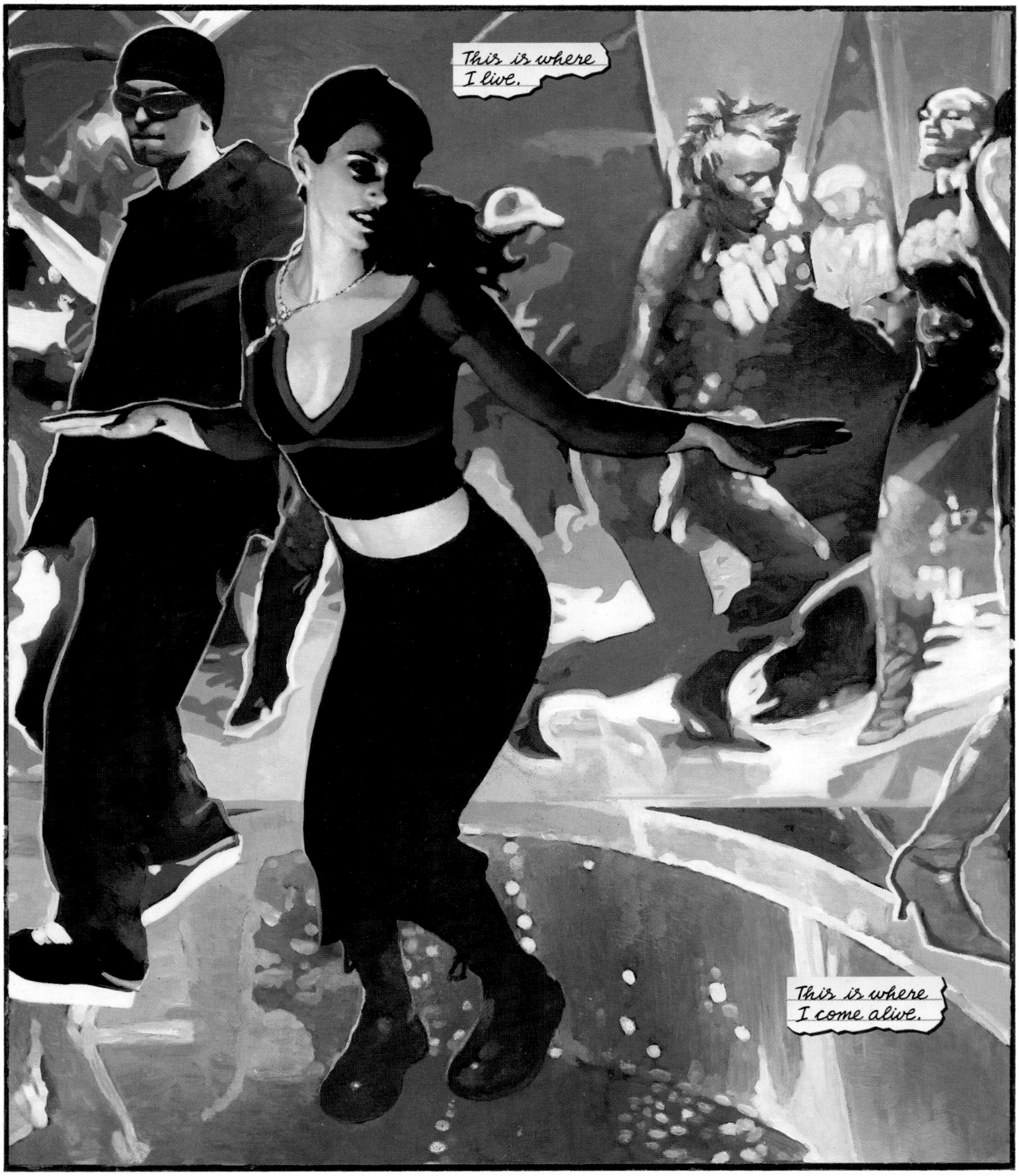
This is where I live.
This is where I come alive.

"WE'RE *LOYAL*," THEY SQUEAL. "LOYAL TO TITANIA."

THE VOICES GET *HOARSER*, THE TUNE STAYS THE *SAME*.

HAH.

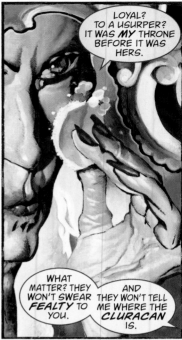

LOYAL? TO A USURPER? IT WAS *MY* THRONE BEFORE IT WAS HERS.

WHAT MATTER? THEY WON'T SWEAR *FEALTY* TO YOU.

AND THEY WON'T TELL ME WHERE THE *CLURACAN* IS.

HE WAS TITANIA'S *EMISSARY*. HER AMBASSADOR.

I REQUIRE EITHER HIS *DEATH* OR HIS *OATH*.

AND MORE *POWDER*.

MY HUSBAND MUST SEE ME AT MY *BEST*.

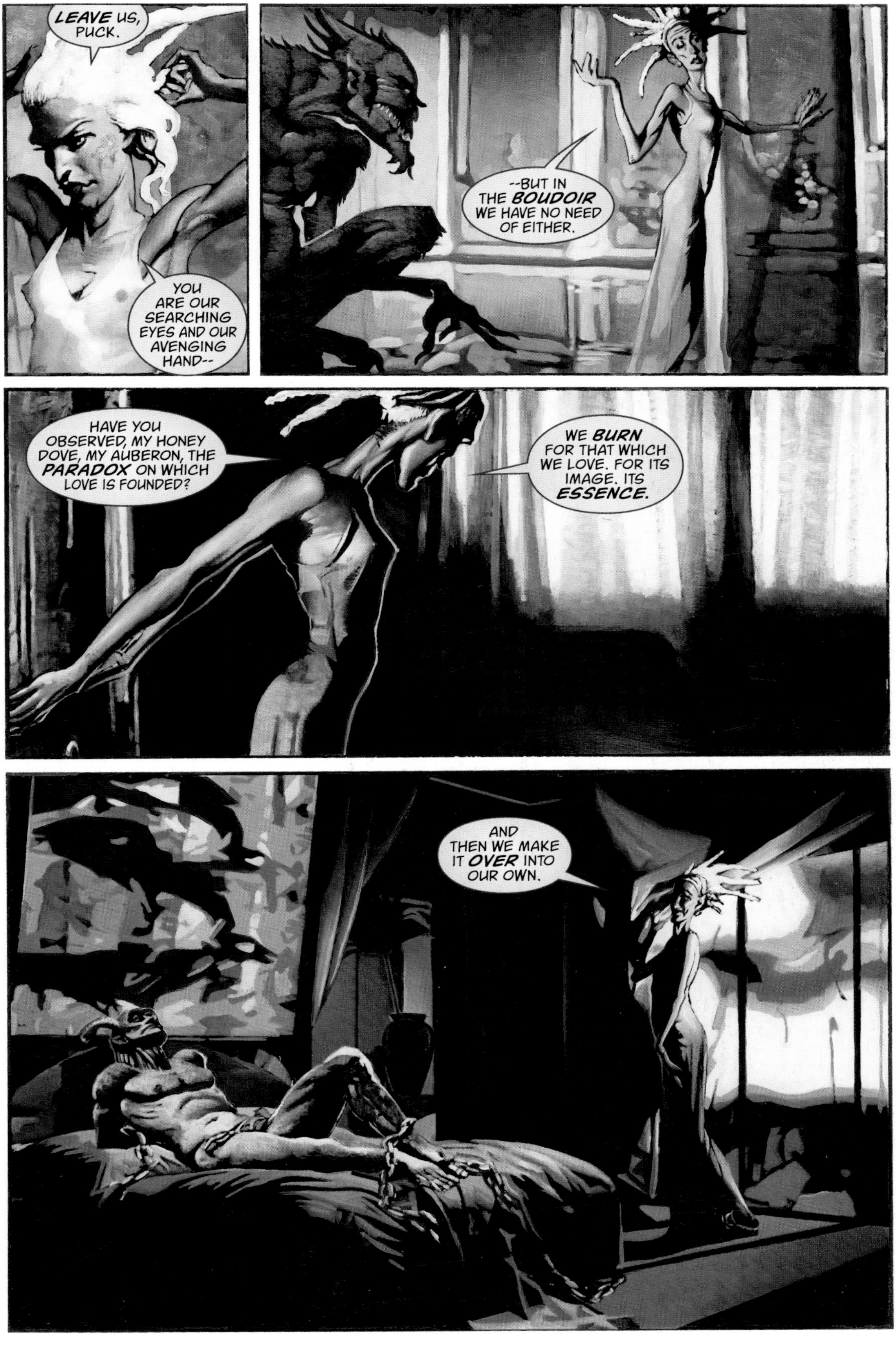
LEAVE US, PUCK.
YOU ARE OUR SEARCHING EYES AND OUR AVENGING HAND--
--BUT IN THE BOUDOIR WE HAVE NO NEED OF EITHER.
HAVE YOU OBSERVED, MY HONEY DOVE, MY AUBERON, THE PARADOX ON WHICH LOVE IS FOUNDED?
WE BURN FOR THAT WHICH WE LOVE. FOR ITS IMAGE. ITS ESSENCE.
AND THEN WE MAKE IT OVER INTO OUR OWN.

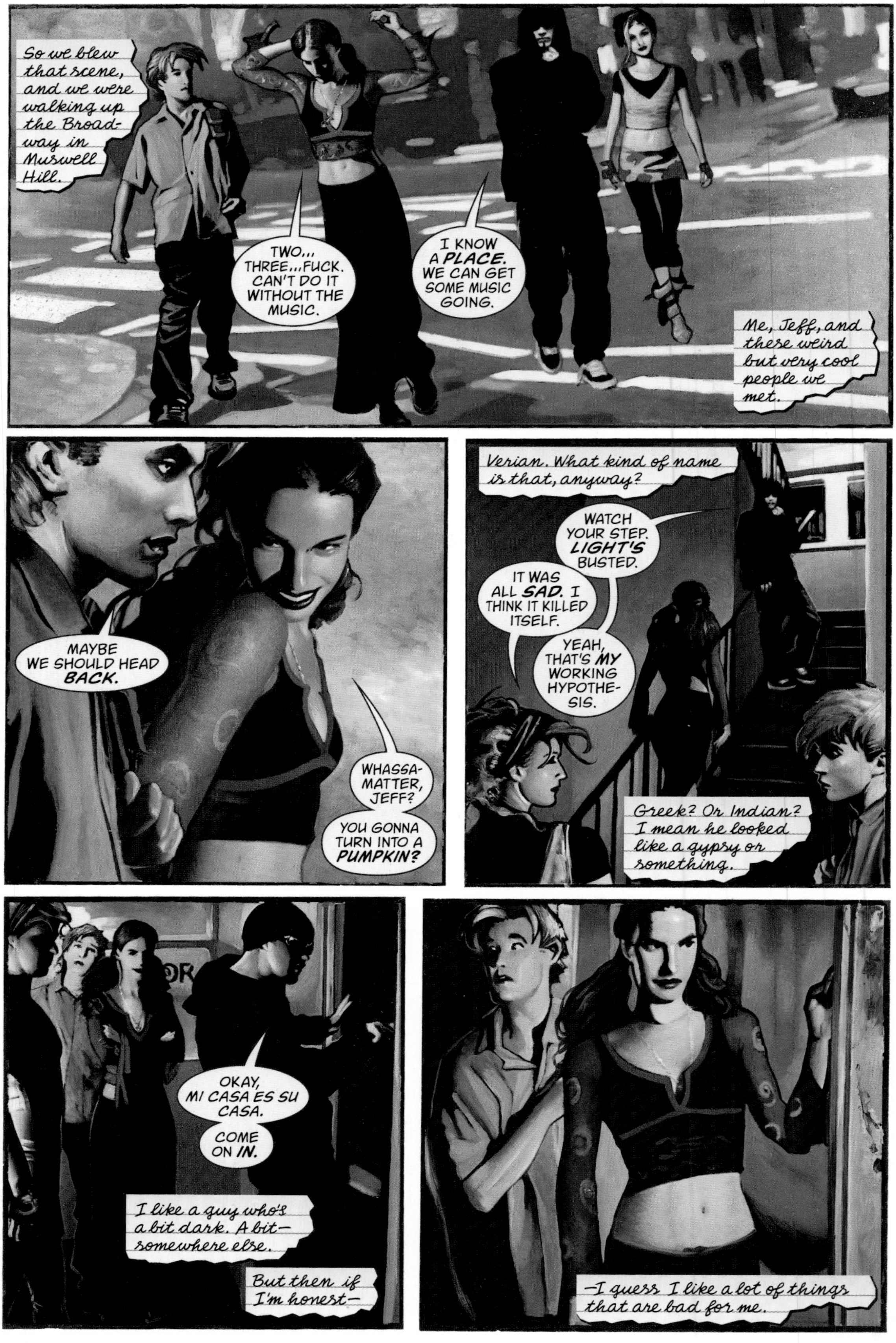

So we blew that scene, and we were walking up the Broadway in Muswell Hill.
TWO... THREE...FUCK. CAN'T DO IT WITHOUT THE MUSIC.
I KNOW A PLACE. WE CAN GET SOME MUSIC GOING.
Me, Jeff, and these weird but very cool people we met.
MAYBE WE SHOULD HEAD BACK.
WHASSA-MATTER, JEFF?
YOU GONNA TURN INTO A PUMPKIN?
Verian. What kind of name is that, anyway?
WATCH YOUR STEP. LIGHT'S BUSTED.
IT WAS ALL SAD. I THINK IT KILLED ITSELF.
YEAH, THAT'S MY WORKING HYPOTHE-SIS.
Greek? Or Indian? I mean he looked like a gypsy or something.
OKAY, MI CASA ES SU CASA.
COME ON IN.
I like a guy who's a bit dark. A bit—somewhere else.
But then if I'm honest—
—I guess I like a lot of things that are bad for me.

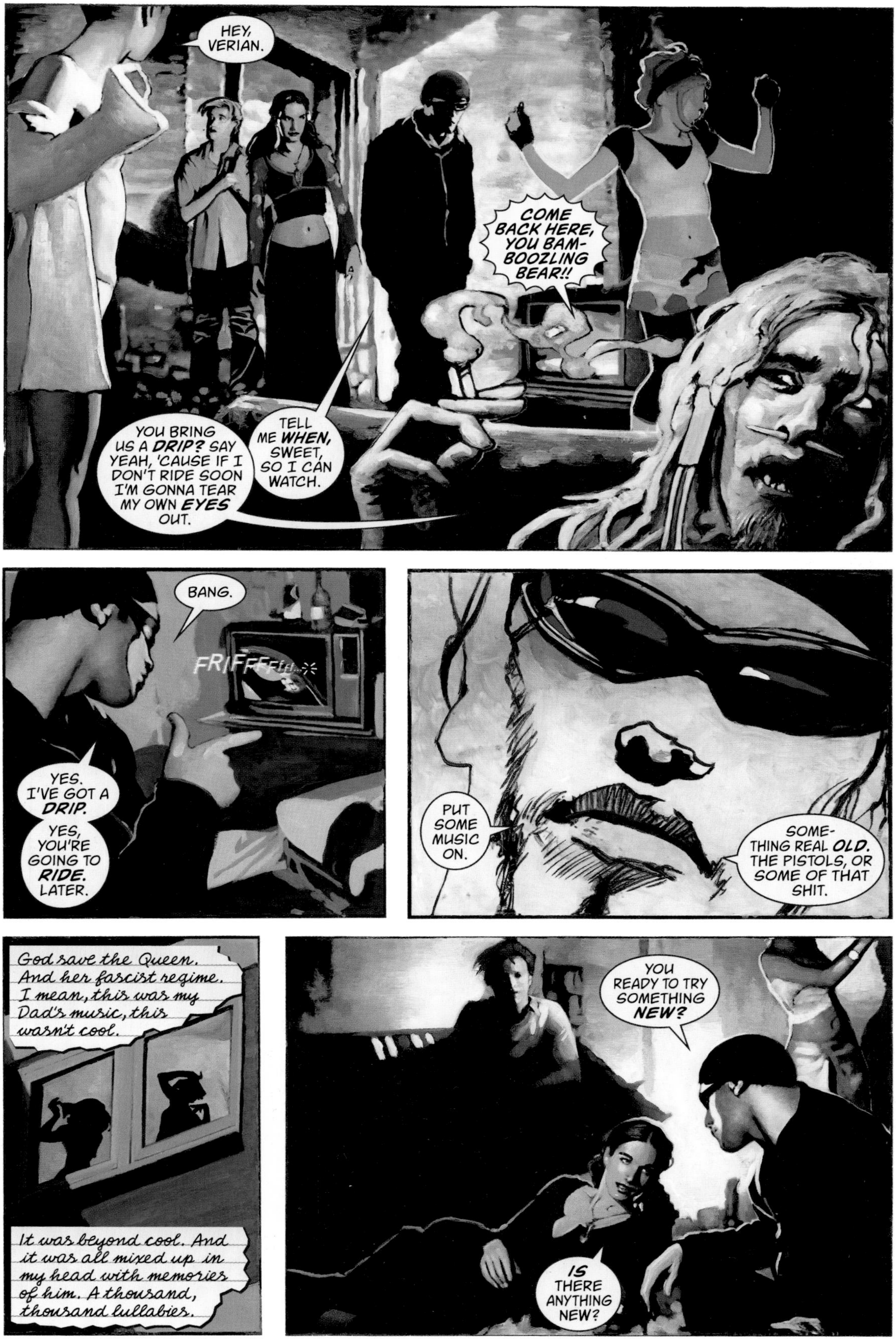
HEY, VERIAN.
COME BACK HERE, YOU BAMBOOZLING BEAR!!
YOU BRING US A **DRIP?** SAY YEAH, 'CAUSE IF I DON'T RIDE SOON I'M GONNA TEAR MY OWN **EYES** OUT.
TELL ME **WHEN,** SWEET, SO I CAN WATCH.
BANG.
FRIFFFFfft...
YES. I'VE GOT A **DRIP.**
YES, YOU'RE GOING TO **RIDE.** LATER.
PUT SOME MUSIC ON.
SOMETHING REAL **OLD.** THE PISTOLS, OR SOME OF THAT SHIT.
God save the Queen. And her fascist regime. I mean, this was my Dad's music, this wasn't cool.
It was beyond cool. And it was all mixed up in my head with memories of him. A thousand, thousand lullabies.
YOU READY TO TRY SOMETHING **NEW?**
IS THERE ANYTHING NEW?

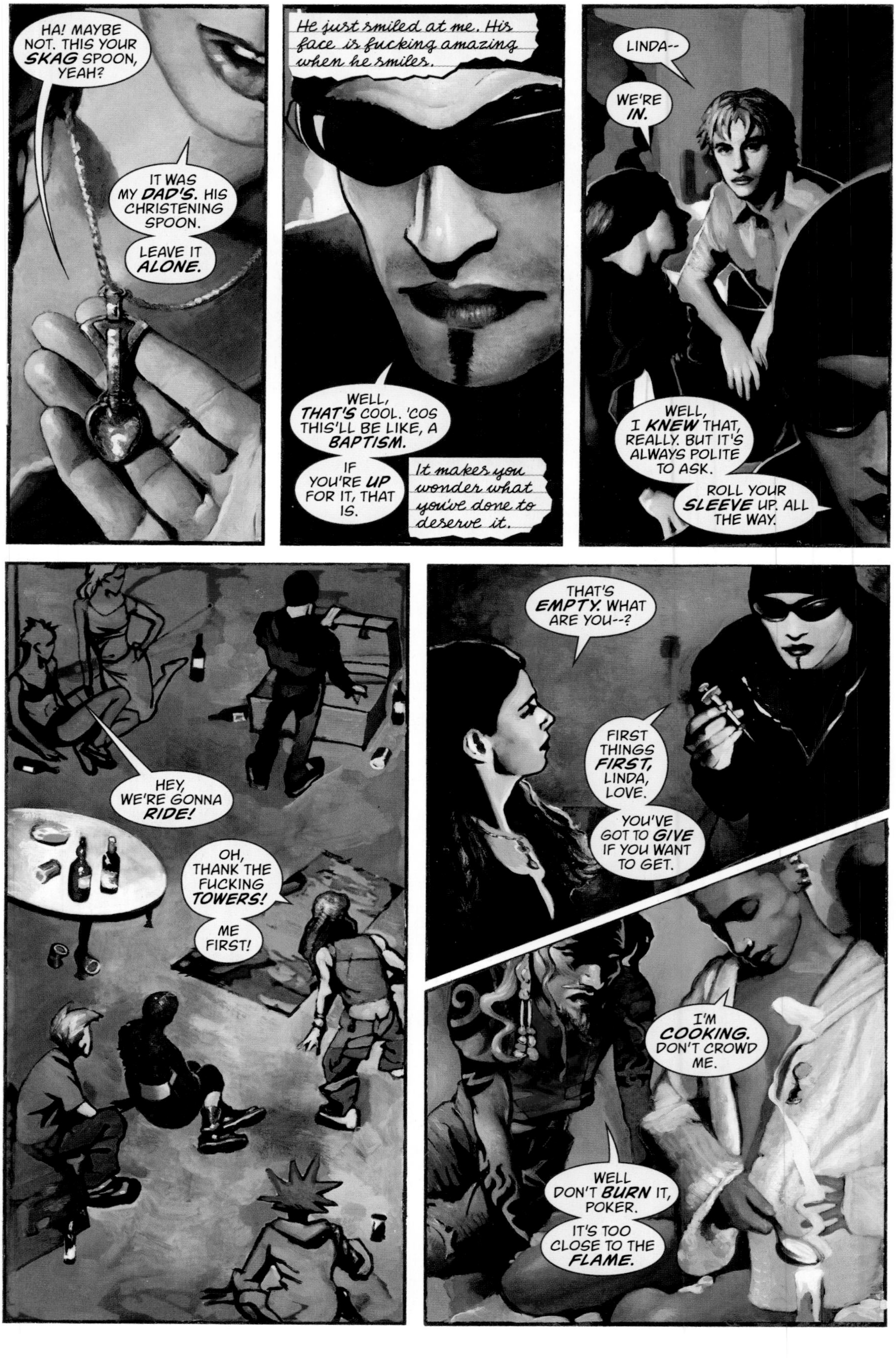
HA! MAYBE NOT. THIS YOUR SKAG SPOON, YEAH?
IT WAS MY DAD'S. HIS CHRISTENING SPOON.
LEAVE IT ALONE.
He just smiled at me. His face is fucking amazing when he smiles.
WELL, THAT'S COOL. 'COS THIS'LL BE LIKE, A BAPTISM.
IF YOU'RE UP FOR IT, THAT IS.
It makes you wonder what you've done to deserve it.
LINDA--
WE'RE IN.
WELL, I KNEW THAT, REALLY. BUT IT'S ALWAYS POLITE TO ASK.
ROLL YOUR SLEEVE UP. ALL THE WAY.
HEY, WE'RE GONNA RIDE!
OH, THANK THE FUCKING TOWERS!
ME FIRST!
THAT'S EMPTY. WHAT ARE YOU--?
FIRST THINGS FIRST, LINDA, LOVE.
YOU'VE GOT TO GIVE IF YOU WANT TO GET.
I'M COOKING. DON'T CROWD ME.
WELL DON'T BURN IT, POKER.
IT'S TOO CLOSE TO THE FLAME.

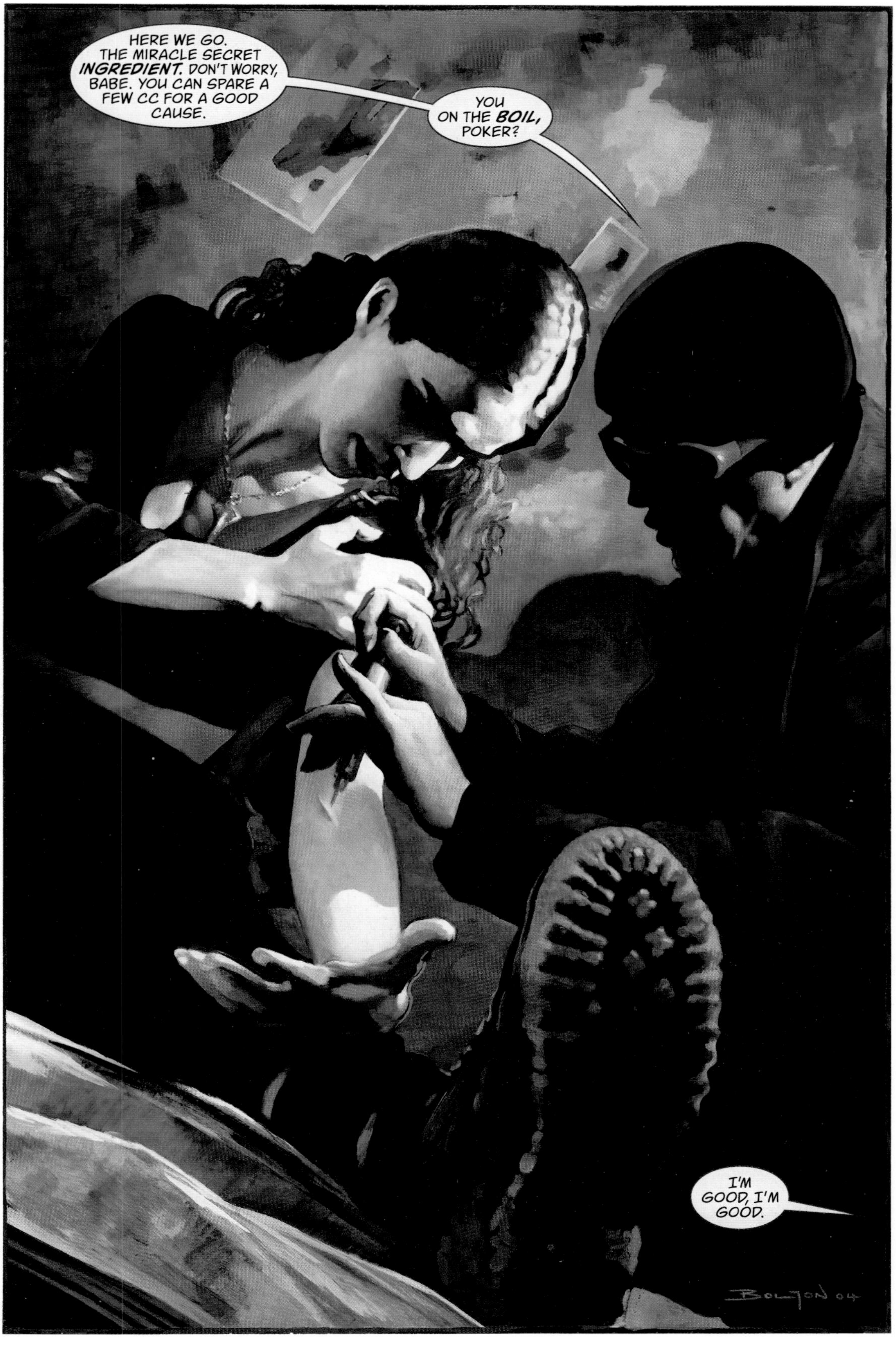
HERE WE GO. THE MIRACLE SECRET INGREDIENT. DON'T WORRY, BABE. YOU CAN SPARE A FEW CC FOR A GOOD CAUSE.
YOU ON THE BOIL, POKER?
I'M GOOD, I'M GOOD.
BOLTON 04

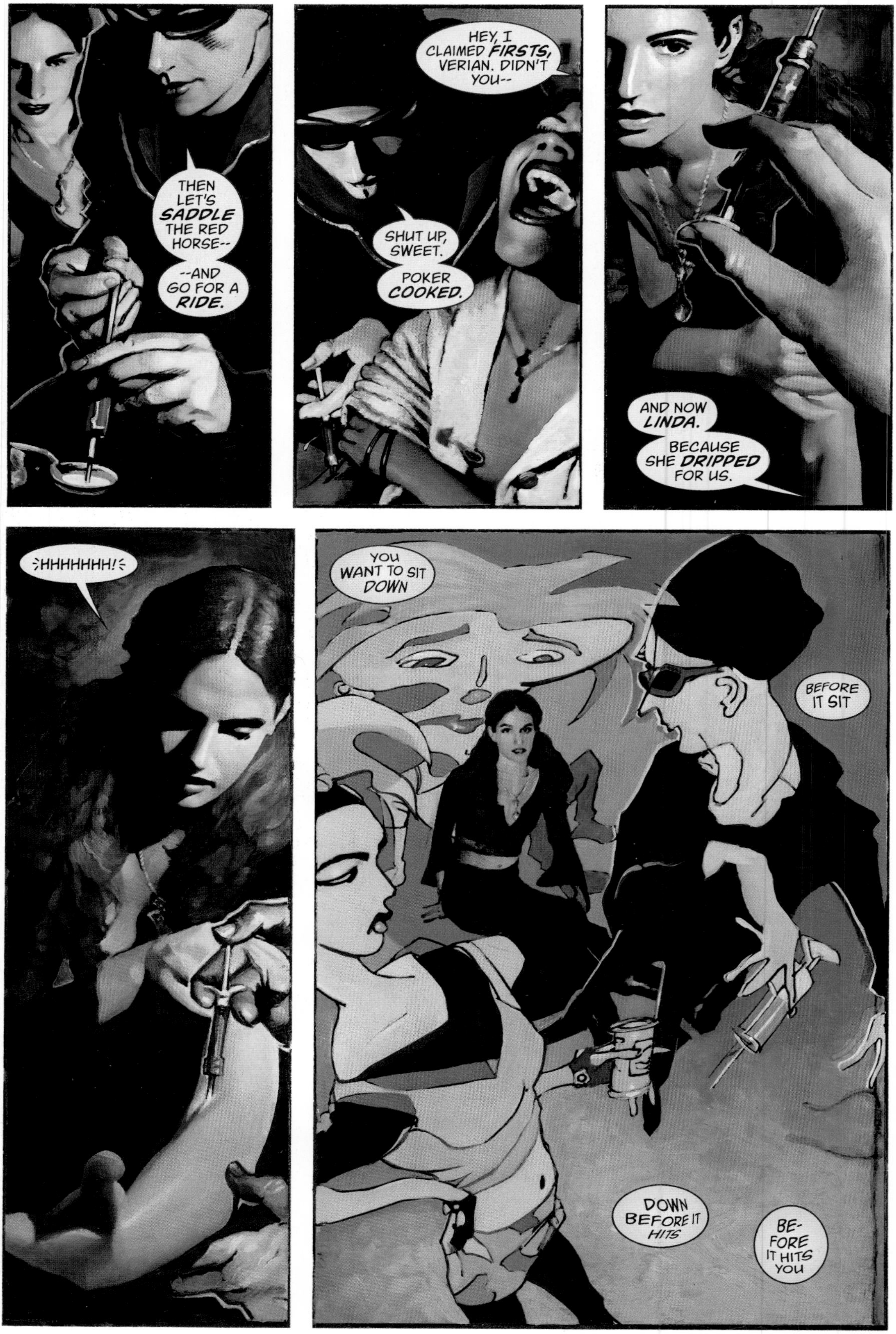
THEN LET'S SADDLE THE RED HORSE--
--AND GO FOR A RIDE.
HEY, I CLAIMED FIRSTS, VERIAN. DIDN'T YOU--
SHUT UP, SWEET.
POKER COOKED.
AND NOW LINDA.
BECAUSE SHE DRIPPED FOR US.
HHHHHHH!
YOU WANT TO SIT DOWN
BEFORE IT SIT
DOWN BEFORE IT HITS
BE-FORE IT HITS YOU

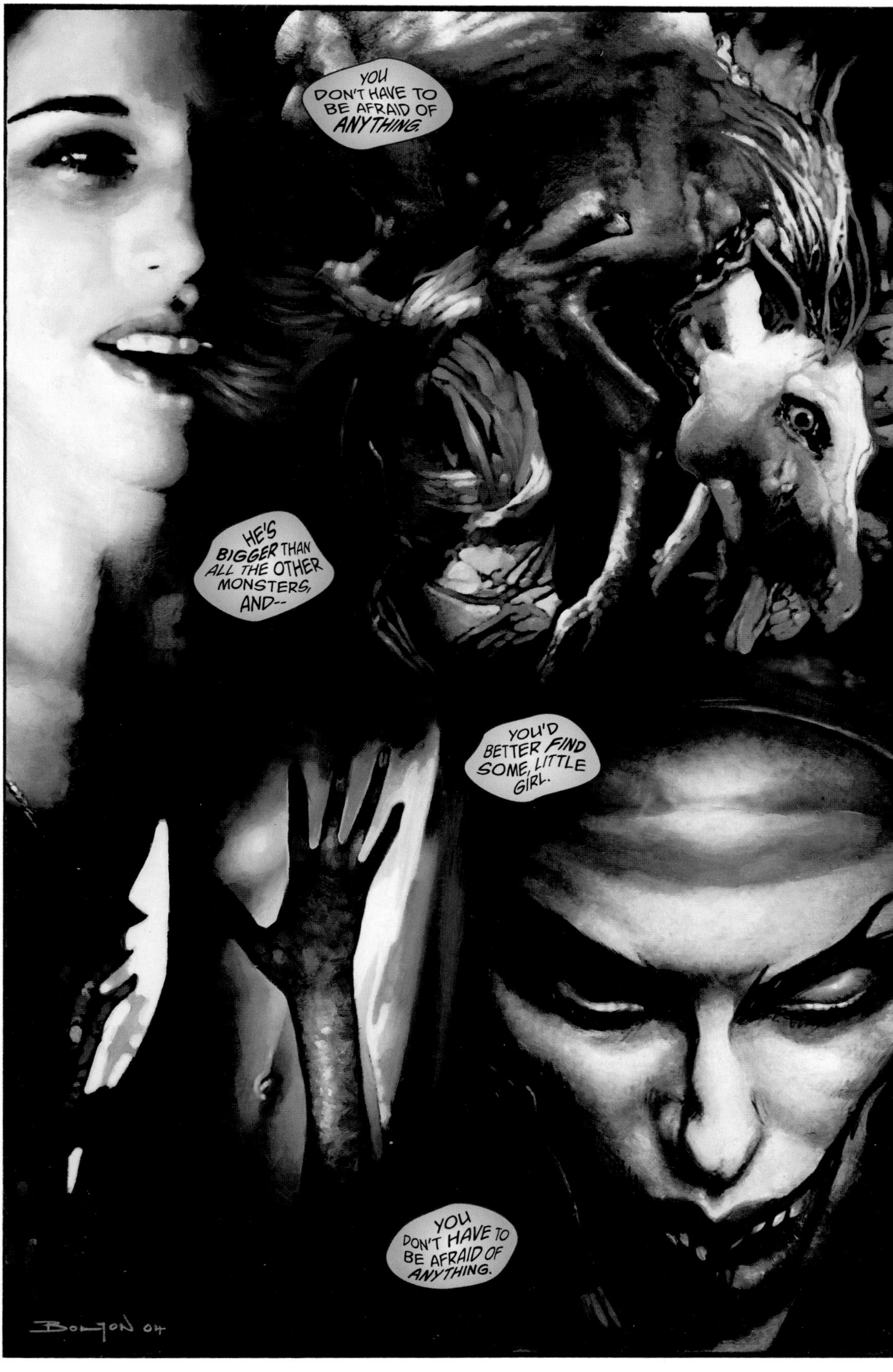
YOU DON'T HAVE TO BE AFRAID OF ANYTHING.
HE'S BIGGER THAN ALL THE OTHER MONSTERS, AND--
YOU'D BETTER FIND SOME, LITTLE GIRL.
YOU DON'T HAVE TO BE AFRAID OF ANYTHING.
BOLTON 04

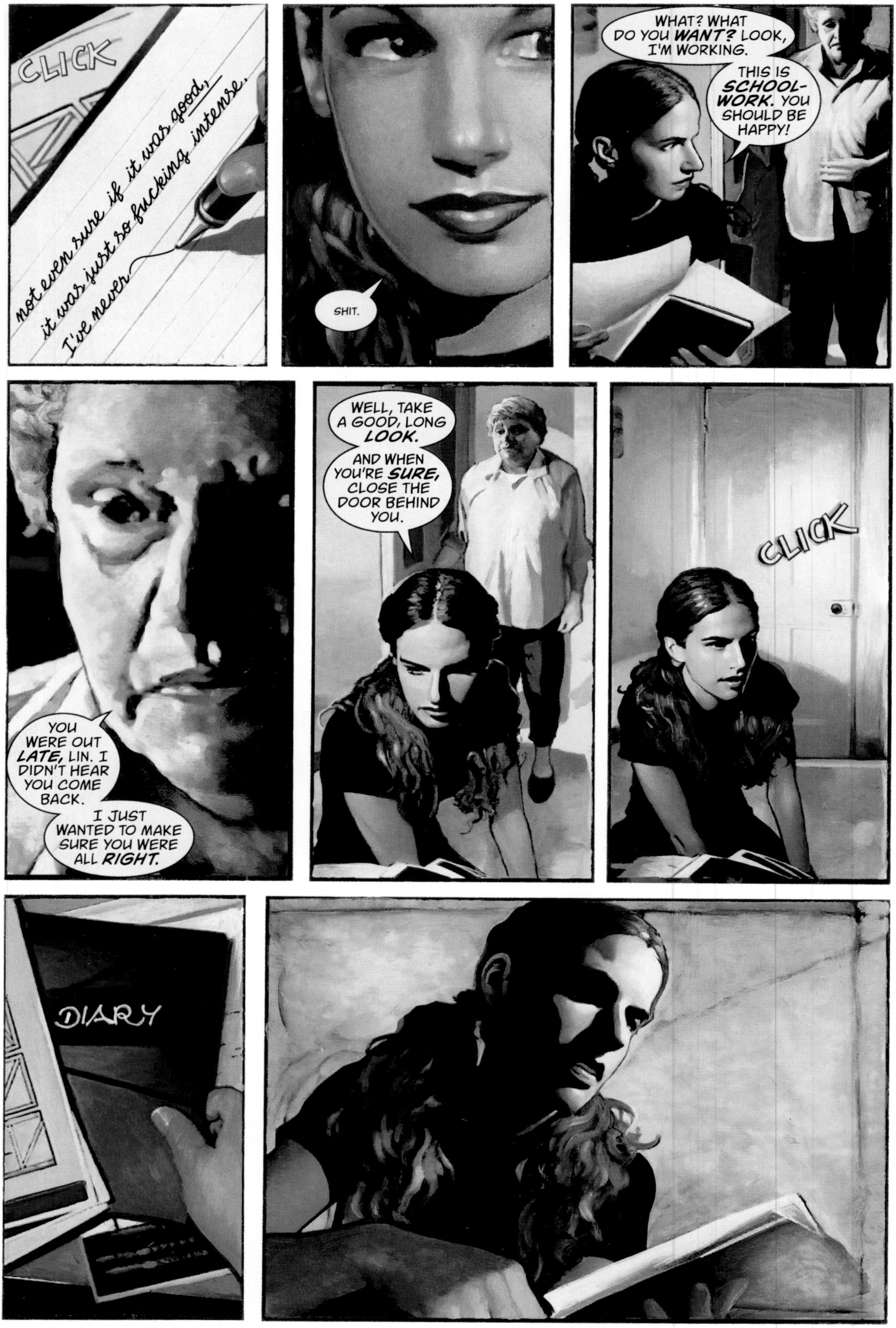
CLICK
not even sure if it was good,
it was just so fucking intense.
I've never
SHIT.
WHAT? WHAT DO YOU WANT? LOOK, I'M WORKING.
THIS IS SCHOOL-WORK. YOU SHOULD BE HAPPY!
YOU WERE OUT LATE, LIN. I DIDN'T HEAR YOU COME BACK.
I JUST WANTED TO MAKE SURE YOU WERE ALL RIGHT.
WELL, TAKE A GOOD, LONG LOOK.
AND WHEN YOU'RE SURE, CLOSE THE DOOR BEHIND YOU.
CLICK
DIARY

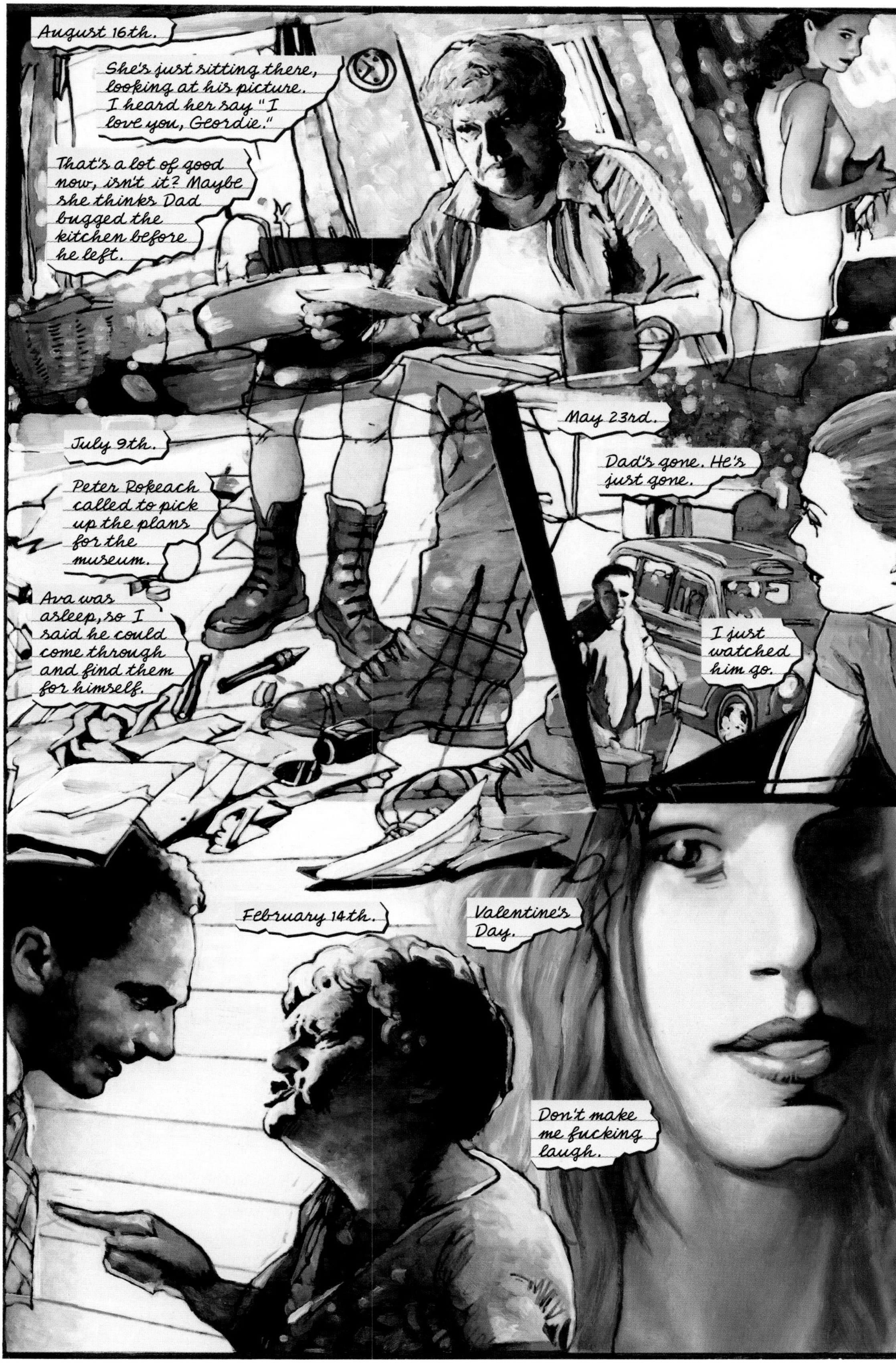
August 16th.
She's just sitting there, looking at his picture. I heard her say "I love you, Geordie."
That's a lot of good now, isn't it? Maybe she thinks Dad bugged the kitchen before he left.
July 9th.
Peter Rokeach called to pick up the plans for the museum.
Ava was asleep, so I said he could come through and find them for himself.
May 23rd.
Dad's gone. He's just gone.
I just watched him go.
February 14th.
Valentine's Day.
Don't make me fucking laugh.

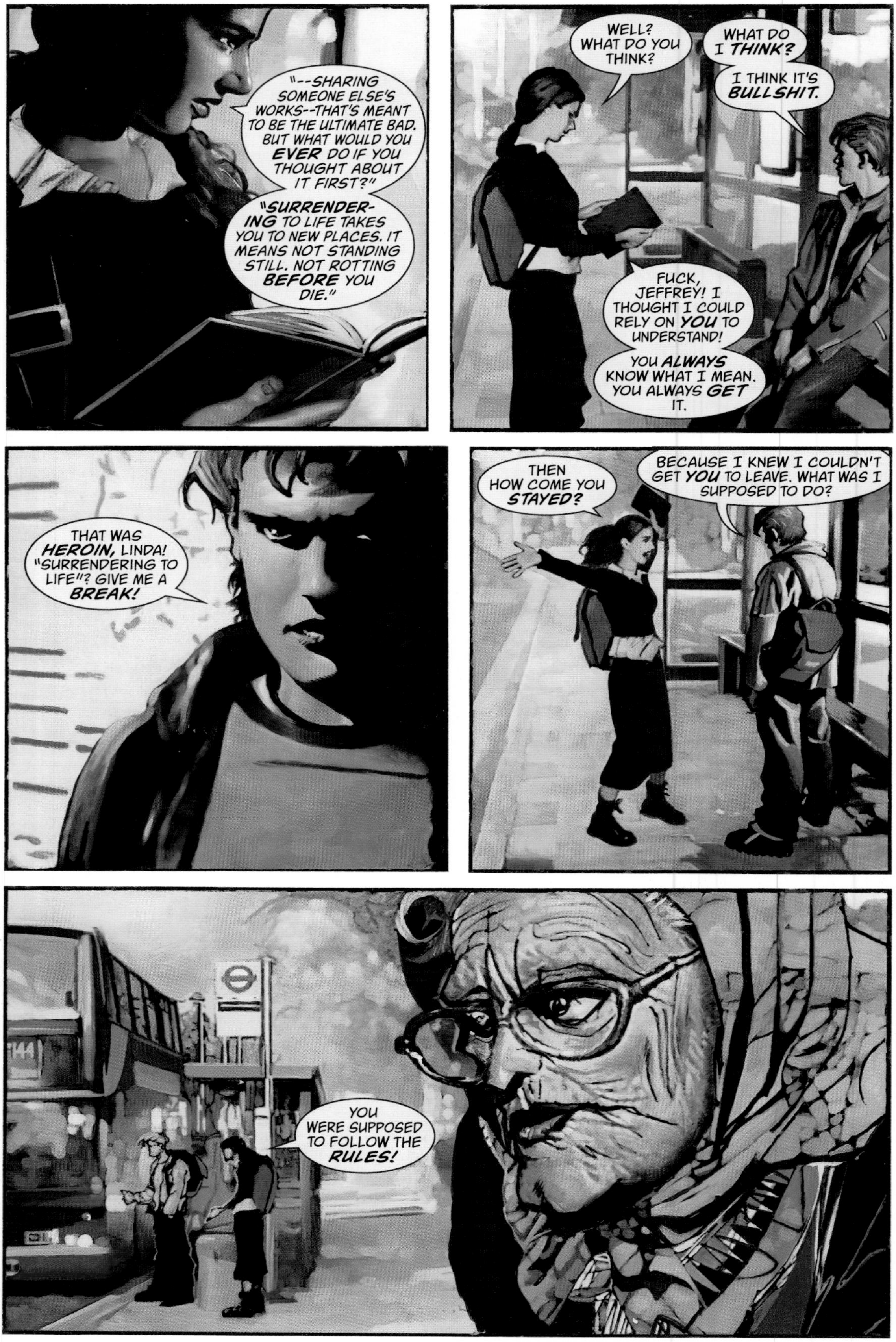
"--SHARING SOMEONE ELSE'S WORKS--THAT'S MEANT TO BE THE ULTIMATE BAD. BUT WHAT WOULD YOU EVER DO IF YOU THOUGHT ABOUT IT FIRST?"
"SURRENDERING TO LIFE TAKES YOU TO NEW PLACES. IT MEANS NOT STANDING STILL. NOT ROTTING BEFORE YOU DIE."
WELL? WHAT DO YOU THINK?
WHAT DO I THINK?
I THINK IT'S BULLSHIT.
FUCK, JEFFREY! I THOUGHT I COULD RELY ON YOU TO UNDERSTAND!
YOU ALWAYS KNOW WHAT I MEAN. YOU ALWAYS GET IT.
THAT WAS HEROIN, LINDA! "SURRENDERING TO LIFE"? GIVE ME A BREAK!
THEN HOW COME YOU STAYED?
BECAUSE I KNEW I COULDN'T GET YOU TO LEAVE. WHAT WAS I SUPPOSED TO DO?
YOU WERE SUPPOSED TO FOLLOW THE RULES!

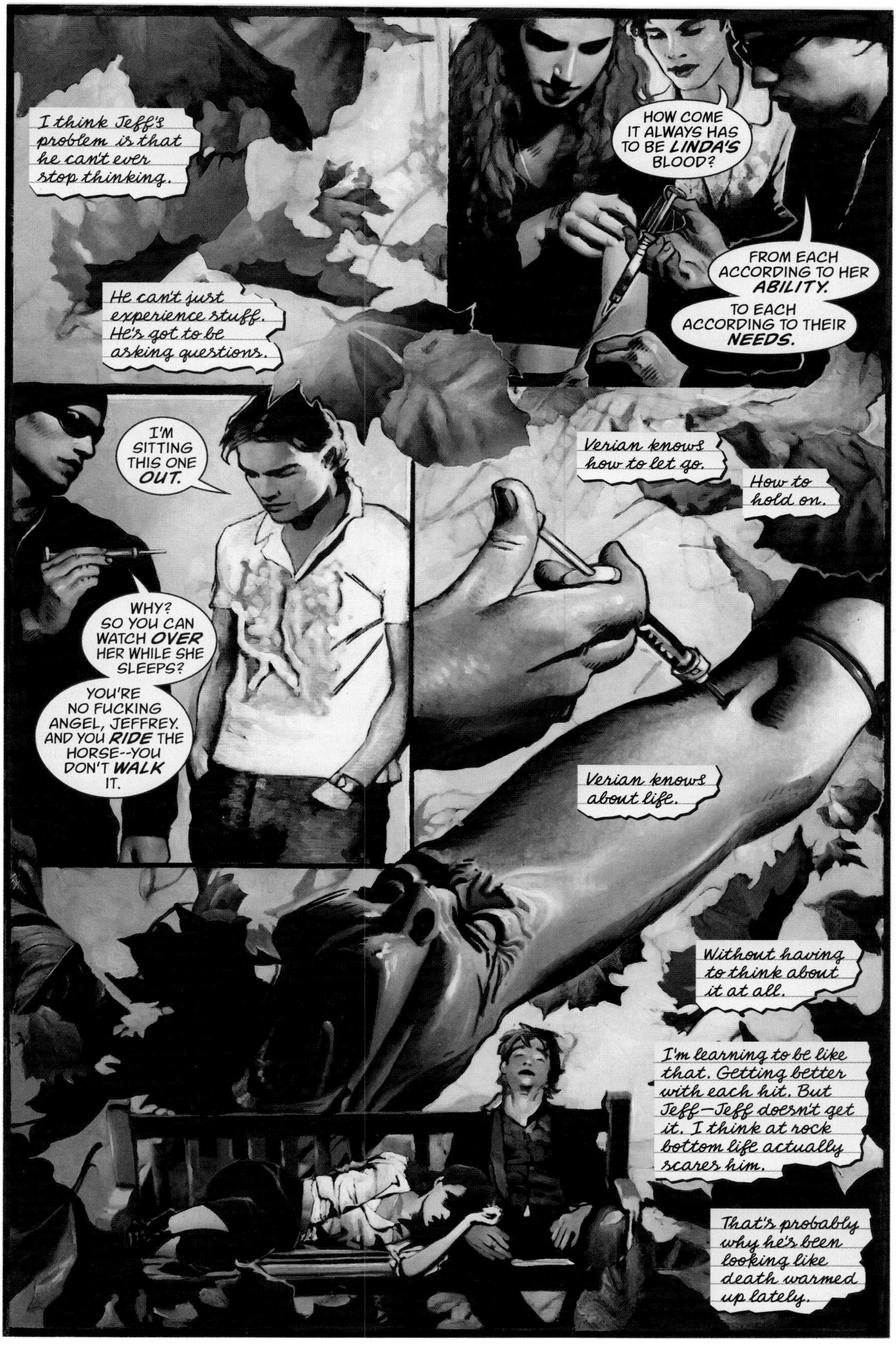
I think Jeff's problem is that he can't ever stop thinking.
He can't just experience stuff. He's got to be asking questions.
HOW COME IT ALWAYS HAS TO BE LINDA'S BLOOD?
FROM EACH ACCORDING TO HER ABILITY.
TO EACH ACCORDING TO THEIR NEEDS.
I'M SITTING THIS ONE OUT.
WHY? SO YOU CAN WATCH OVER HER WHILE SHE SLEEPS?
YOU'RE NO FUCKING ANGEL, JEFFREY. AND YOU RIDE THE HORSE--YOU DON'T WALK IT.
Verian knows how to let go.
How to hold on.
Verian knows about life.
Without having to think about it at all.
I'm learning to be like that. Getting better with each hit. But Jeff—Jeff doesn't get it. I think at rock bottom life actually scares him.
That's probably why he's been looking like death warmed up lately.

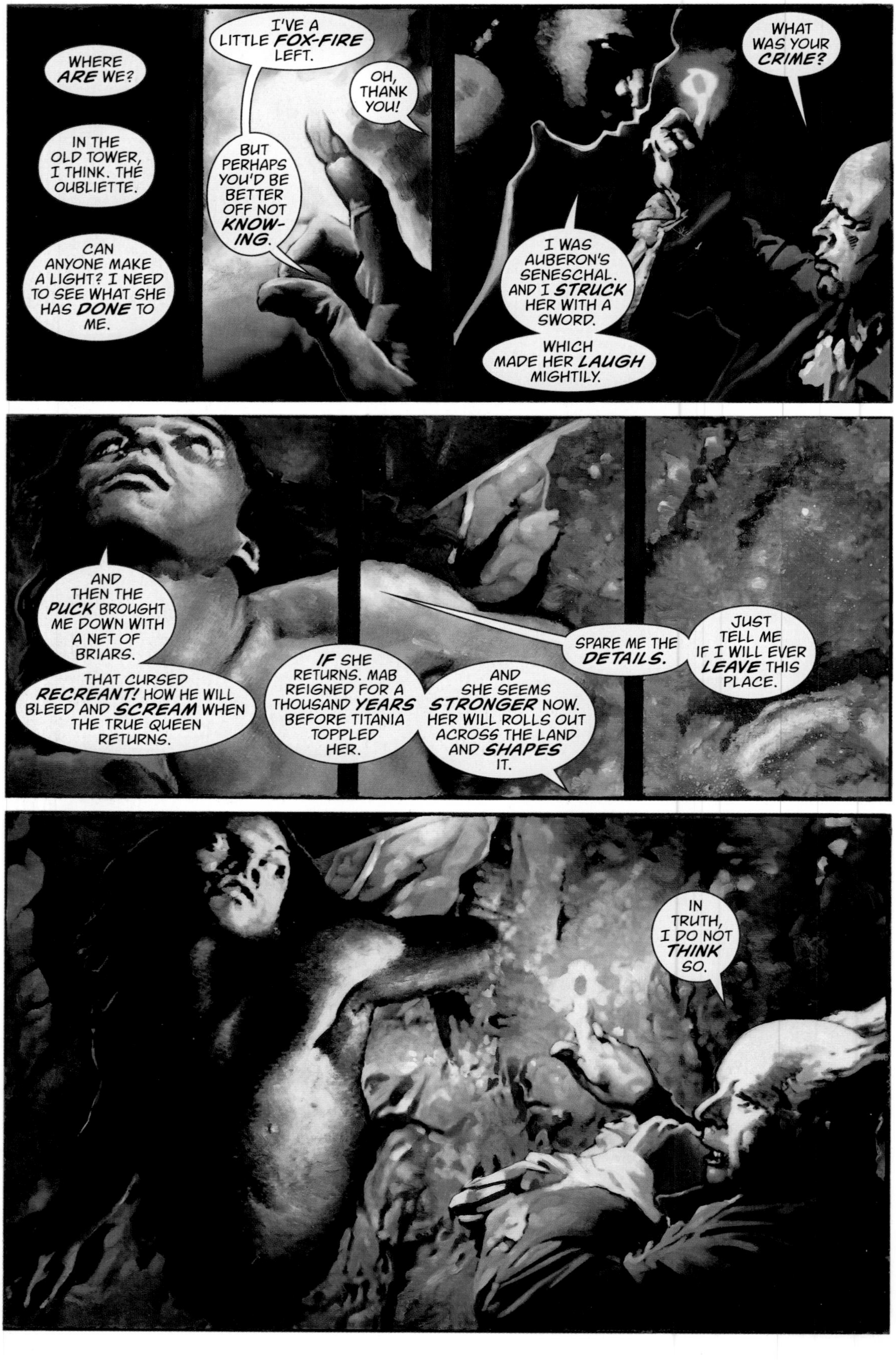
WHERE ARE WE?
IN THE OLD TOWER, I THINK. THE OUBLIETTE.
CAN ANYONE MAKE A LIGHT? I NEED TO SEE WHAT SHE HAS DONE TO ME.
I'VE A LITTLE FOX-FIRE LEFT.
OH, THANK YOU!
BUT PERHAPS YOU'D BE BETTER OFF NOT KNOWING.
WHAT WAS YOUR CRIME?
I WAS AUBERON'S SENESCHAL. AND I STRUCK HER WITH A SWORD.
WHICH MADE HER LAUGH MIGHTILY.
AND THEN THE PUCK BROUGHT ME DOWN WITH A NET OF BRIARS.
THAT CURSED RECREANT! HOW HE WILL BLEED AND SCREAM WHEN THE TRUE QUEEN RETURNS.
IF SHE RETURNS. MAB REIGNED FOR A THOUSAND YEARS BEFORE TITANIA TOPPLED HER.
AND SHE SEEMS STRONGER NOW. HER WILL ROLLS OUT ACROSS THE LAND AND SHAPES IT.
SPARE ME THE DETAILS.
JUST TELL ME IF I WILL EVER LEAVE THIS PLACE.
IN TRUTH, I DO NOT THINK SO.

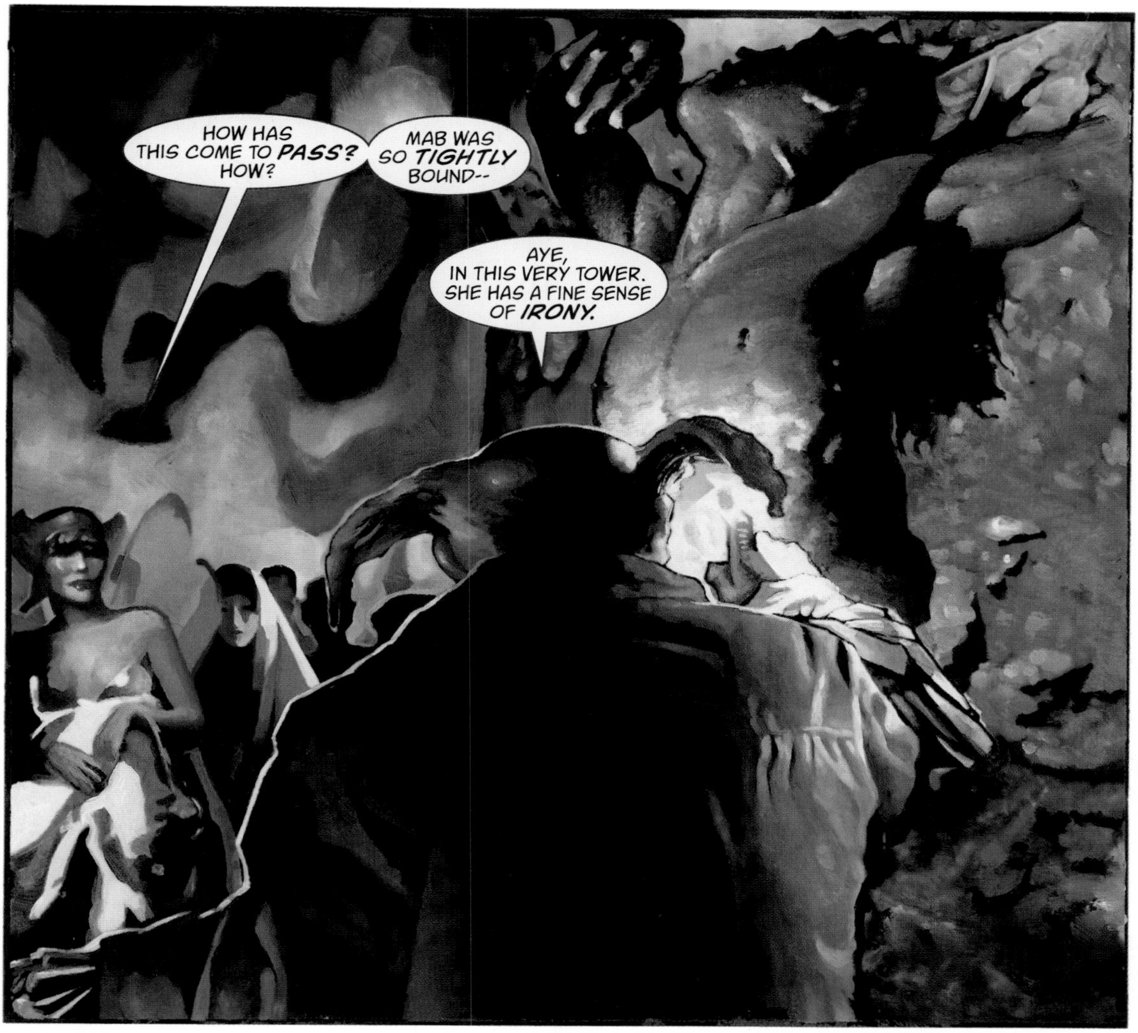
HOW HAS THIS COME TO PASS? HOW?
MAB WAS SO TIGHTLY BOUND--
AYE, IN THIS VERY TOWER. SHE HAS A FINE SENSE OF IRONY.

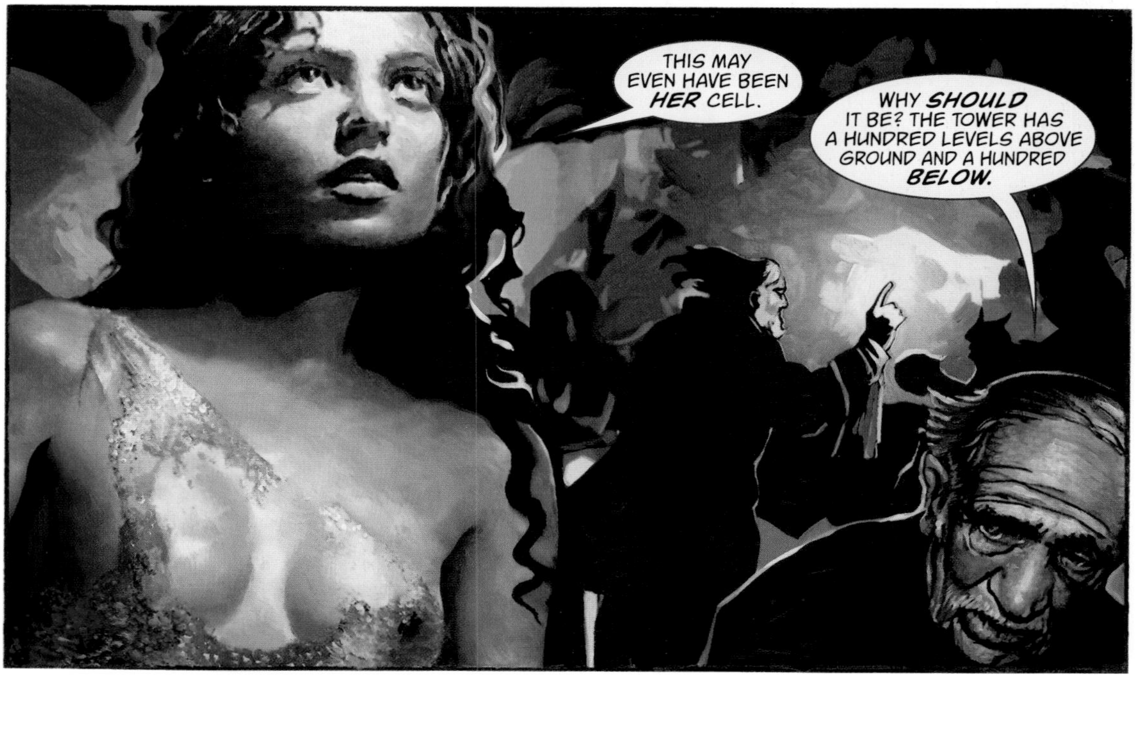
THIS MAY EVEN HAVE BEEN HER CELL.
WHY SHOULD IT BE? THE TOWER HAS A HUNDRED LEVELS ABOVE GROUND AND A HUNDRED BELOW.

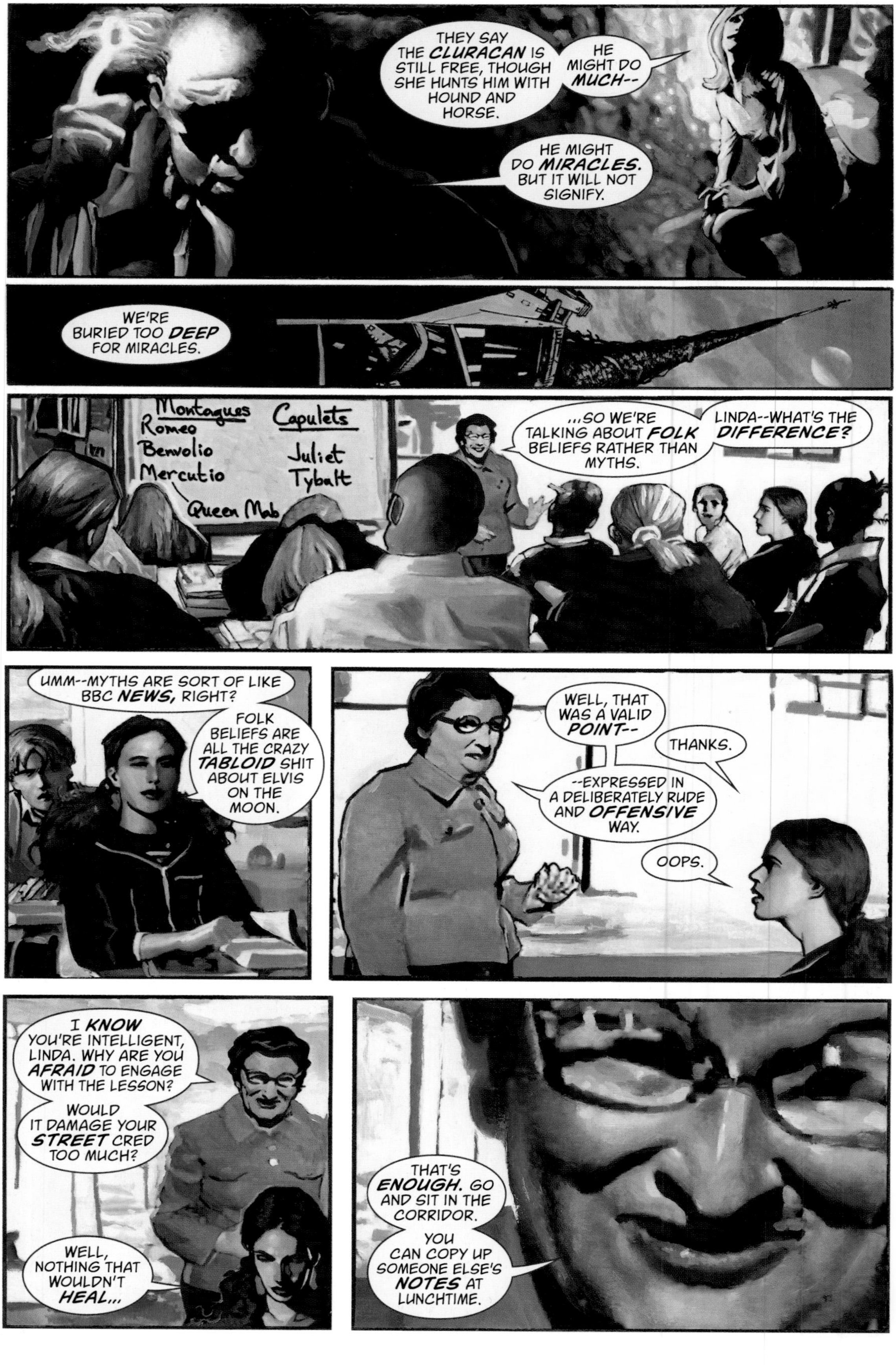
THEY SAY THE CLURACAN IS STILL FREE, THOUGH SHE HUNTS HIM WITH HOUND AND HORSE.
HE MIGHT DO MUCH--
HE MIGHT DO MIRACLES. BUT IT WILL NOT SIGNIFY.
WE'RE BURIED TOO DEEP FOR MIRACLES.
Montagues
Romeo
Benvolio
Mercutio
Queen Mab
Capulets
Juliet
Tybalt
...SO WE'RE TALKING ABOUT FOLK BELIEFS RATHER THAN MYTHS.
LINDA--WHAT'S THE DIFFERENCE?
UMM--MYTHS ARE SORT OF LIKE BBC NEWS, RIGHT?
FOLK BELIEFS ARE ALL THE CRAZY TABLOID SHIT ABOUT ELVIS ON THE MOON.
WELL, THAT WAS A VALID POINT--
THANKS.
--EXPRESSED IN A DELIBERATELY RUDE AND OFFENSIVE WAY.
OOPS.
I KNOW YOU'RE INTELLIGENT, LINDA. WHY ARE YOU AFRAID TO ENGAGE WITH THE LESSON?
WOULD IT DAMAGE YOUR STREET CRED TOO MUCH?
WELL, NOTHING THAT WOULDN'T HEAL...
THAT'S ENOUGH. GO AND SIT IN THE CORRIDOR.
YOU CAN COPY UP SOMEONE ELSE'S NOTES AT LUNCHTIME.

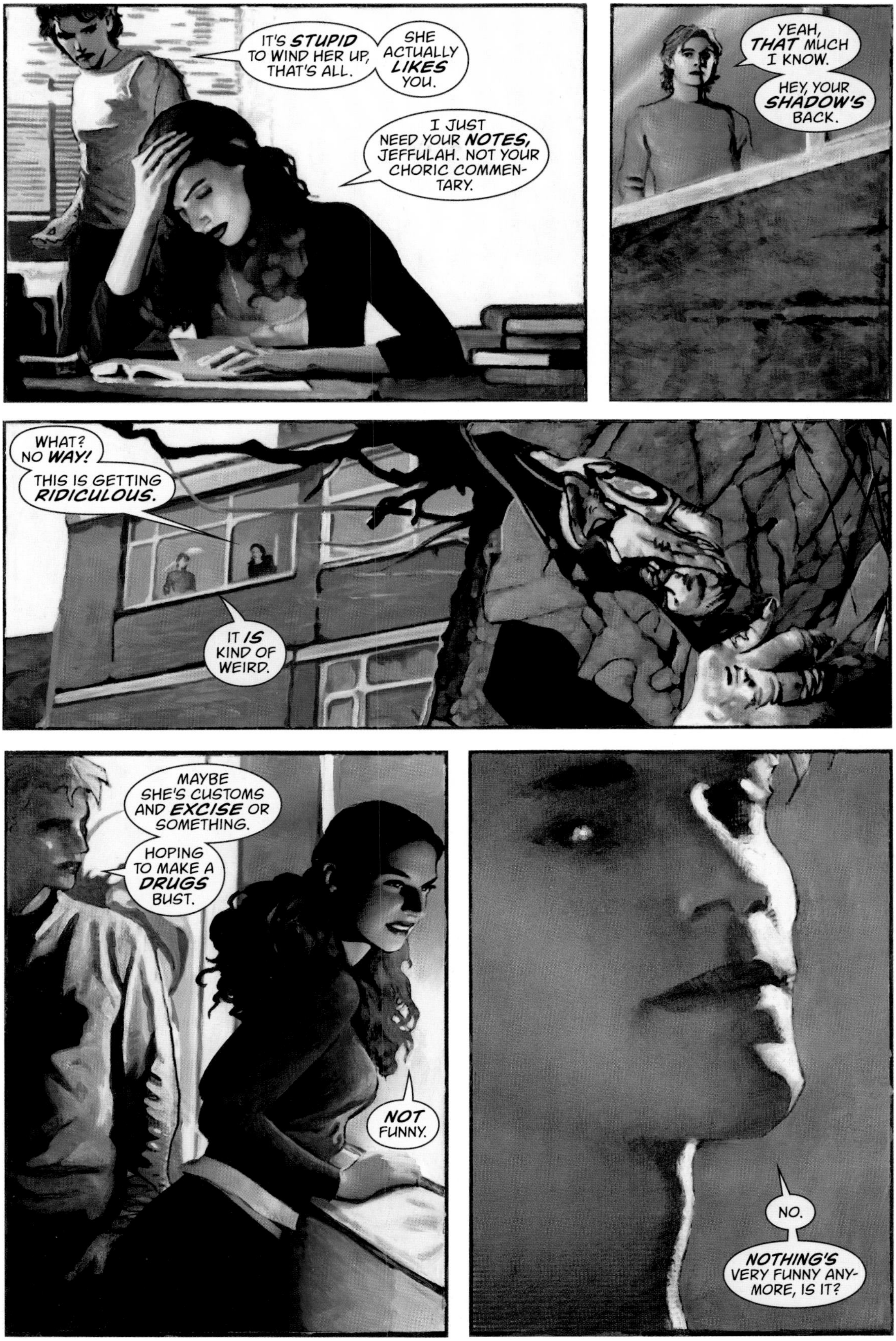
IT'S STUPID TO WIND HER UP, THAT'S ALL.
SHE ACTUALLY LIKES YOU.
I JUST NEED YOUR NOTES, JEFFULAH. NOT YOUR CHORIC COMMENTARY.
YEAH, THAT MUCH I KNOW.
HEY, YOUR SHADOW'S BACK.
WHAT? NO WAY!
THIS IS GETTING RIDICULOUS.
IT IS KIND OF WEIRD.
MAYBE SHE'S CUSTOMS AND EXCISE OR SOMETHING.
HOPING TO MAKE A DRUGS BUST.
NOT FUNNY.
NO.
NOTHING'S VERY FUNNY ANY-MORE, IS IT?

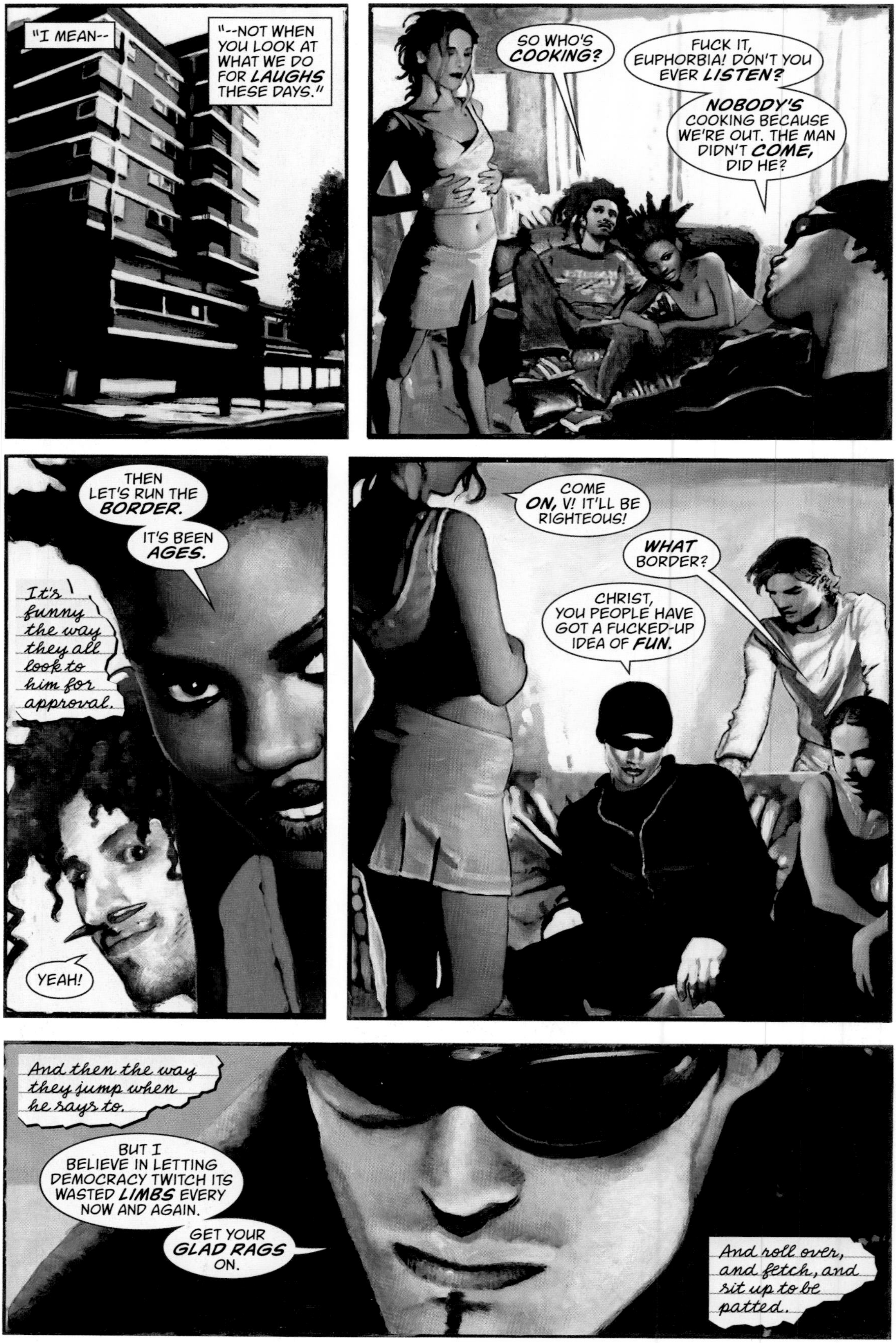
"I MEAN--
"--NOT WHEN YOU LOOK AT WHAT WE DO FOR LAUGHS THESE DAYS."
SO WHO'S COOKING?
FUCK IT, EUPHORBIA! DON'T YOU EVER LISTEN?
NOBODY'S COOKING BECAUSE WE'RE OUT. THE MAN DIDN'T COME, DID HE?
THEN LET'S RUN THE BORDER.
IT'S BEEN AGES.
It's funny the way they all look to him for approval.
YEAH!
COME ON, V! IT'LL BE RIGHTEOUS!
WHAT BORDER?
CHRIST, YOU PEOPLE HAVE GOT A FUCKED-UP IDEA OF FUN.
And then the way they jump when he says to.
BUT I BELIEVE IN LETTING DEMOCRACY TWITCH ITS WASTED LIMBS EVERY NOW AND AGAIN.
GET YOUR GLAD RAGS ON.
And roll over, and fetch, and sit up to be patted.

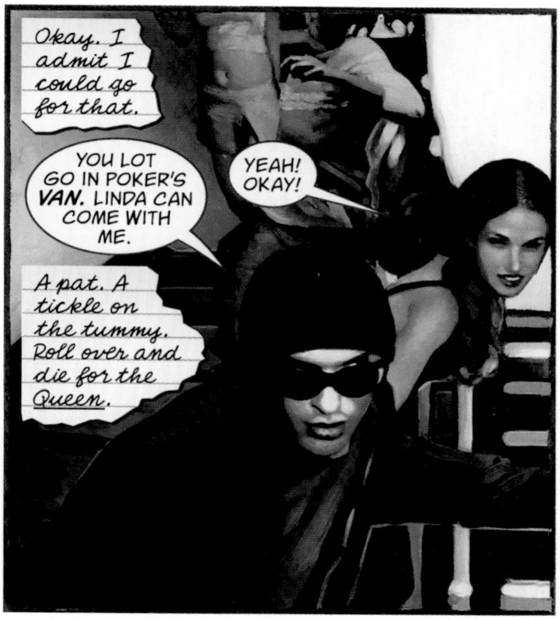
Okay. I admit I could go for that.
YOU LOT GO IN POKER'S VAN. LINDA CAN COME WITH ME.
YEAH! OKAY!
A pat. A tickle on the tummy. Roll over and die for the Queen.

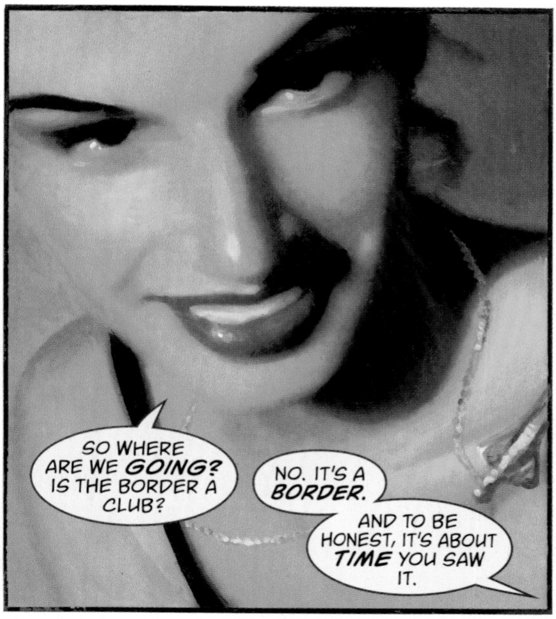
SO WHERE ARE WE GOING? IS THE BORDER A CLUB?
NO. IT'S A BORDER.
AND TO BE HONEST, IT'S ABOUT TIME YOU SAW IT.

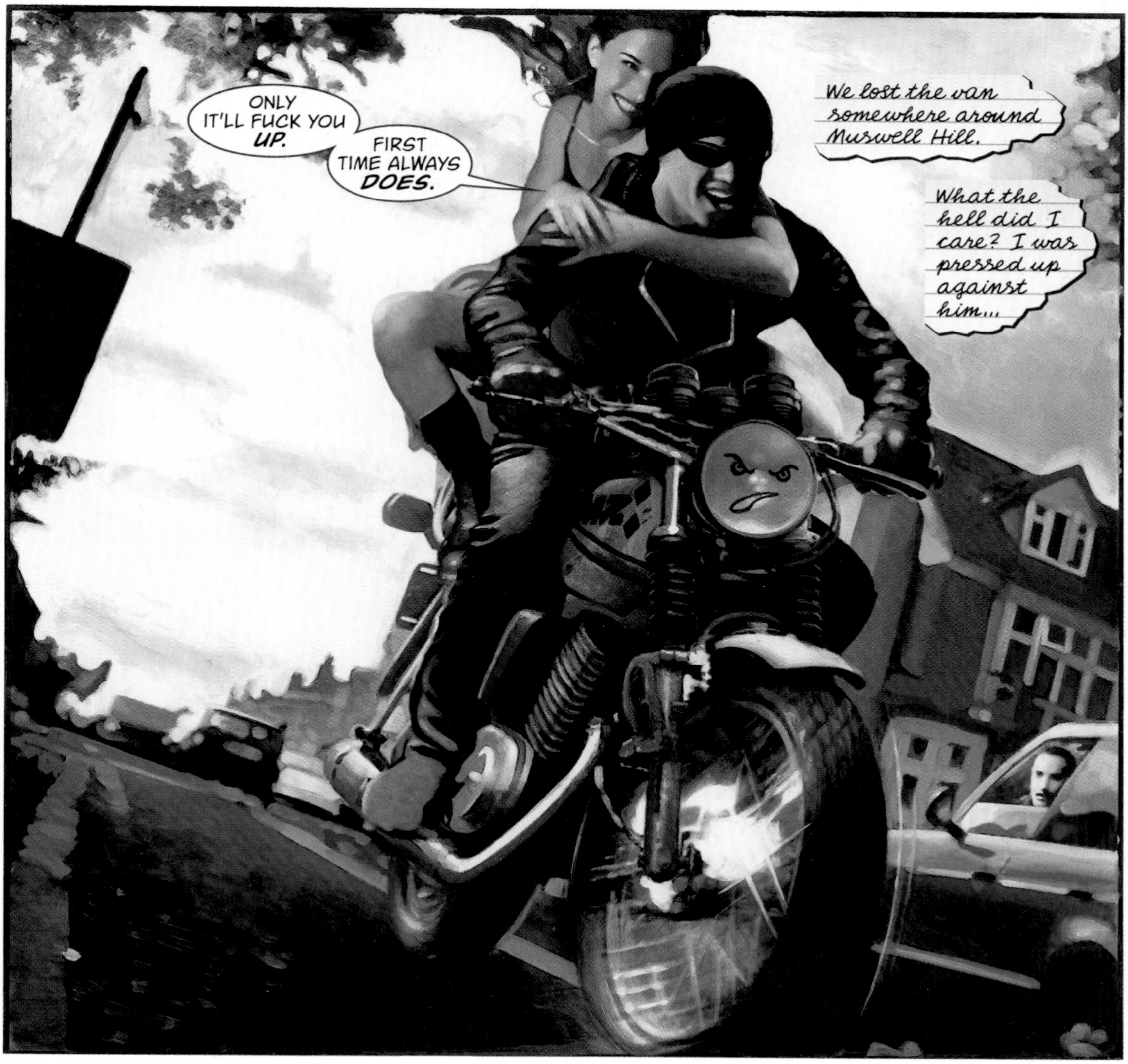
ONLY IT'LL FUCK YOU UP.
FIRST TIME ALWAYS DOES.
We lost the van somewhere around Muswell Hill.
What the hell did I care? I was pressed up against him...

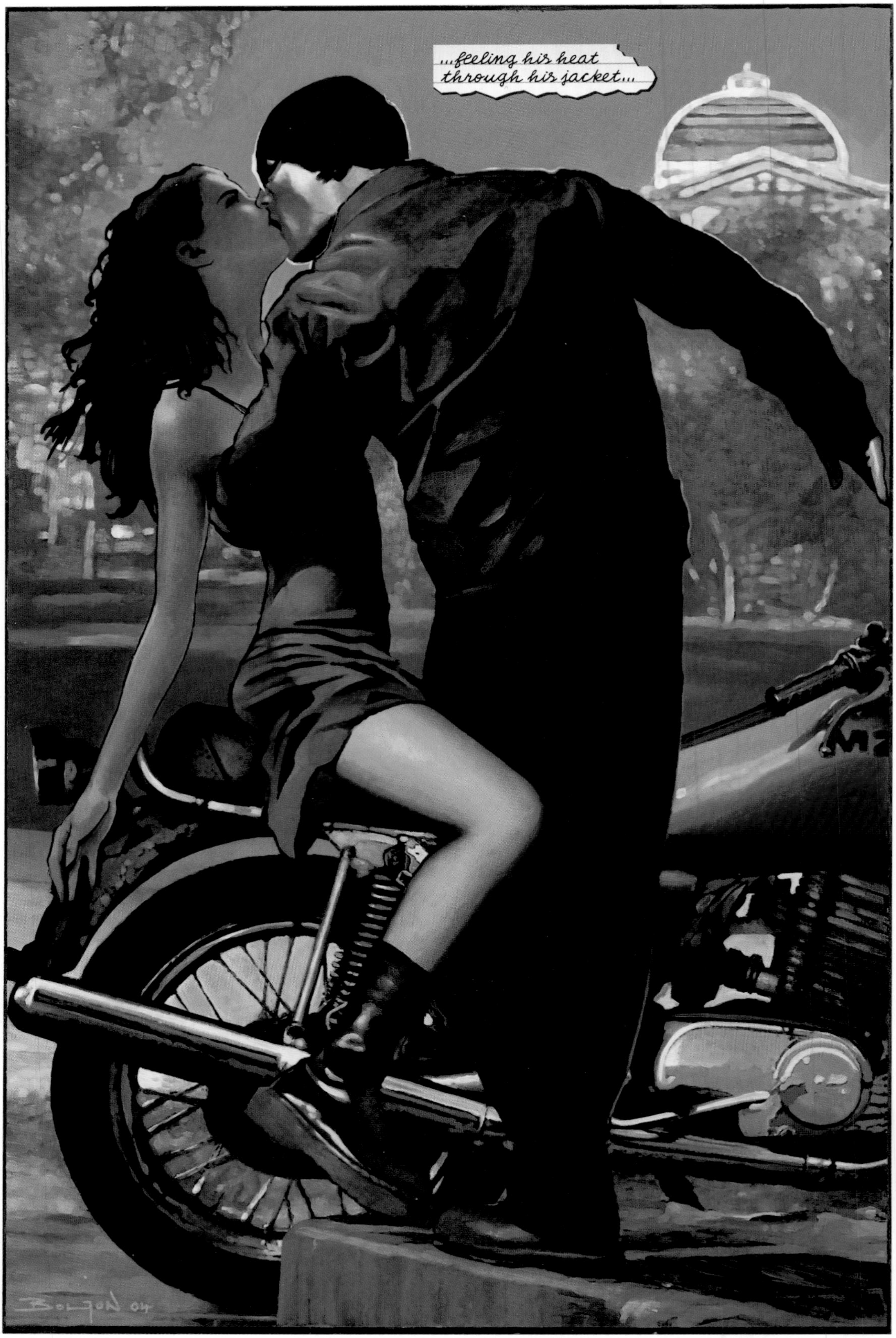
...feeling his heat through his jacket...
BOLTON 04

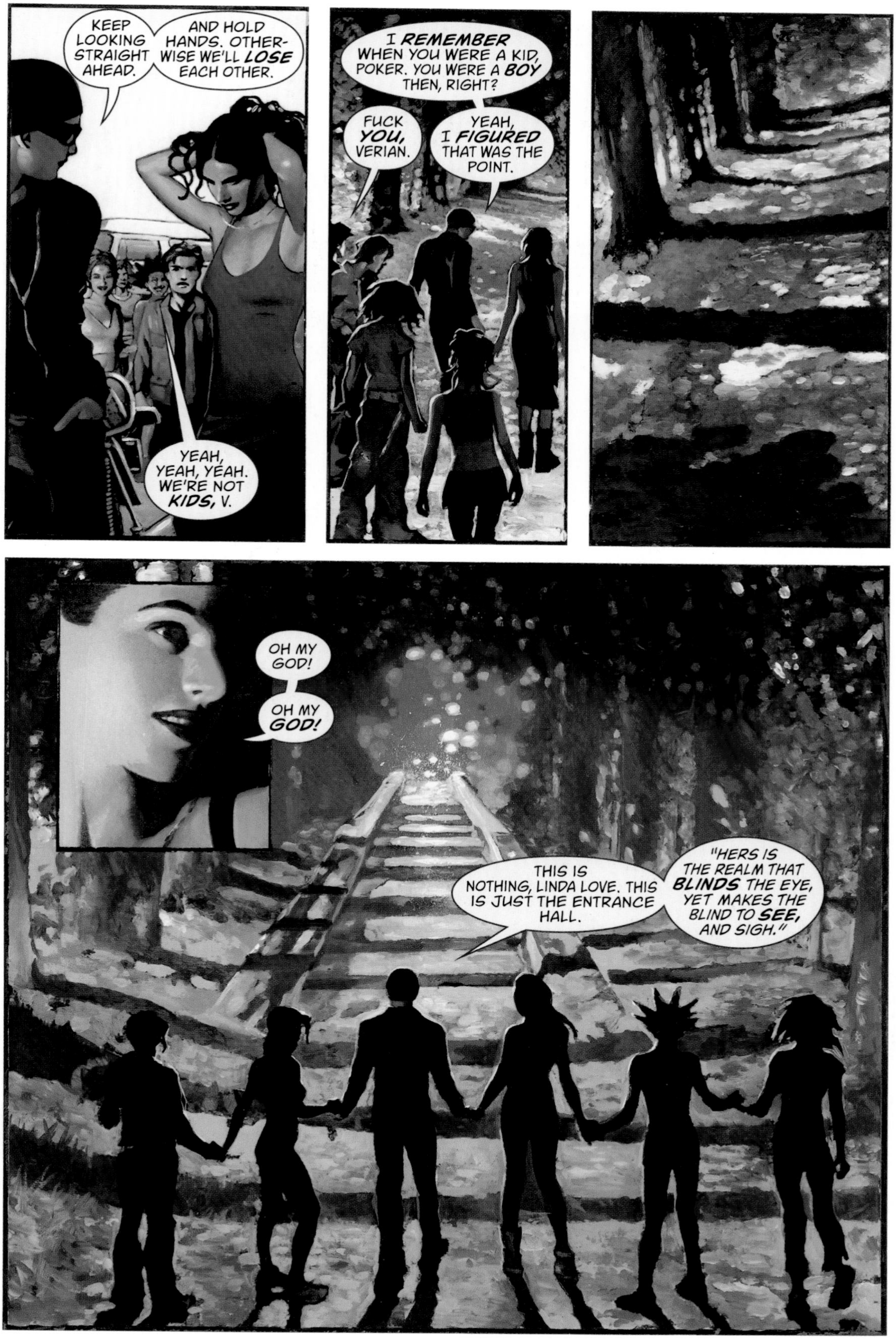
KEEP LOOKING STRAIGHT AHEAD.
AND HOLD HANDS. OTHER-WISE WE'LL **LOSE** EACH OTHER.
YEAH, YEAH, YEAH. WE'RE NOT **KIDS,** V.
I **REMEMBER** WHEN YOU WERE A KID, POKER. YOU WERE A **BOY** THEN, RIGHT?
FUCK **YOU,** VERIAN.
YEAH, I **FIGURED** THAT WAS THE POINT.
OH MY GOD!
OH MY **GOD!**
THIS IS NOTHING, LINDA LOVE. THIS IS JUST THE ENTRANCE HALL.
"HERS IS THE REALM THAT **BLINDS** THE EYE, YET MAKES THE BLIND TO **SEE,** AND SIGH."

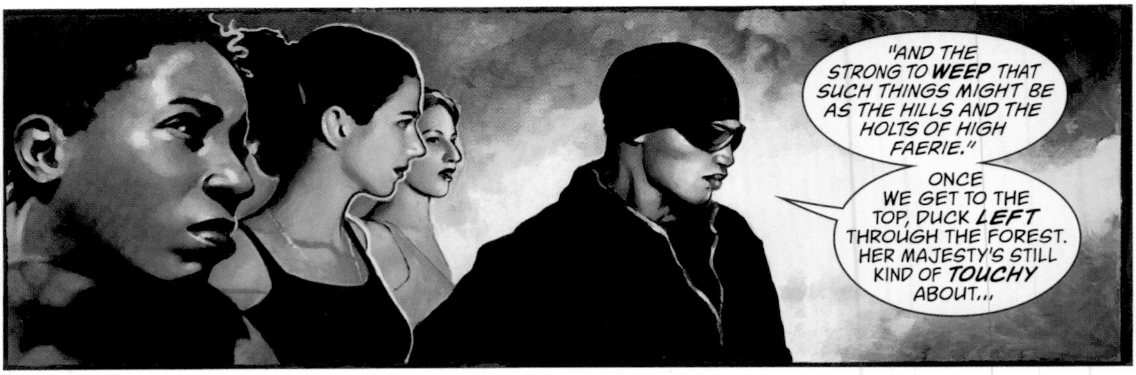
"AND THE STRONG TO WEEP THAT SUCH THINGS MIGHT BE AS THE HILLS AND THE HOLTS OF HIGH FAERIE."
ONCE WE GET TO THE TOP, DUCK LEFT THROUGH THE FOREST. HER MAJESTY'S STILL KIND OF TOUCHY ABOUT...

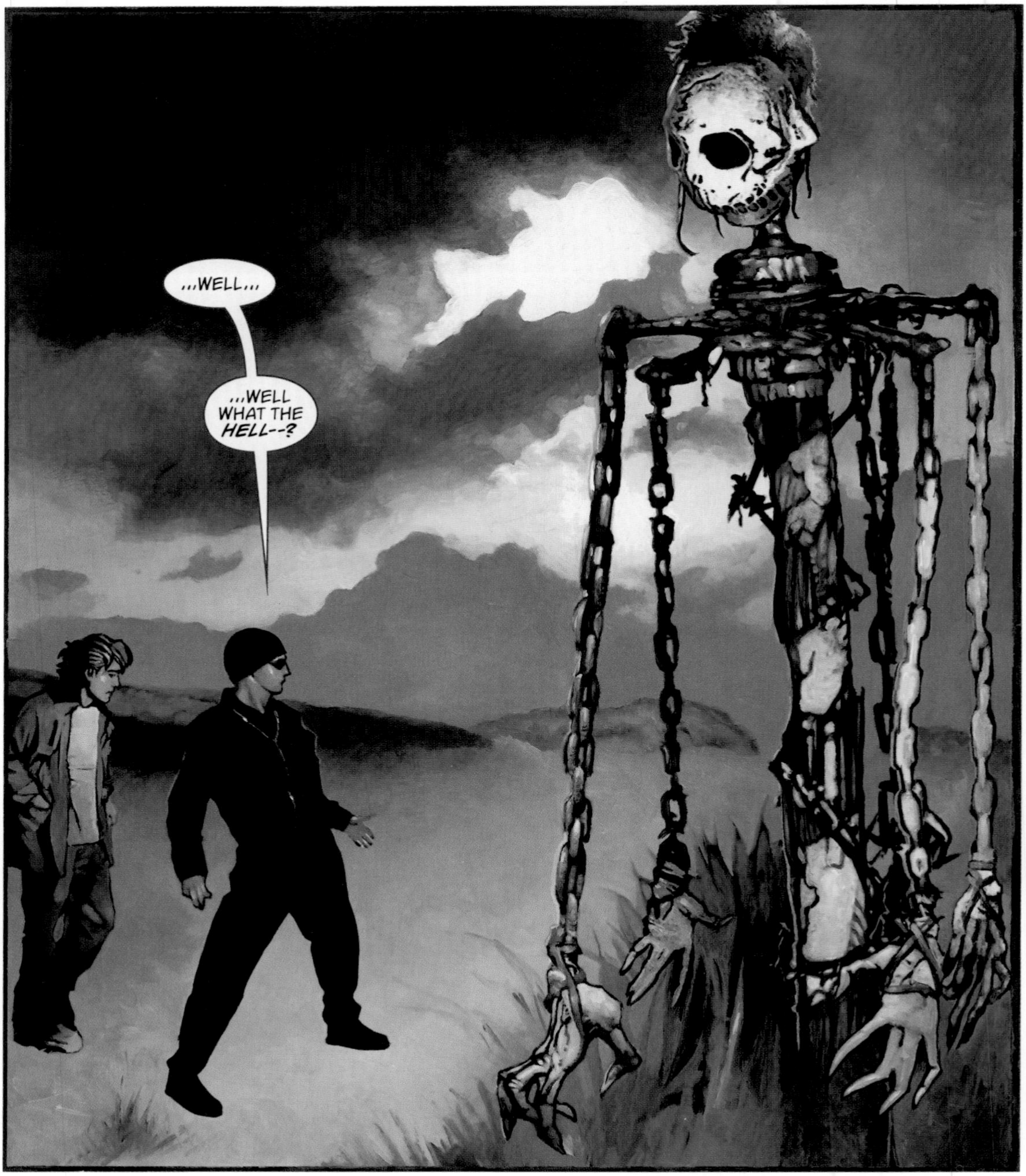
...WELL...
...WELL WHAT THE HELL--?

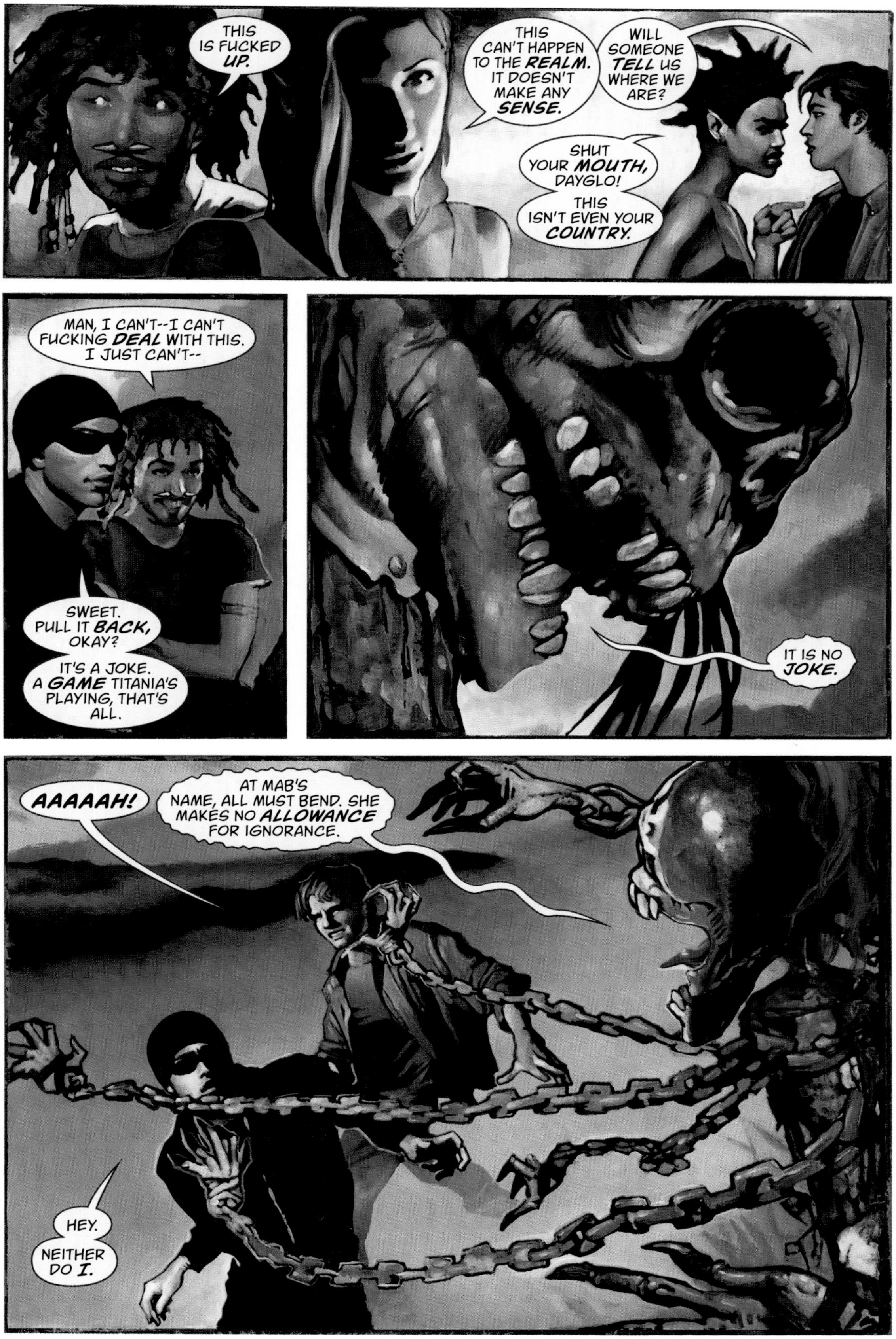
THIS IS FUCKED UP.
THIS CAN'T HAPPEN TO THE REALM. IT DOESN'T MAKE ANY SENSE.
WILL SOMEONE TELL US WHERE WE ARE?
SHUT YOUR MOUTH, DAYGLO!
THIS ISN'T EVEN YOUR COUNTRY.
MAN, I CAN'T--I CAN'T FUCKING DEAL WITH THIS. I JUST CAN'T--
SWEET. PULL IT BACK, OKAY?
IT'S A JOKE. A GAME TITANIA'S PLAYING, THAT'S ALL.
IT IS NO JOKE.
AAAAAH!
AT MAB'S NAME, ALL MUST BEND. SHE MAKES NO ALLOWANCE FOR IGNORANCE.
HEY.
NEITHER DO I.

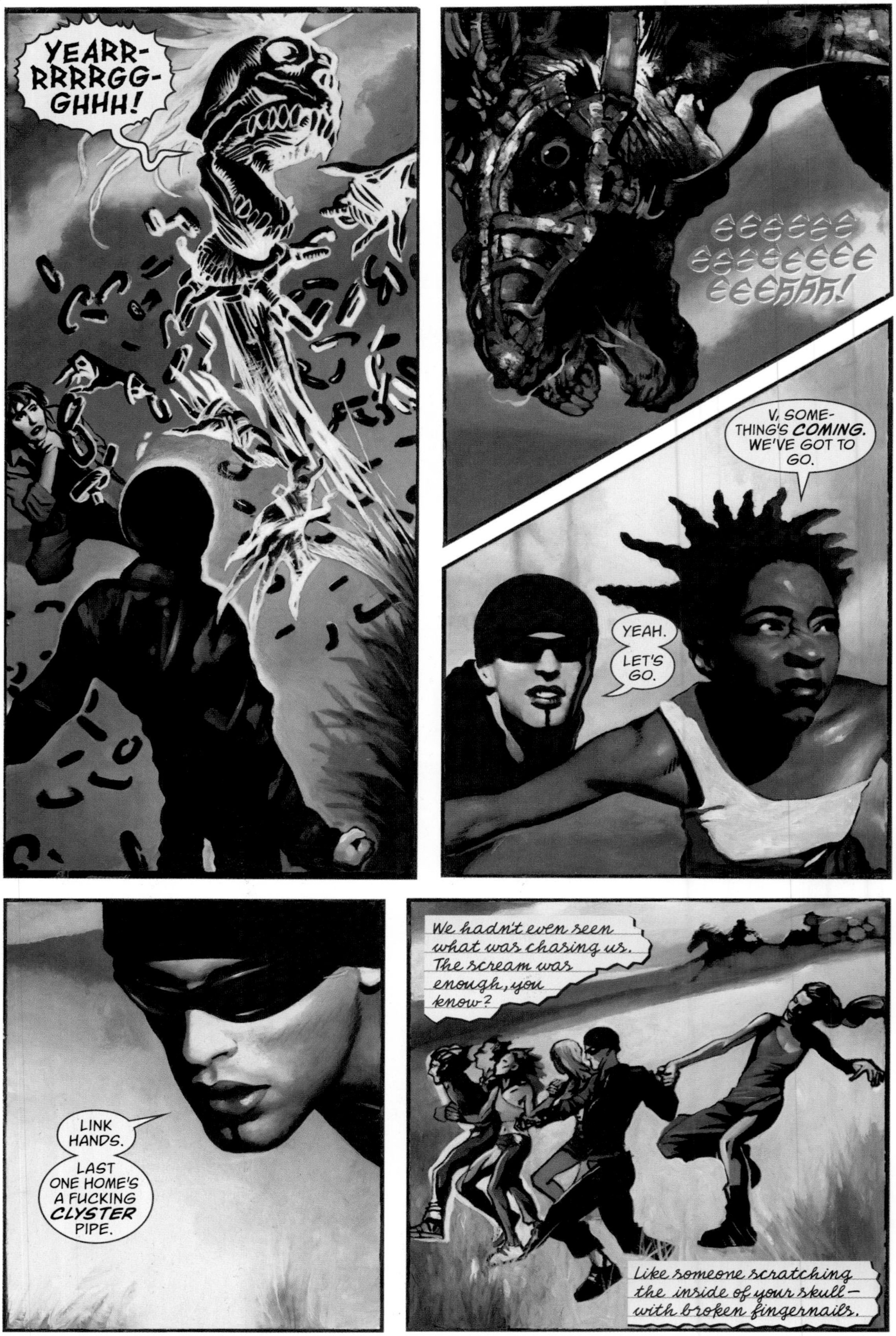
YEARR-RRRRGG-GHHH!
EEEEEE EEEEEEEE EEEEHH!
V, SOME-THING'S **COMING.** WE'VE GOT TO GO.
YEAH.
LET'S GO.
LINK HANDS.
LAST ONE HOME'S A FUCKING **CLYSTER** PIPE.
We hadn't even seen what was chasing us. The scream was enough, you know?
Like someone scratching the inside of your skull— with broken fingernails.

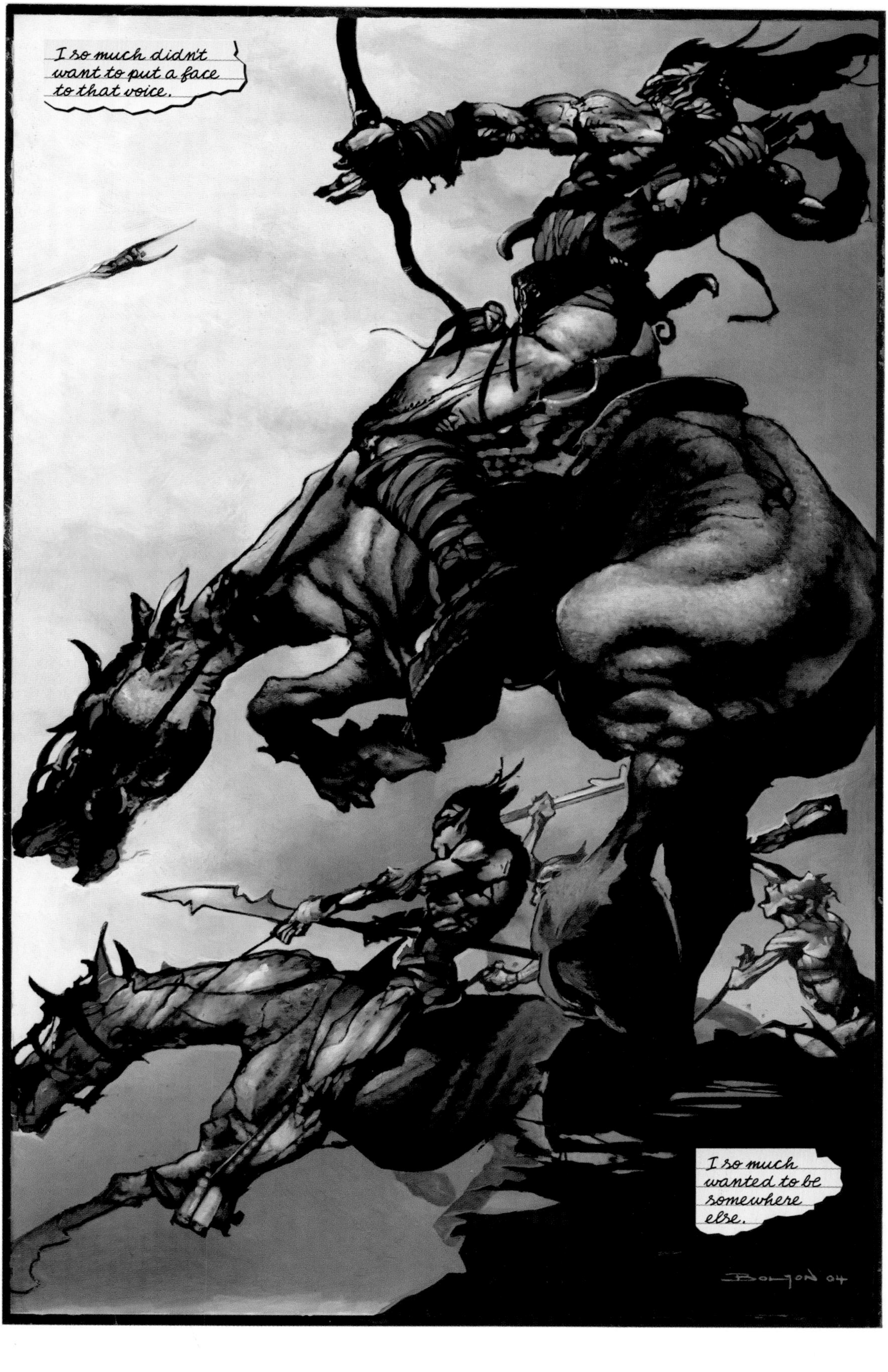
I so much didn't want to put a face to that voice.
I so much wanted to be somewhere else.
BOLTON 04

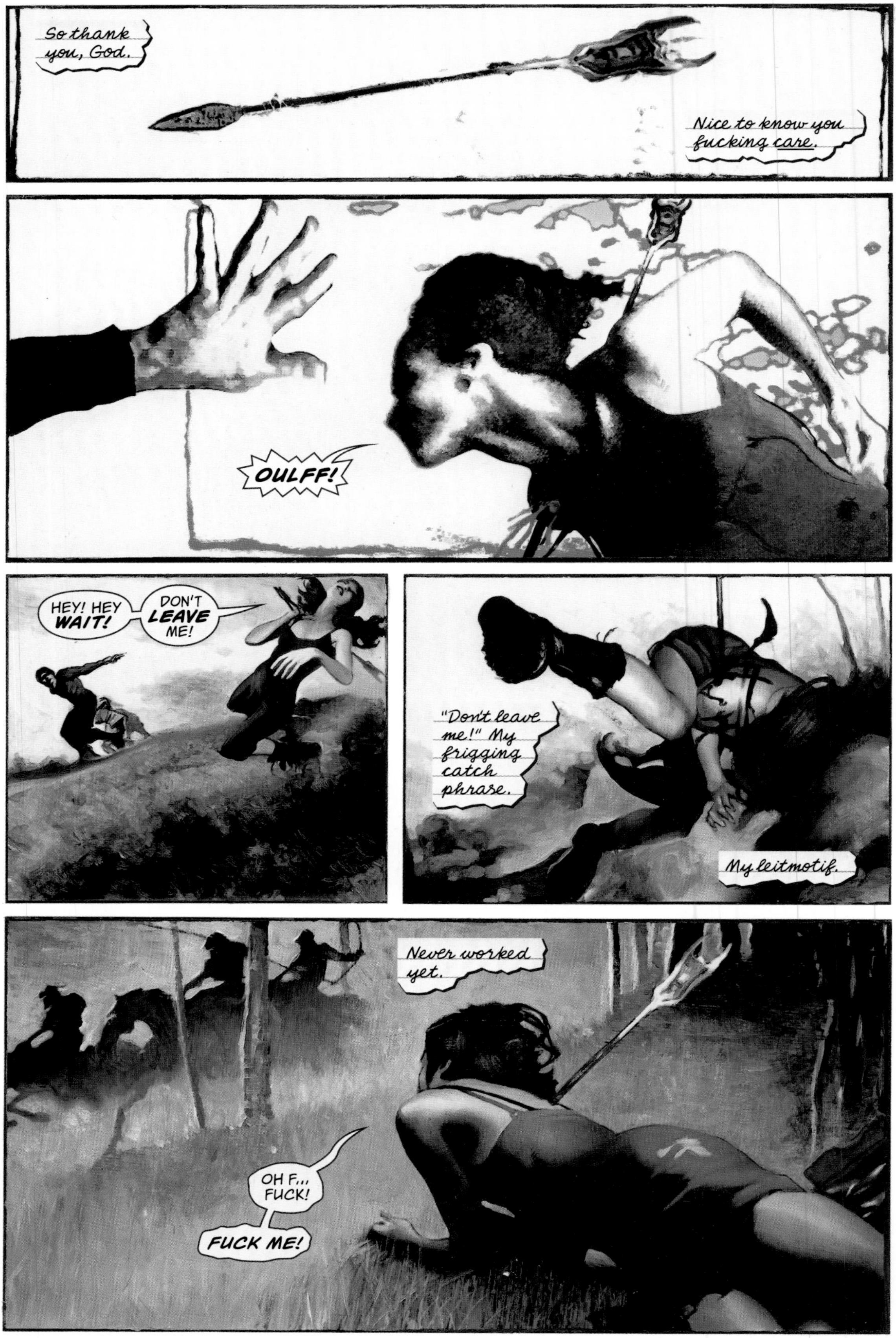
So thank you, God.
Nice to know you fucking care.
OULFF!
HEY! HEY WAIT!
DON'T LEAVE ME!
"Don't leave me!" My frigging catch phrase.
My leitmotif.
Never worked yet.
OH F... FUCK!
FUCK ME!

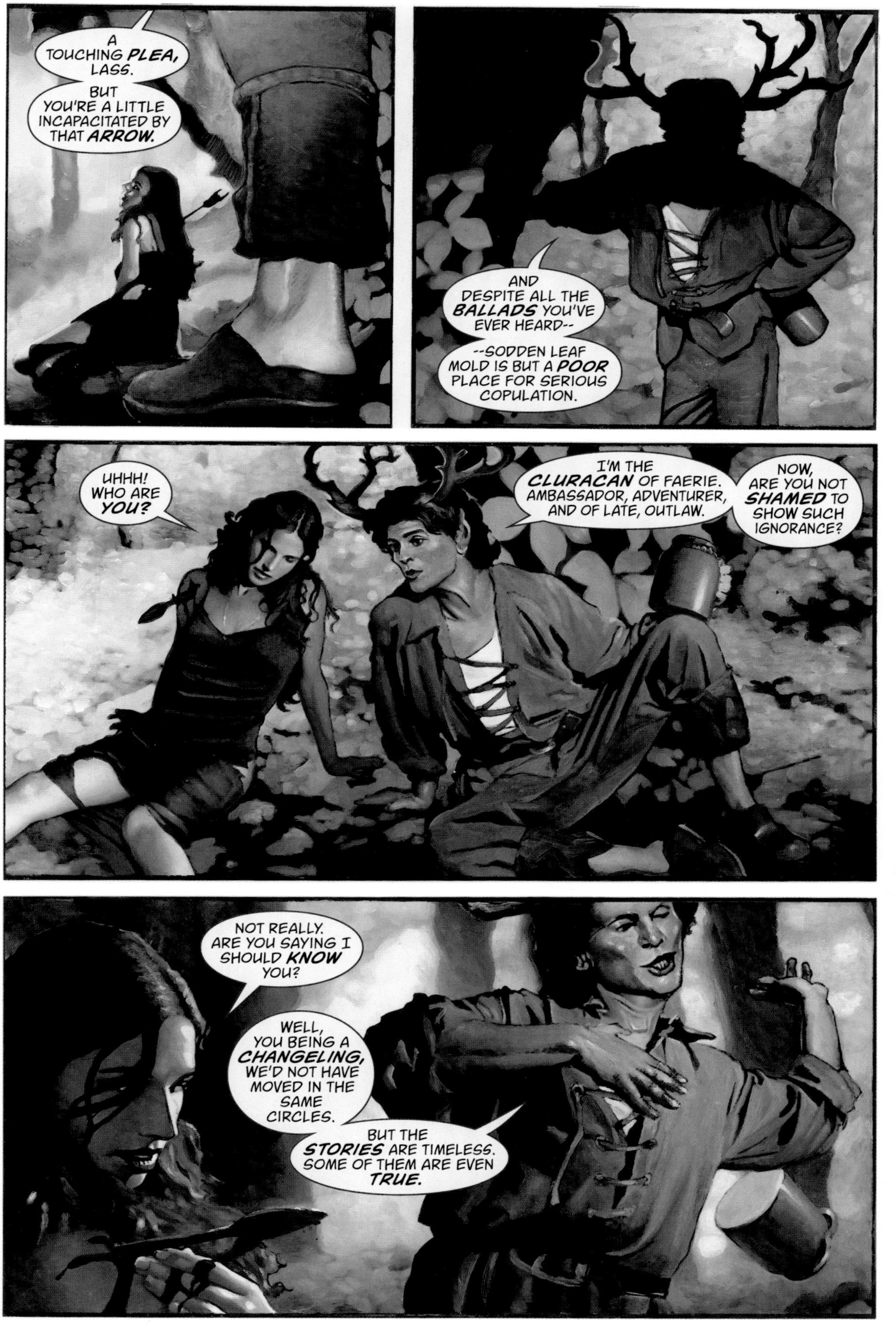
A TOUCHING PLEA, LASS.
BUT YOU'RE A LITTLE INCAPACITATED BY THAT ARROW.
AND DESPITE ALL THE BALLADS YOU'VE EVER HEARD--
--SODDEN LEAF MOLD IS BUT A POOR PLACE FOR SERIOUS COPULATION.
UHHH! WHO ARE YOU?
I'M THE CLURACAN OF FAERIE. AMBASSADOR, ADVENTURER, AND OF LATE, OUTLAW.
NOW, ARE YOU NOT SHAMED TO SHOW SUCH IGNORANCE?
NOT REALLY. ARE YOU SAYING I SHOULD KNOW YOU?
WELL, YOU BEING A CHANGELING, WE'D NOT HAVE MOVED IN THE SAME CIRCLES.
BUT THE STORIES ARE TIMELESS. SOME OF THEM ARE EVEN TRUE.

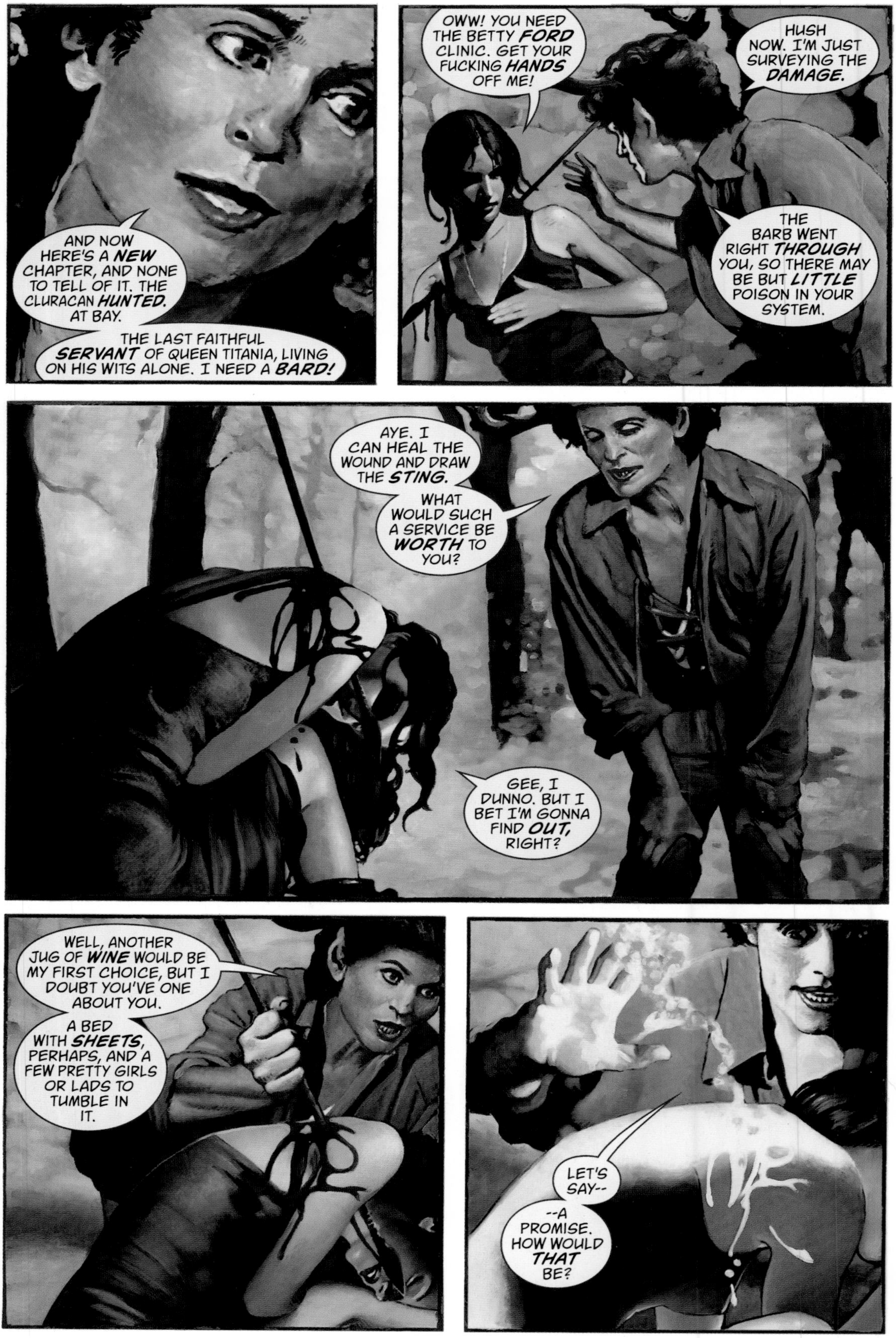
AND NOW HERE'S A NEW CHAPTER, AND NONE TO TELL OF IT. THE CLURACAN HUNTED. AT BAY.
THE LAST FAITHFUL SERVANT OF QUEEN TITANIA, LIVING ON HIS WITS ALONE. I NEED A BARD!
OWW! YOU NEED THE BETTY FORD CLINIC. GET YOUR FUCKING HANDS OFF ME!
HUSH NOW. I'M JUST SURVEYING THE DAMAGE.
THE BARB WENT RIGHT THROUGH YOU, SO THERE MAY BE BUT LITTLE POISON IN YOUR SYSTEM.
AYE. I CAN HEAL THE WOUND AND DRAW THE STING.
WHAT WOULD SUCH A SERVICE BE WORTH TO YOU?
GEE, I DUNNO. BUT I BET I'M GONNA FIND OUT, RIGHT?
WELL, ANOTHER JUG OF WINE WOULD BE MY FIRST CHOICE, BUT I DOUBT YOU'VE ONE ABOUT YOU.
A BED WITH SHEETS, PERHAPS, AND A FEW PRETTY GIRLS OR LADS TO TUMBLE IN IT.
LET'S SAY--
--A PROMISE. HOW WOULD THAT BE?

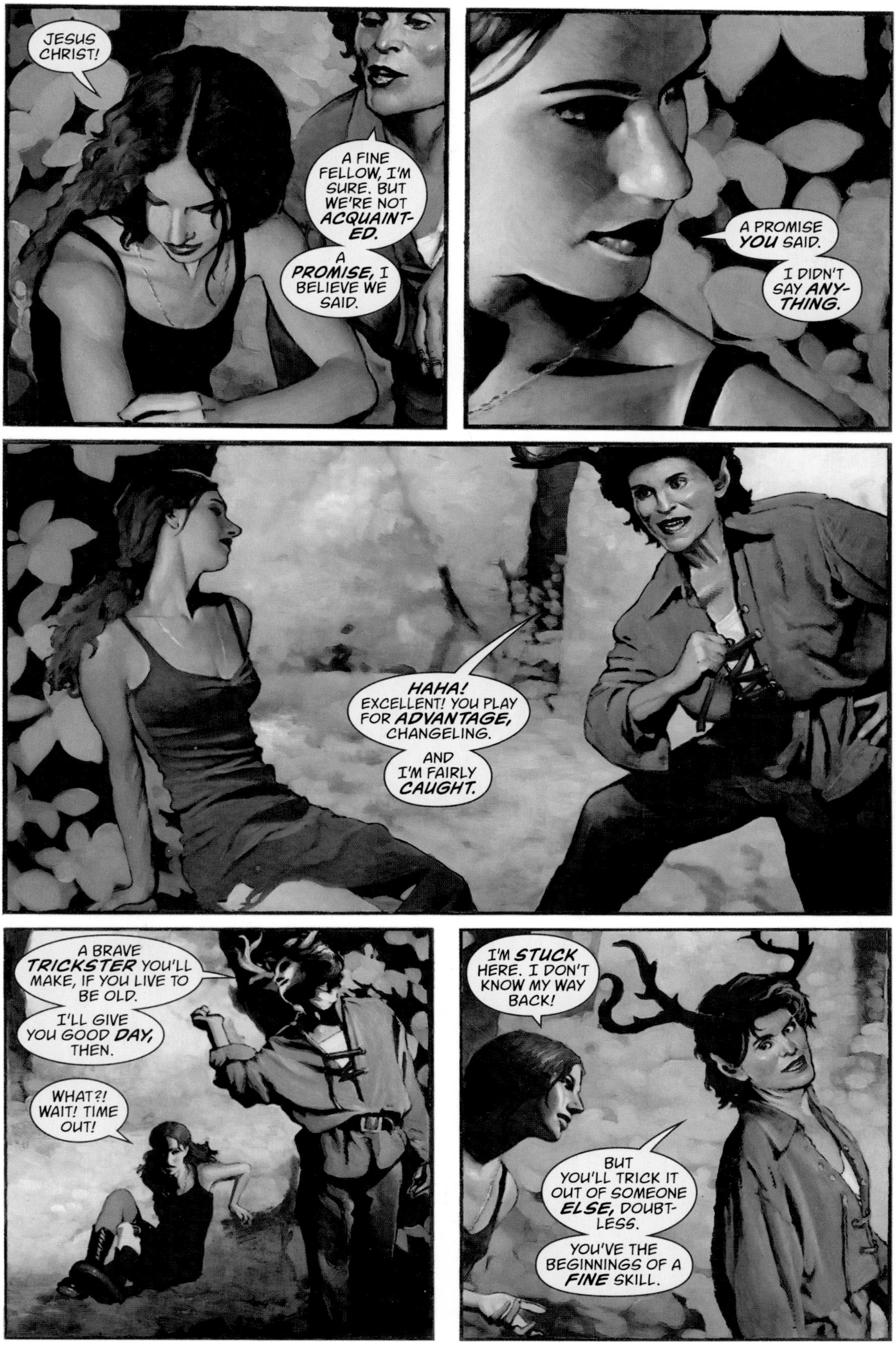
JESUS CHRIST!
A FINE FELLOW, I'M SURE. BUT WE'RE NOT ACQUAINTED.
A PROMISE, I BELIEVE WE SAID.
A PROMISE YOU SAID.
I DIDN'T SAY ANYTHING.
HAHA! EXCELLENT! YOU PLAY FOR ADVANTAGE, CHANGELING.
AND I'M FAIRLY CAUGHT.
A BRAVE TRICKSTER YOU'LL MAKE, IF YOU LIVE TO BE OLD.
I'LL GIVE YOU GOOD DAY, THEN.
WHAT?! WAIT! TIME OUT!
I'M STUCK HERE. I DON'T KNOW MY WAY BACK!
BUT YOU'LL TRICK IT OUT OF SOMEONE ELSE, DOUBTLESS.
YOU'VE THE BEGINNINGS OF A FINE SKILL.

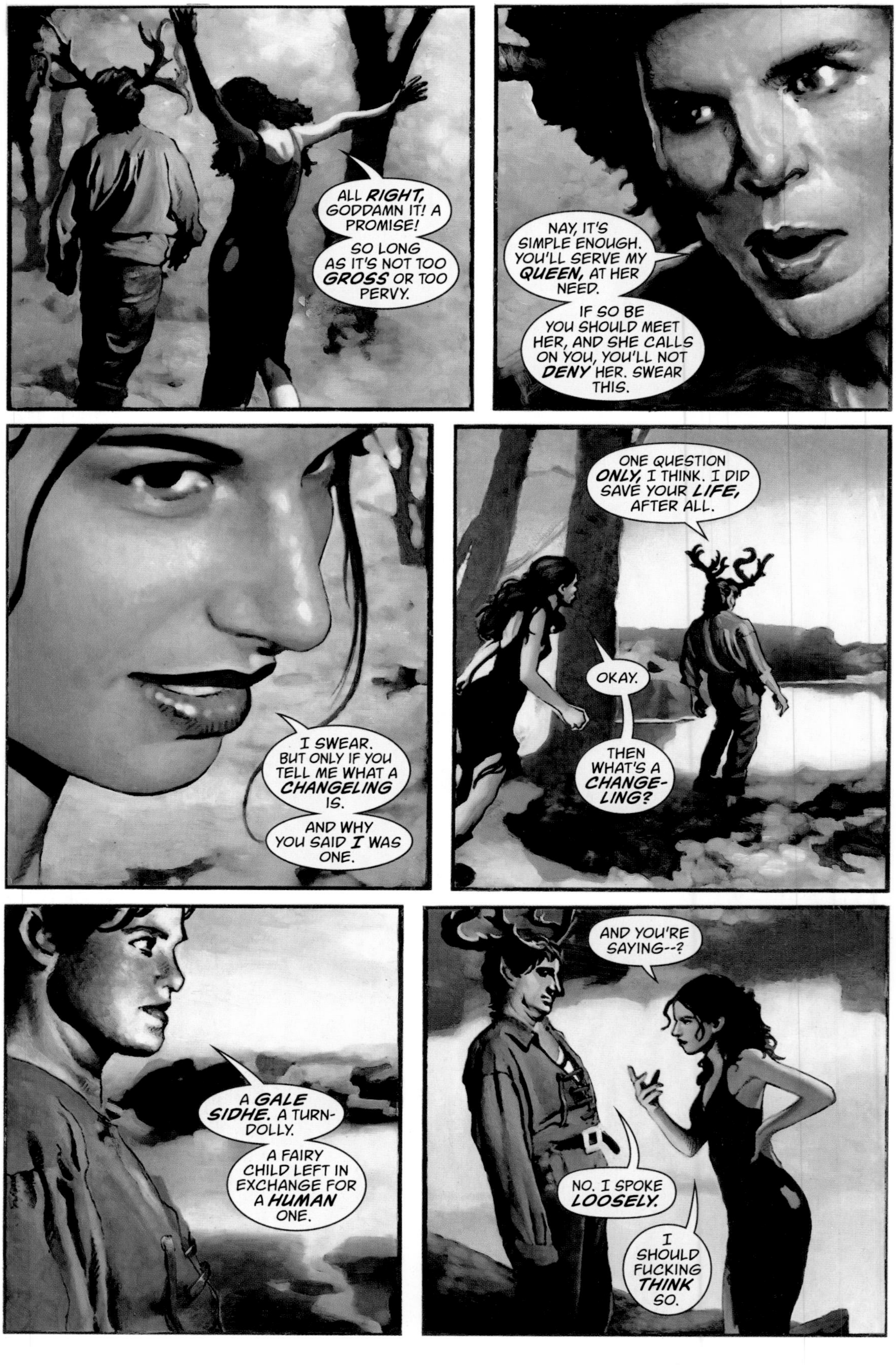

ALL RIGHT, GODDAMN IT! A PROMISE!
SO LONG AS IT'S NOT TOO GROSS OR TOO PERVY.
NAY, IT'S SIMPLE ENOUGH. YOU'LL SERVE MY QUEEN, AT HER NEED.
IF SO BE YOU SHOULD MEET HER, AND SHE CALLS ON YOU, YOU'LL NOT DENY HER. SWEAR THIS.
I SWEAR. BUT ONLY IF YOU TELL ME WHAT A CHANGELING IS.
AND WHY YOU SAID I WAS ONE.
ONE QUESTION ONLY, I THINK. I DID SAVE YOUR LIFE, AFTER ALL.
OKAY.
THEN WHAT'S A CHANGE-LING?
A GALE SIDHE. A TURN-DOLLY.
A FAIRY CHILD LEFT IN EXCHANGE FOR A HUMAN ONE.
AND YOU'RE SAYING--?
NO. I SPOKE LOOSELY.
I SHOULD FUCKING THINK SO.

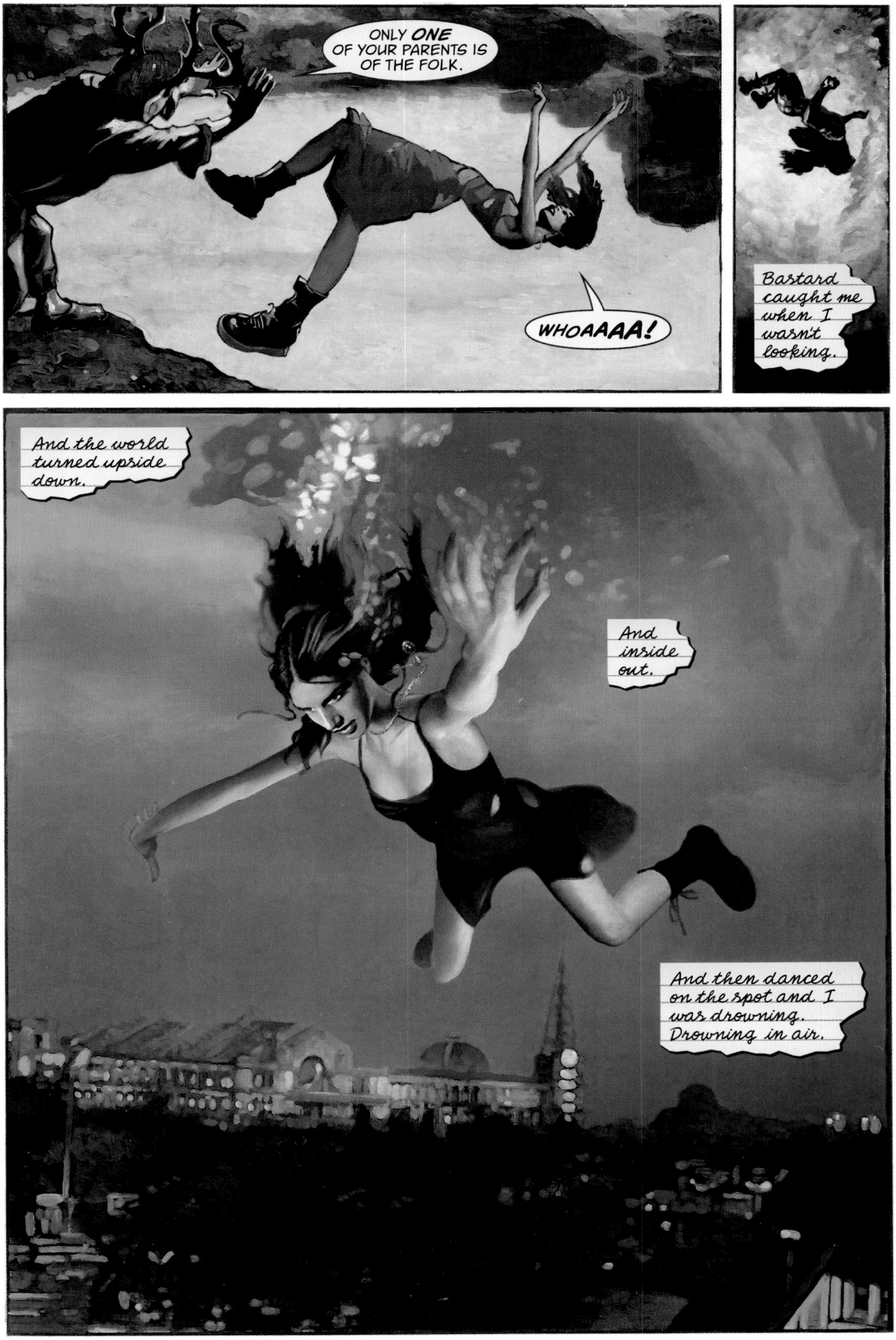
ONLY ONE OF YOUR PARENTS IS OF THE FOLK.
WHOAAAA!
Bastard caught me when I wasn't looking.
And the world turned upside down.
And inside out.
And then danced on the spot and I was drowning. Drowning in air.

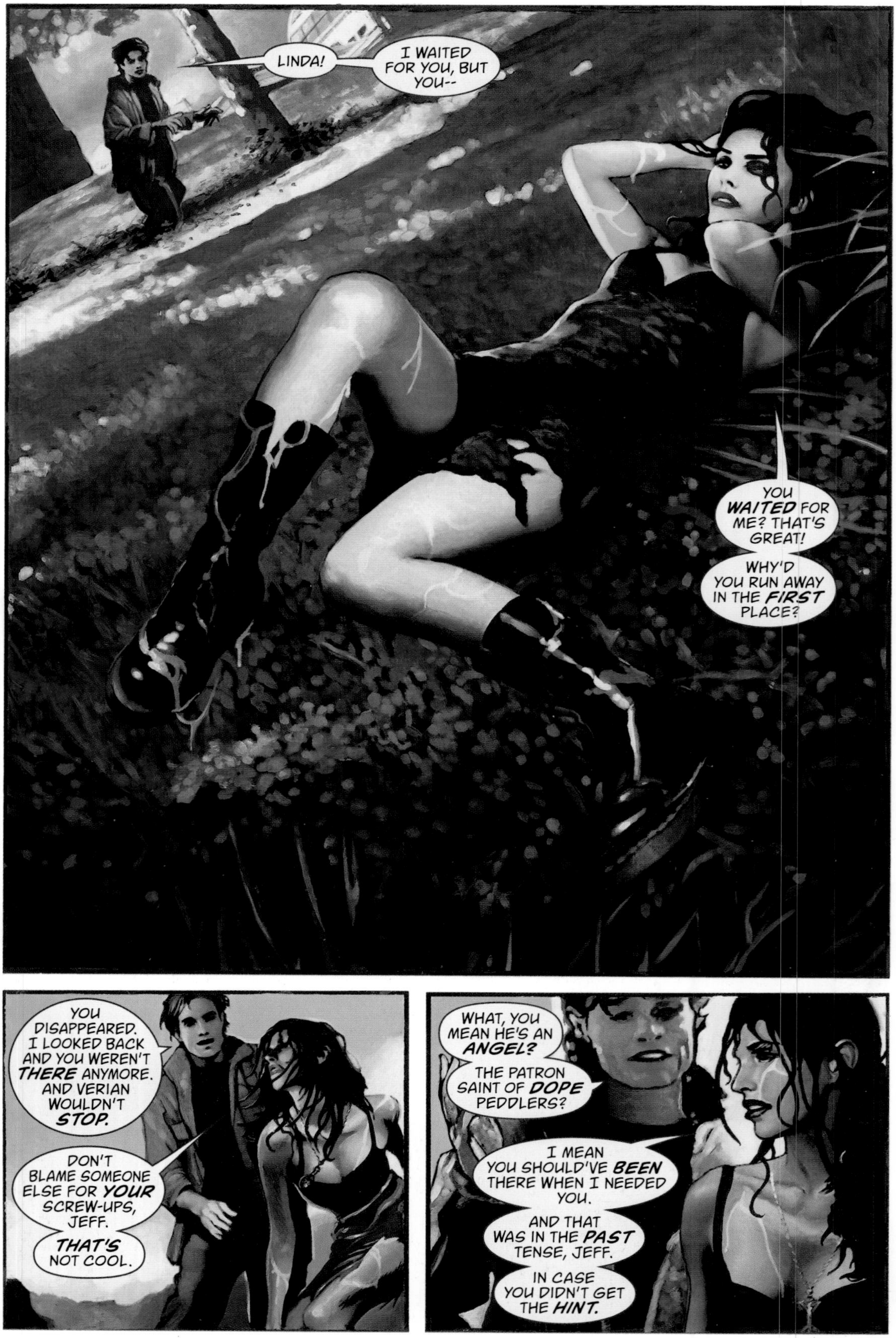
LINDA!
I WAITED FOR YOU, BUT YOU--
YOU WAITED FOR ME? THAT'S GREAT!
WHY'D YOU RUN AWAY IN THE FIRST PLACE?
YOU DISAPPEARED. I LOOKED BACK AND YOU WEREN'T THERE ANYMORE. AND VERIAN WOULDN'T STOP.
DON'T BLAME SOMEONE ELSE FOR YOUR SCREW-UPS, JEFF.
THAT'S NOT COOL.
WHAT, YOU MEAN HE'S AN ANGEL?
THE PATRON SAINT OF DOPE PEDDLERS?
I MEAN YOU SHOULD'VE BEEN THERE WHEN I NEEDED YOU.
AND THAT WAS IN THE PAST TENSE, JEFF.
IN CASE YOU DIDN'T GET THE HINT.

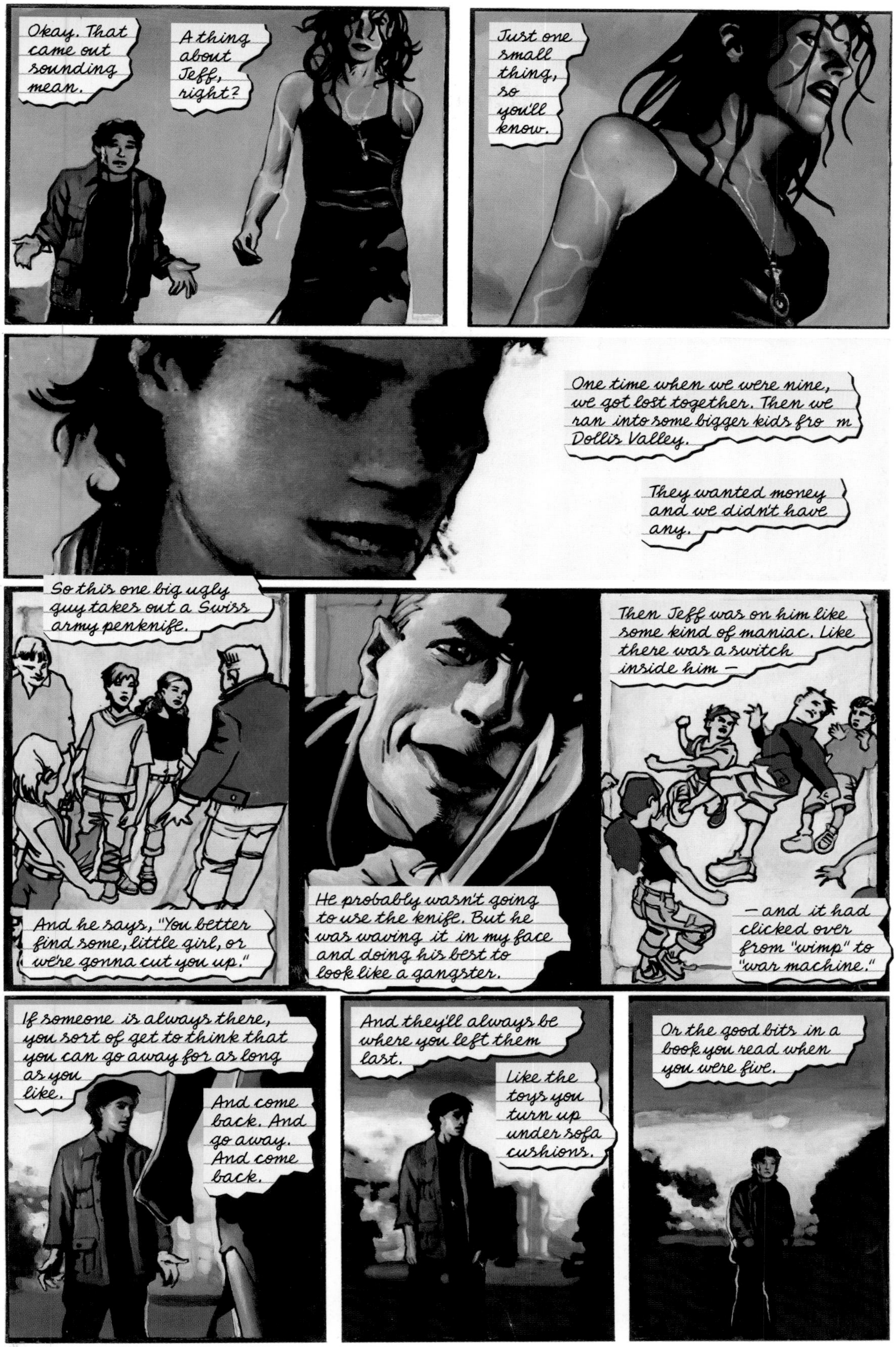
Okay. That came out sounding mean.
A thing about Jeff, right?
Just one small thing, so you'll know.
One time when we were nine, we got lost together. Then we ran into some bigger kids fro m Dollis Valley.
They wanted money and we didn't have any.
So this one big ugly guy takes out a Swiss army penknife.
And he says, "You better find some, little girl, or we're gonna cut you up."
He probably wasn't going to use the knife. But he was waving it in my face and doing his best to look like a gangster.
Then Jeff was on him like some kind of maniac. Like there was a switch inside him —
— and it had clicked over from "wimp" to "war machine."
If someone is always there, you sort of get to think that you can go away for as long as you like.
And come back. And go away. And come back.
And they'll always be where you left them last.
Like the toys you turn up under sofa cushions.
Or the good bits in a book you read when you were five.

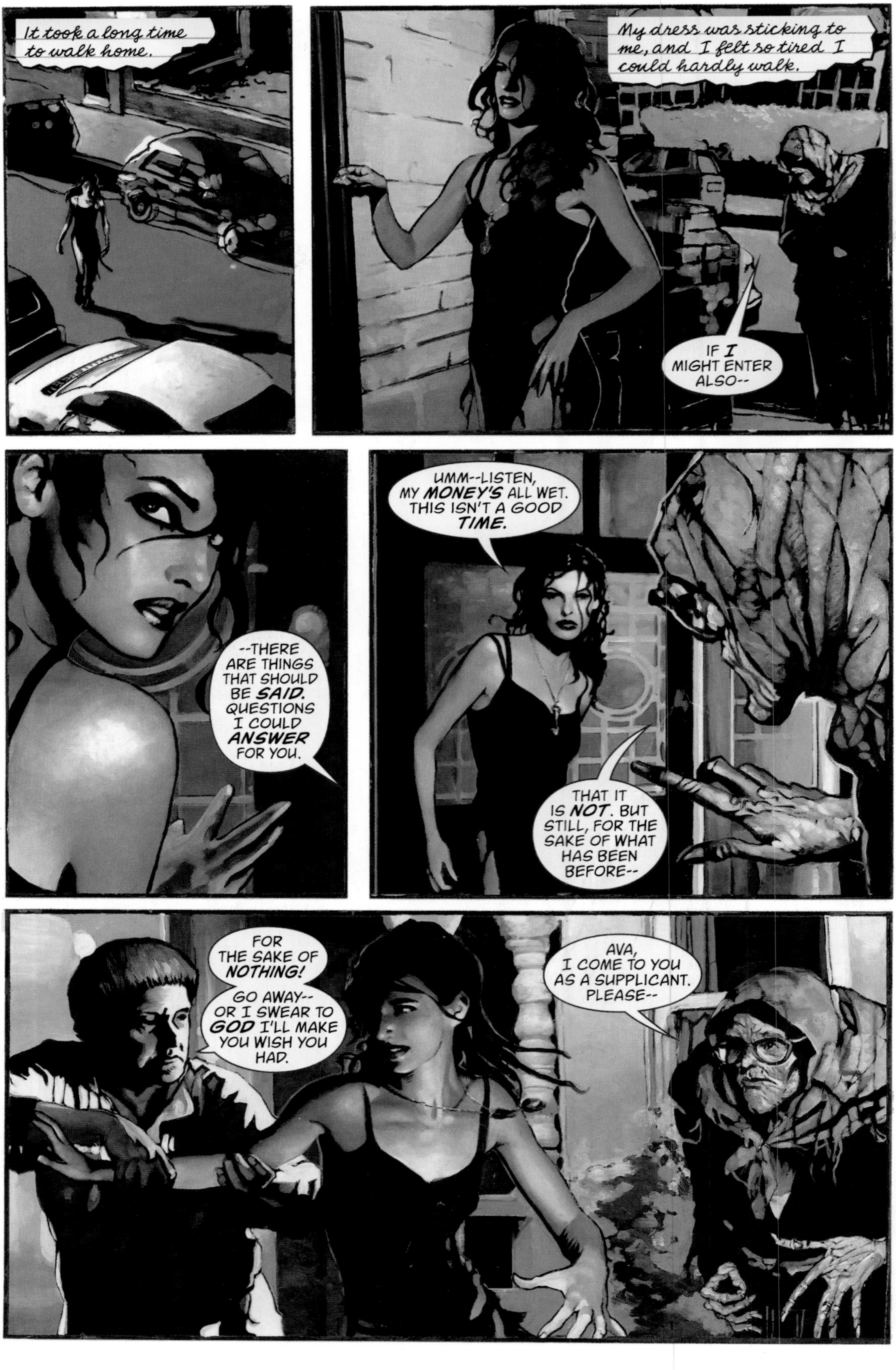

It took a long time to walk home.
My dress was sticking to me, and I felt so tired I could hardly walk.
IF I MIGHT ENTER ALSO--
UMM--LISTEN, MY MONEY'S ALL WET. THIS ISN'T A GOOD TIME.
THAT IT IS NOT. BUT STILL, FOR THE SAKE OF WHAT HAS BEEN BEFORE--
--THERE ARE THINGS THAT SHOULD BE SAID. QUESTIONS I COULD ANSWER FOR YOU.
FOR THE SAKE OF NOTHING!
GO AWAY--OR I SWEAR TO GOD I'LL MAKE YOU WISH YOU HAD.
AVA, I COME TO YOU AS A SUPPLICANT. PLEASE--

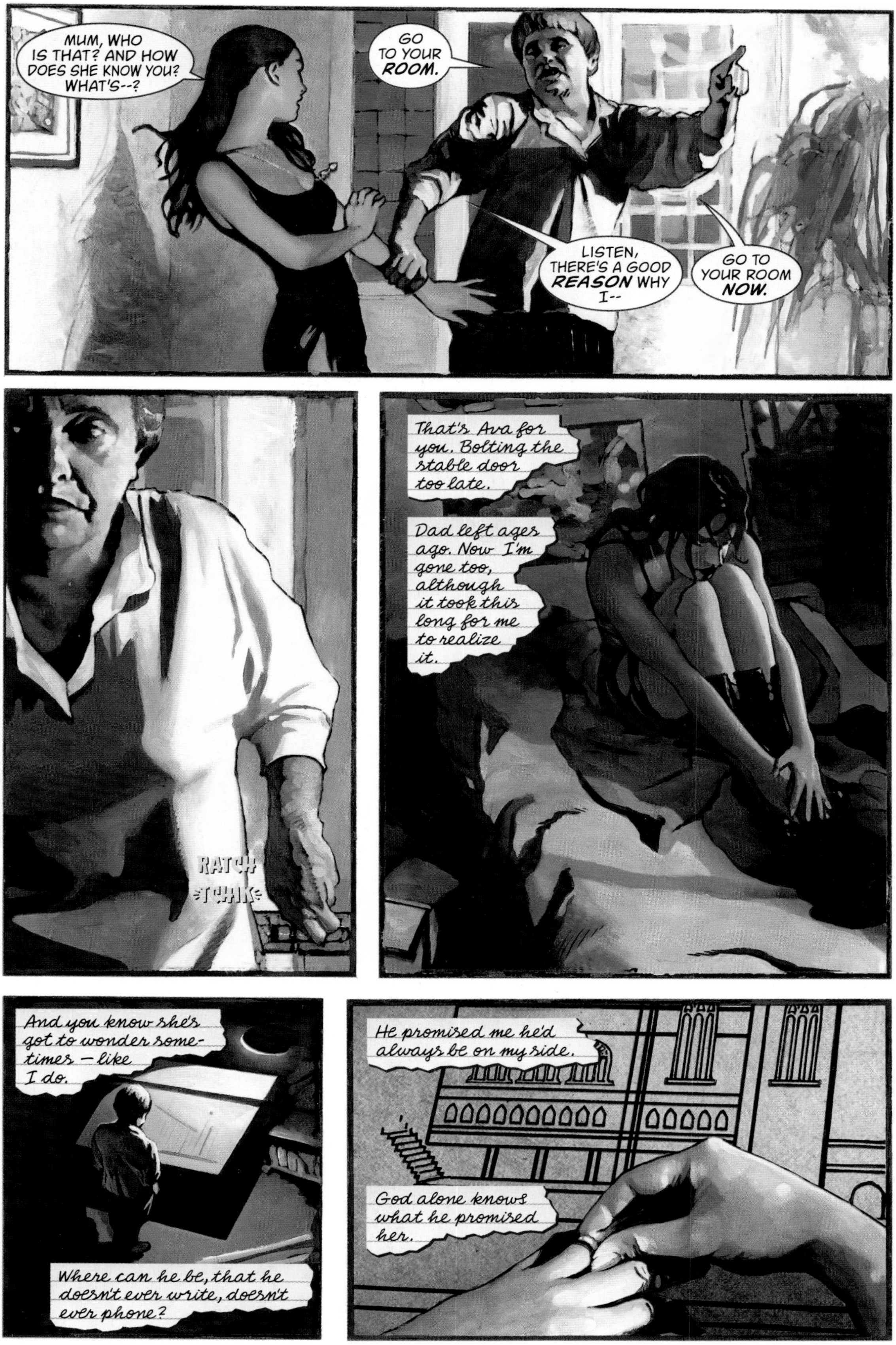
MUM, WHO IS THAT? AND HOW DOES SHE KNOW YOU? WHAT'S--?
GO TO YOUR **ROOM.**
LISTEN, THERE'S A GOOD **REASON** WHY I--
GO TO YOUR ROOM **NOW.**
RATCH
TCHAK
That's Ava for you. Bolting the stable door too late.
Dad left ages ago. Now I'm gone too, although it took this long for me to realize it.
And you know she's got to wonder some-times — like I do.
Where can he be, that he doesn't ever write, doesn't ever phone?
He promised me he'd always be on my side.
God alone knows what he promised her.

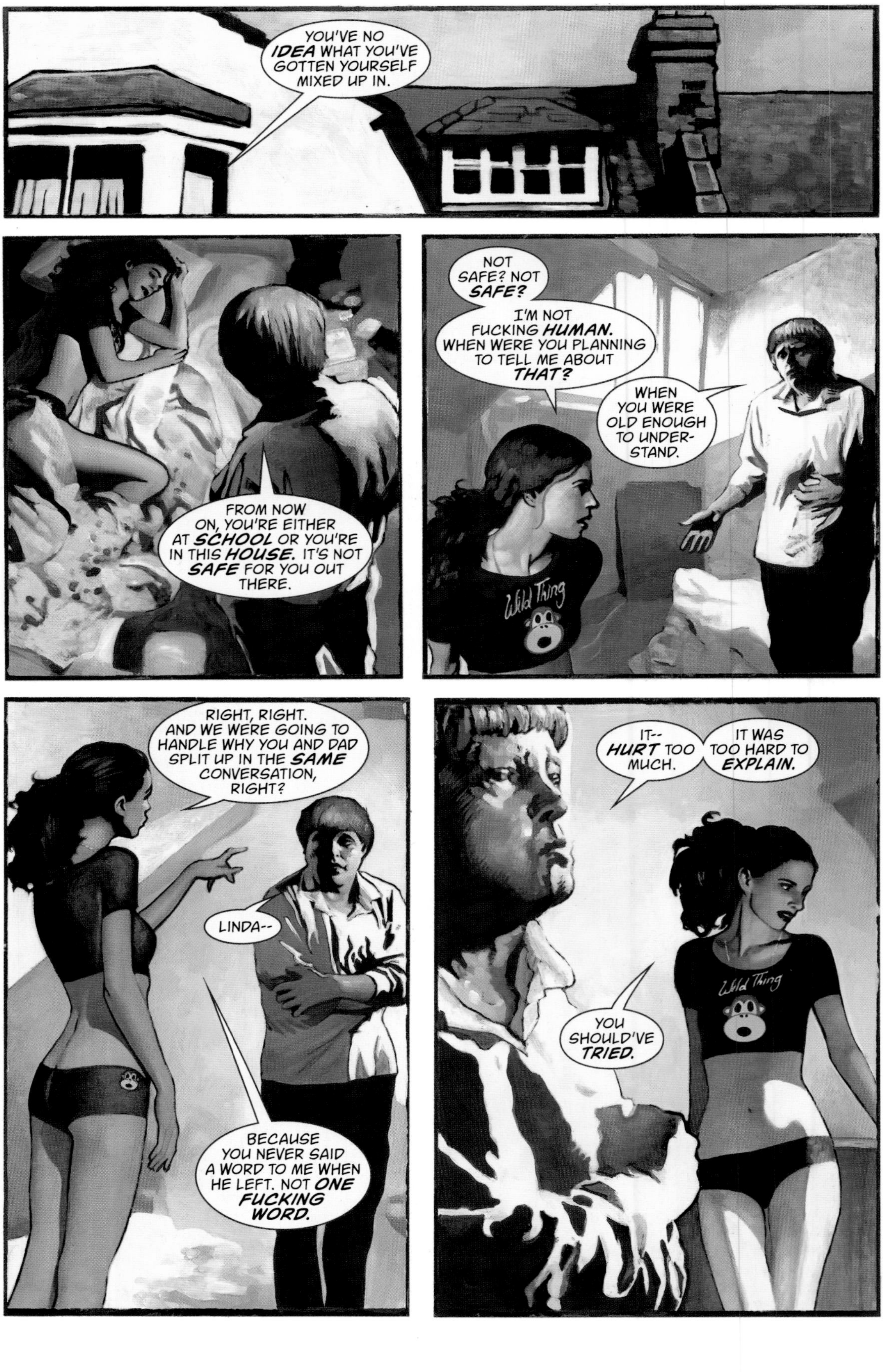
YOU'VE NO IDEA WHAT YOU'VE GOTTEN YOURSELF MIXED UP IN.
FROM NOW ON, YOU'RE EITHER AT SCHOOL OR YOU'RE IN THIS HOUSE. IT'S NOT SAFE FOR YOU OUT THERE.
NOT SAFE? NOT SAFE?
I'M NOT FUCKING HUMAN. WHEN WERE YOU PLANNING TO TELL ME ABOUT THAT?
WHEN YOU WERE OLD ENOUGH TO UNDER-STAND.
Wild Thing
RIGHT, RIGHT. AND WE WERE GOING TO HANDLE WHY YOU AND DAD SPLIT UP IN THE SAME CONVERSATION, RIGHT?
LINDA--
BECAUSE YOU NEVER SAID A WORD TO ME WHEN HE LEFT. NOT ONE FUCKING WORD.
IT--HURT TOO MUCH.
IT WAS TOO HARD TO EXPLAIN.
Wild Thing
YOU SHOULD'VE TRIED.

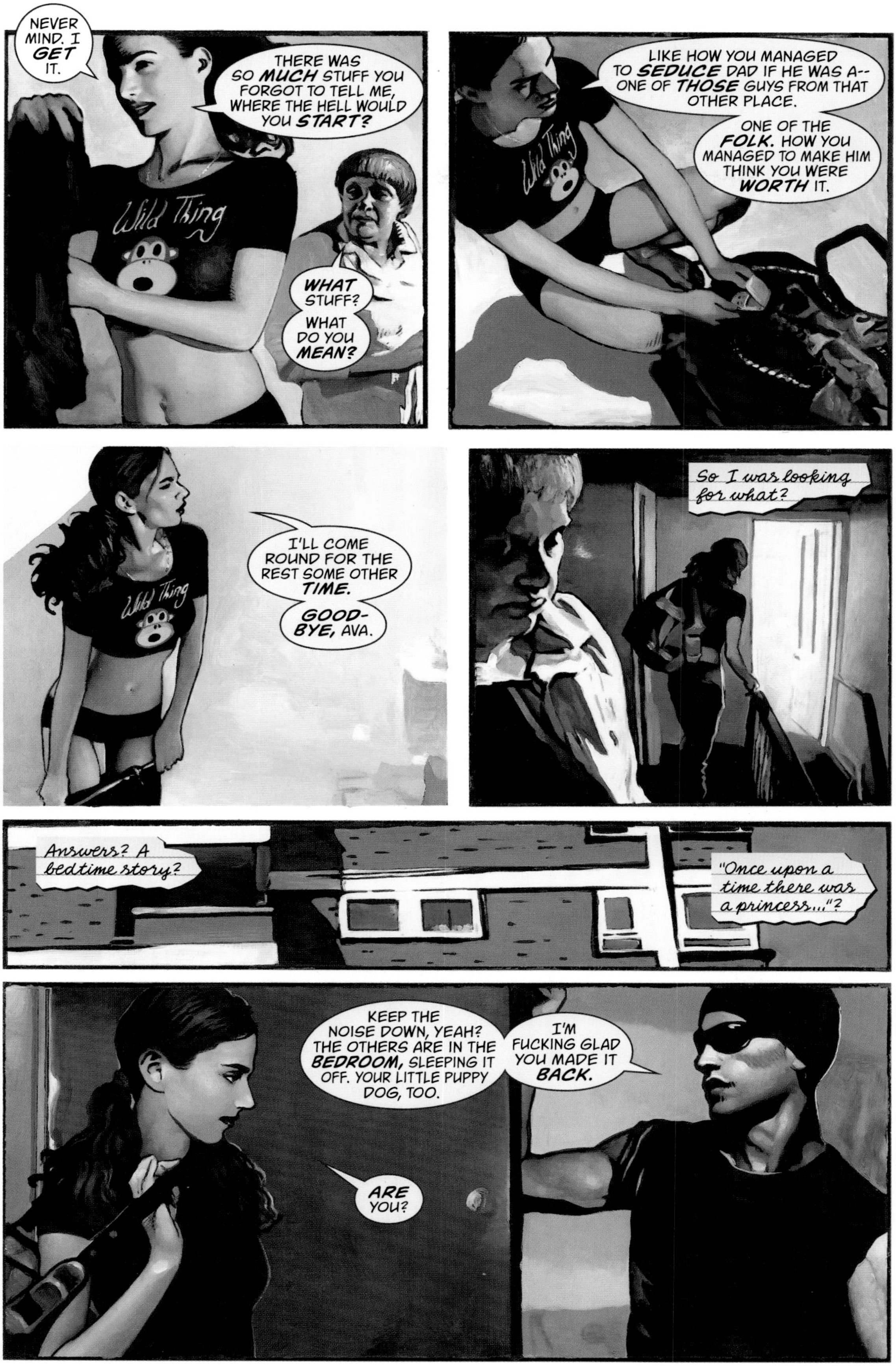
NEVER MIND. I GET IT.
THERE WAS SO MUCH STUFF YOU FORGOT TO TELL ME, WHERE THE HELL WOULD YOU START?
WHAT STUFF?
WHAT DO YOU MEAN?
LIKE HOW YOU MANAGED TO SEDUCE DAD IF HE WAS A-- ONE OF THOSE GUYS FROM THAT OTHER PLACE.
ONE OF THE FOLK. HOW YOU MANAGED TO MAKE HIM THINK YOU WERE WORTH IT.
I'LL COME ROUND FOR THE REST SOME OTHER TIME.
GOOD-BYE, AVA.
So I was looking for what?
Answers? A bedtime story?
"Once upon a time there was a princess..."?
KEEP THE NOISE DOWN, YEAH? THE OTHERS ARE IN THE BEDROOM, SLEEPING IT OFF. YOUR LITTLE PUPPY DOG, TOO.
I'M FUCKING GLAD YOU MADE IT BACK.
ARE YOU?

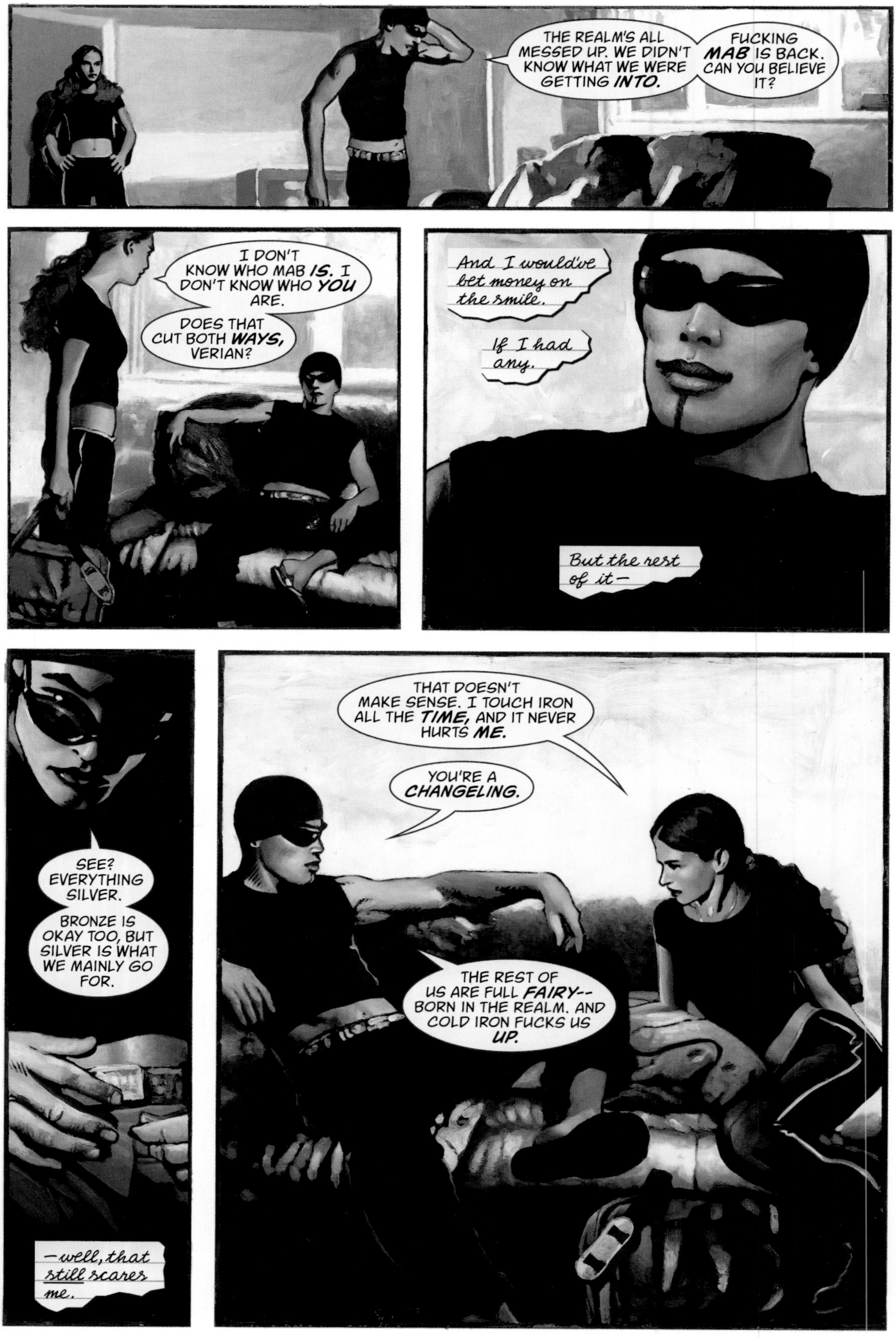
THE REALM'S ALL MESSED UP. WE DIDN'T KNOW WHAT WE WERE GETTING INTO.
FUCKING MAB IS BACK. CAN YOU BELIEVE IT?
I DON'T KNOW WHO MAB IS. I DON'T KNOW WHO YOU ARE.
DOES THAT CUT BOTH WAYS, VERIAN?
And I would've bet money on the smile.
If I had any.
But the rest of it—
SEE? EVERYTHING SILVER.
BRONZE IS OKAY TOO, BUT SILVER IS WHAT WE MAINLY GO FOR.
—well, that still scares me.
THAT DOESN'T MAKE SENSE. I TOUCH IRON ALL THE TIME, AND IT NEVER HURTS ME.
YOU'RE A CHANGELING.
THE REST OF US ARE FULL FAIRY--BORN IN THE REALM. AND COLD IRON FUCKS US UP.

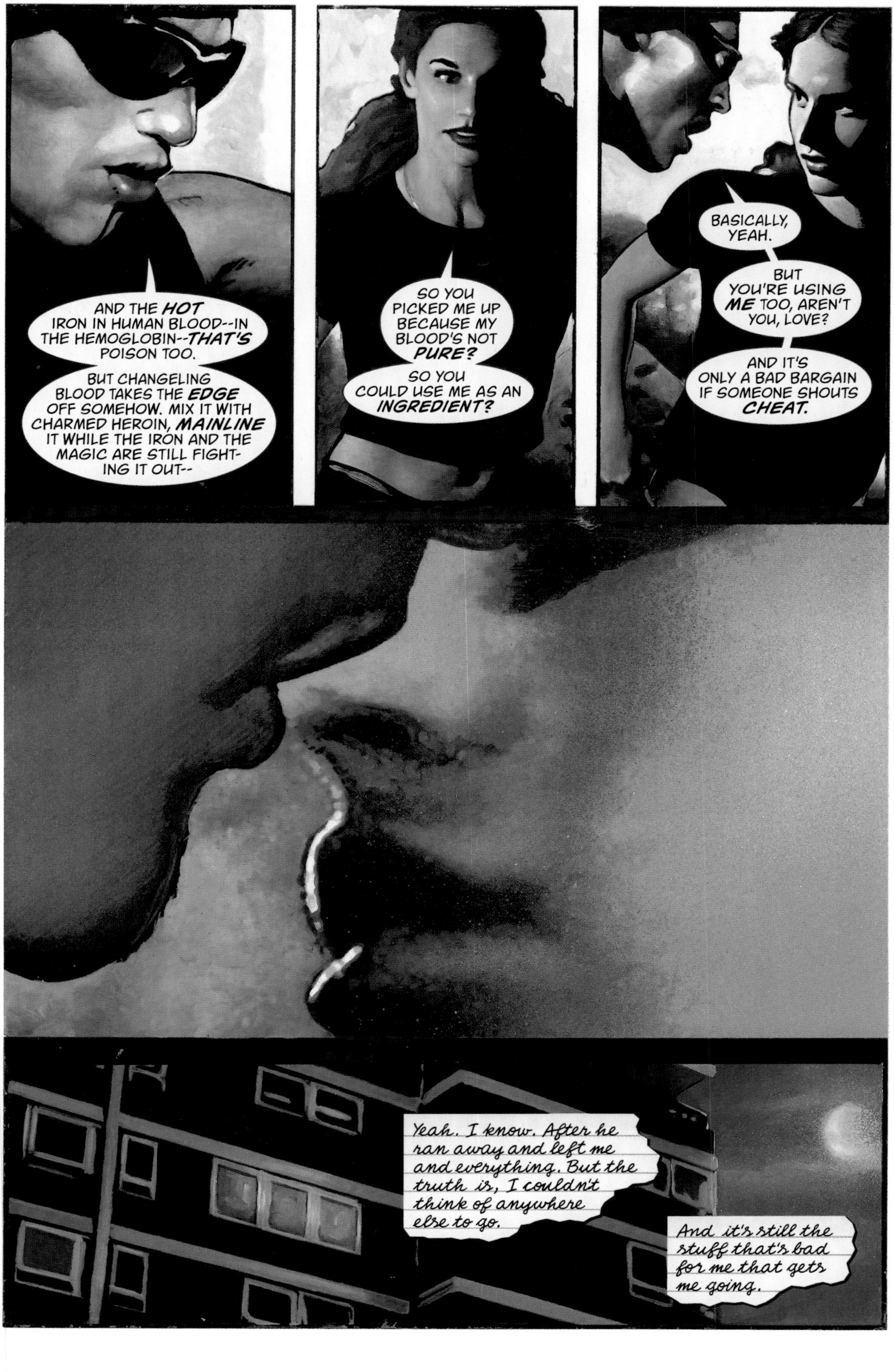
AND THE HOT IRON IN HUMAN BLOOD--IN THE HEMOGLOBIN--THAT'S POISON TOO.
BUT CHANGELING BLOOD TAKES THE EDGE OFF SOMEHOW. MIX IT WITH CHARMED HEROIN, MAINLINE IT WHILE THE IRON AND THE MAGIC ARE STILL FIGHTING IT OUT--
SO YOU PICKED ME UP BECAUSE MY BLOOD'S NOT PURE?
SO YOU COULD USE ME AS AN INGREDIENT?
BASICALLY, YEAH.
BUT YOU'RE USING ME TOO, AREN'T YOU, LOVE?
AND IT'S ONLY A BAD BARGAIN IF SOMEONE SHOUTS CHEAT.
Yeah. I know. After he ran away and left me and everything. But the truth is, I couldn't think of anywhere else to go.
And it's still the stuff that's bad for me that gets me going.

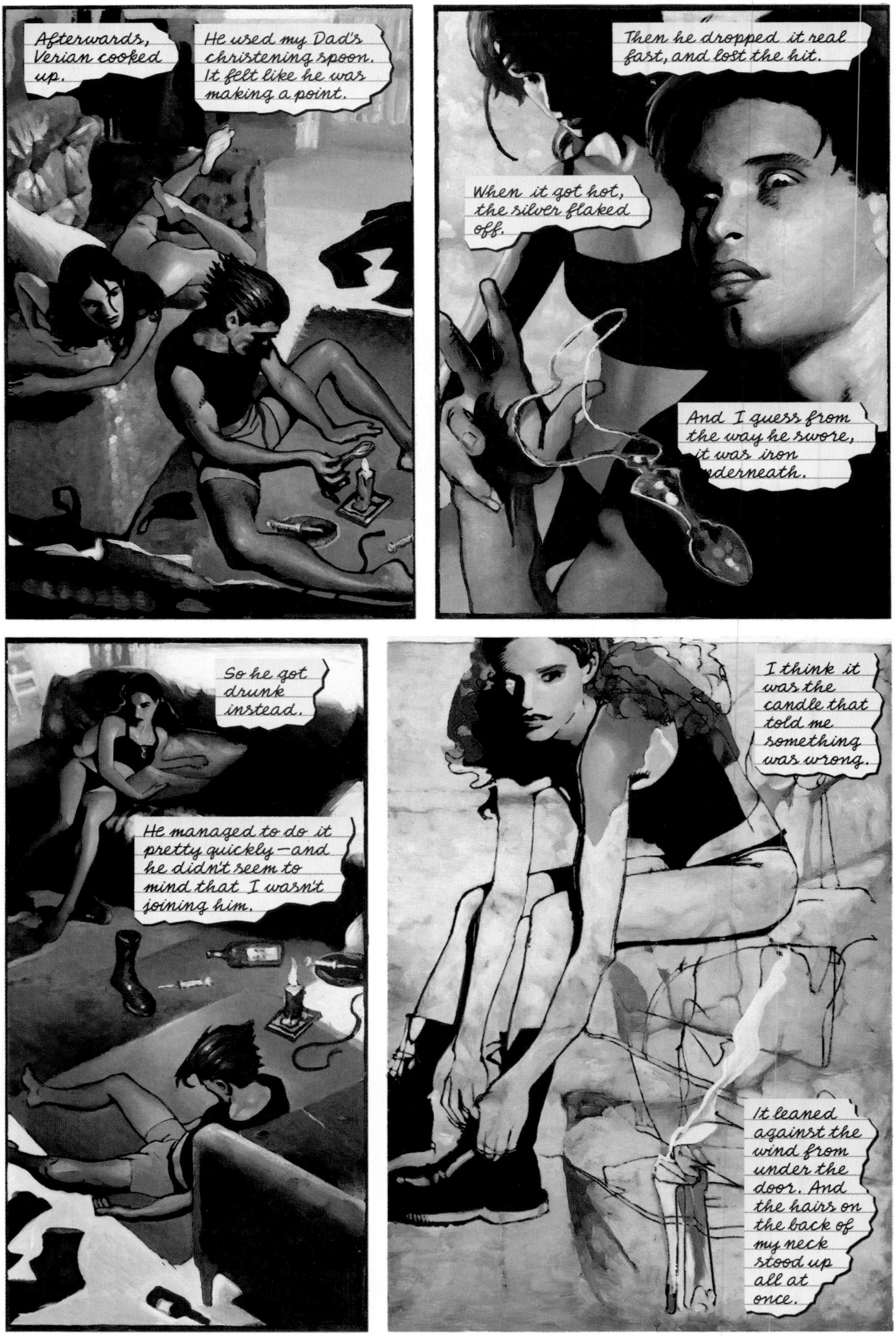

Afterwards, Verian cooked up.
He used my Dad's christening spoon. It felt like he was making a point.
Then he dropped it real fast, and lost the hit.
When it got hot, the silver flaked off.
And I guess from the way he swore, it was iron nderneath.
So he got drunk instead.
He managed to do it pretty quickly—and he didn't seem to mind that I wasn't joining him.
I think it was the candle that told me something was wrong.
It leaned against the wind from under the door. And the hairs on the back of my neck stood up all at once.

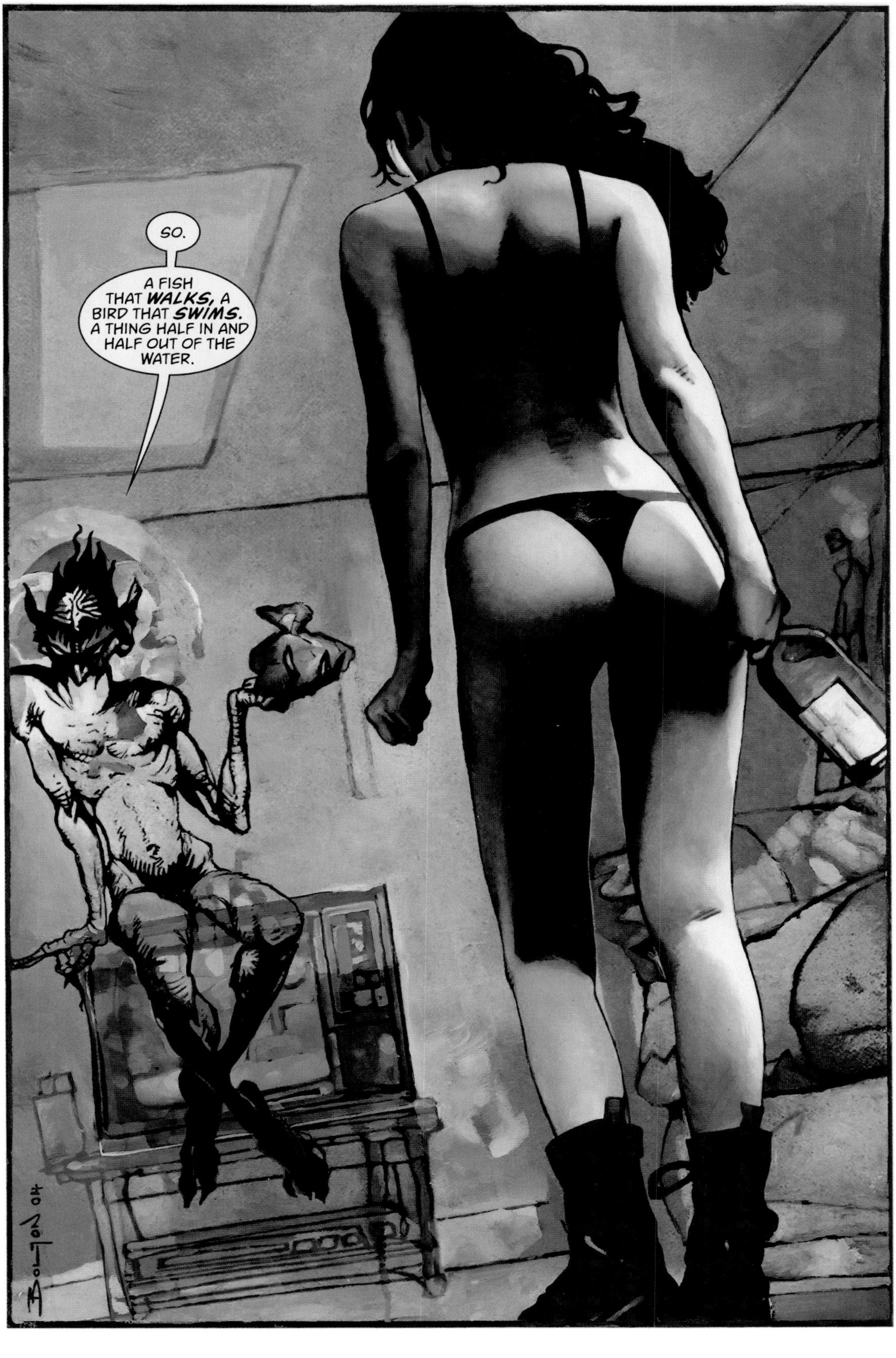
SO.
A FISH THAT WALKS, A BIRD THAT SWIMS. A THING HALF IN AND HALF OUT OF THE WATER.
BOLTON 04

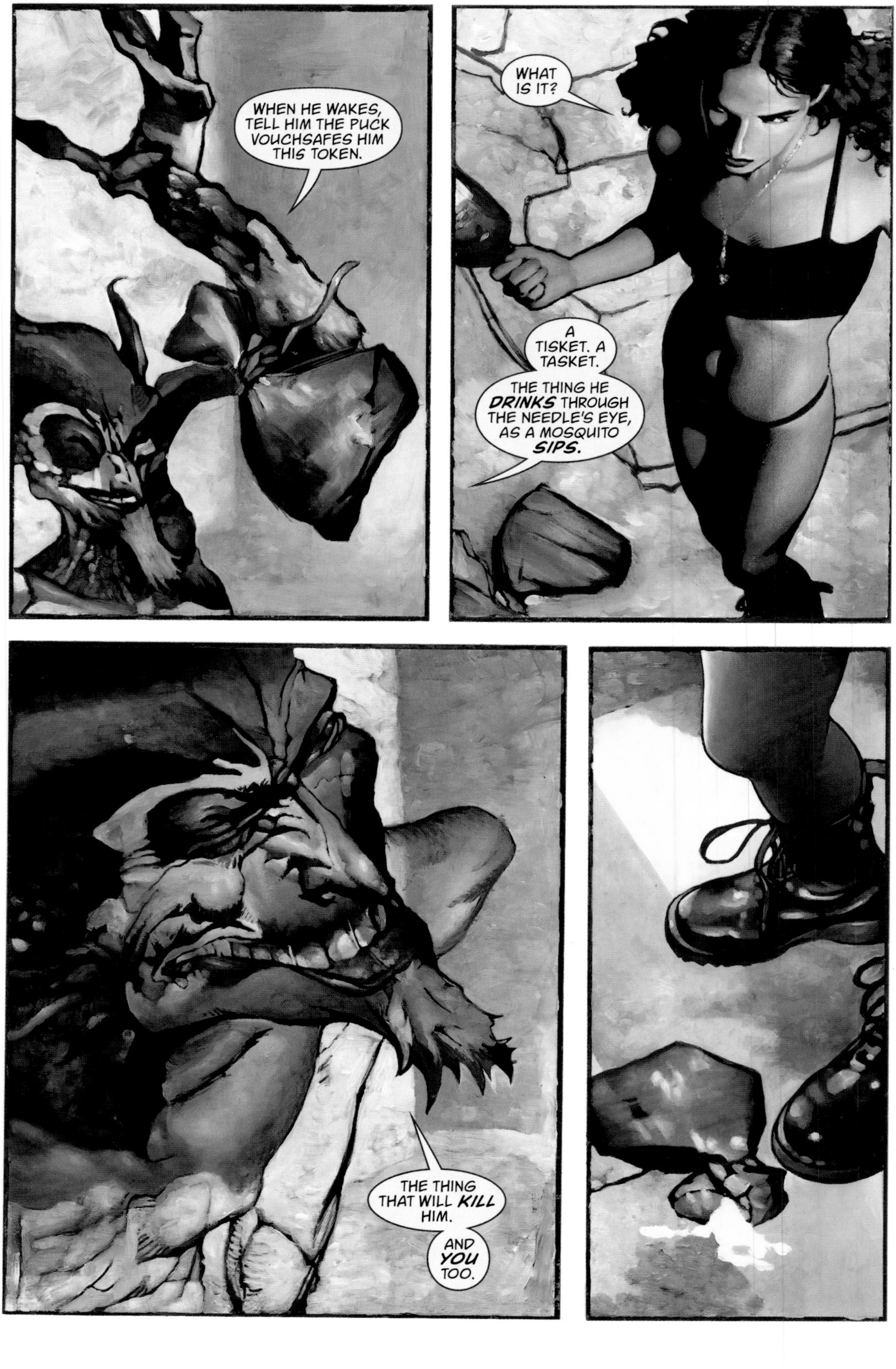
WHEN HE WAKES, TELL HIM THE PUCK VOUCHSAFES HIM THIS TOKEN.
WHAT IS IT?
A TISKET. A TASKET.
THE THING HE DRINKS THROUGH THE NEEDLE'S EYE, AS A MOSQUITO SIPS.
THE THING THAT WILL KILL HIM.
AND YOU TOO.

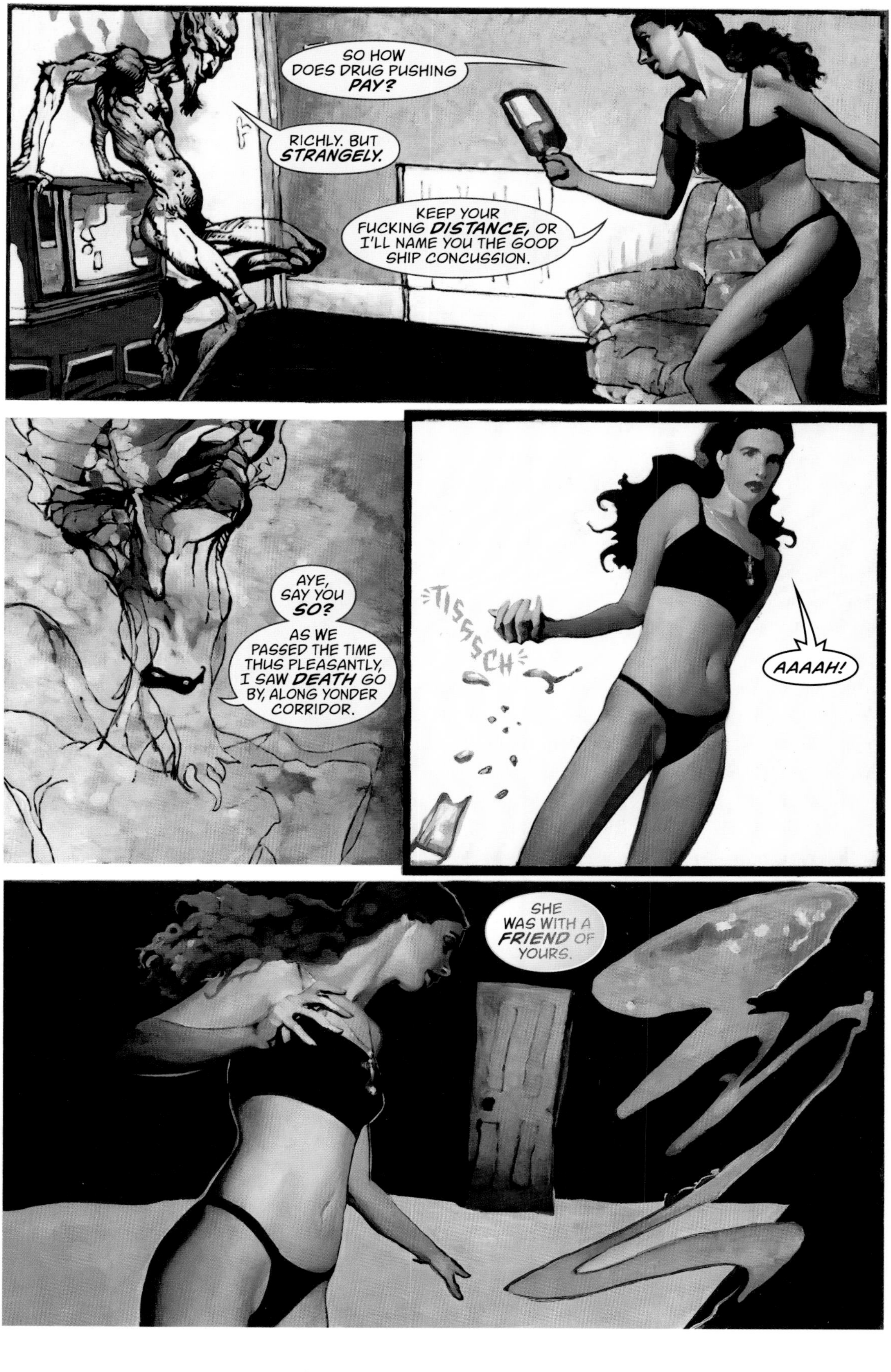
SO HOW DOES DRUG PUSHING PAY?
RICHLY. BUT STRANGELY.
KEEP YOUR FUCKING DISTANCE, OR I'LL NAME YOU THE GOOD SHIP CONCUSSION.
AYE, SAY YOU SO?
AS WE PASSED THE TIME THUS PLEASANTLY, I SAW DEATH GO BY, ALONG YONDER CORRIDOR.
TISSSCH
AAAAH!
SHE WAS WITH A FRIEND OF YOURS.

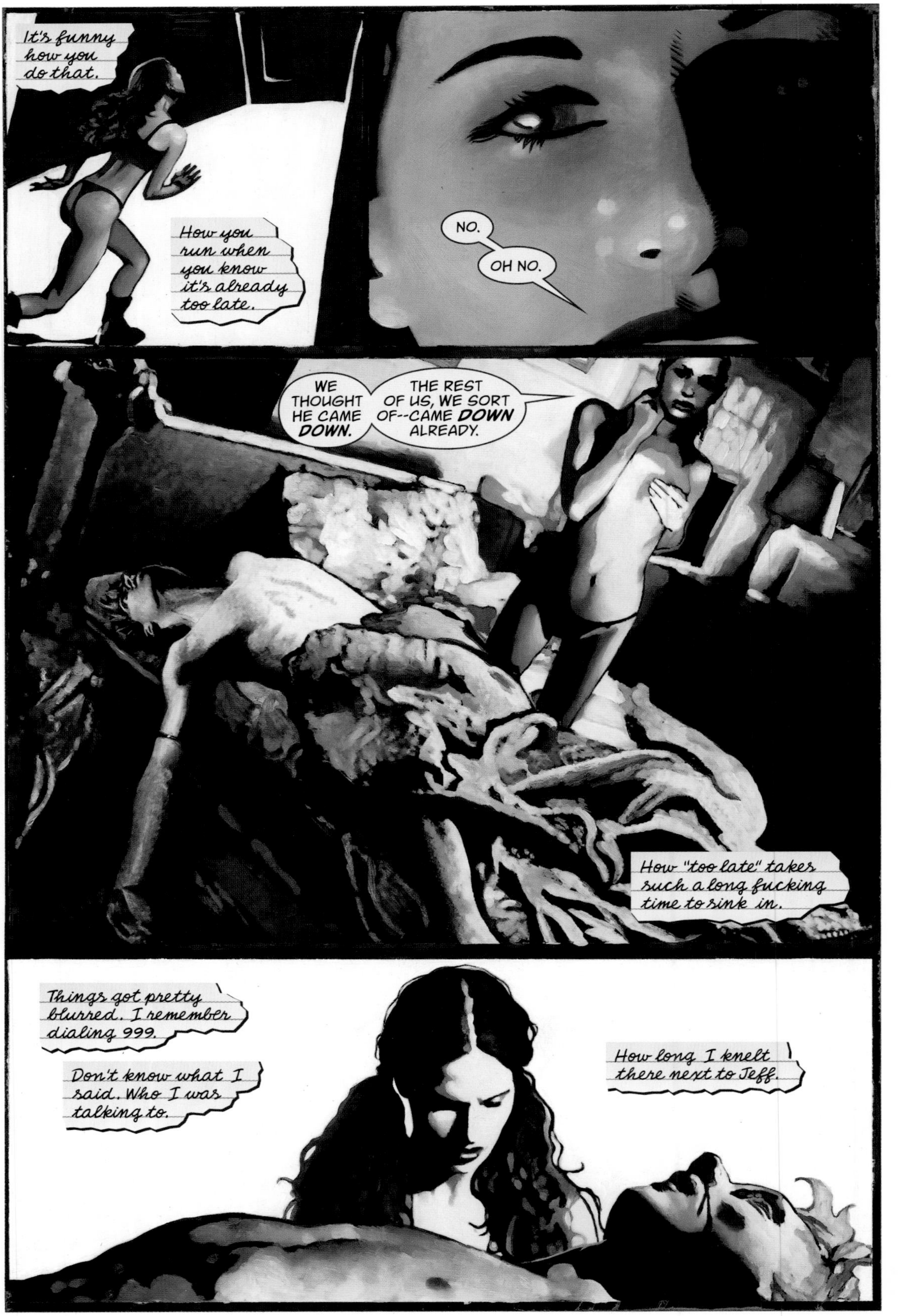
It's funny how you do that.
How you run when you know it's already too late.
NO.
OH NO.
WE THOUGHT HE CAME DOWN.
THE REST OF US, WE SORT OF--CAME DOWN ALREADY.
How "too late" takes such a long fucking time to sink in.
Things got pretty blurred. I remember dialing 999.
Don't know what I said. Who I was talking to.
How long I knelt there next to Jeff.

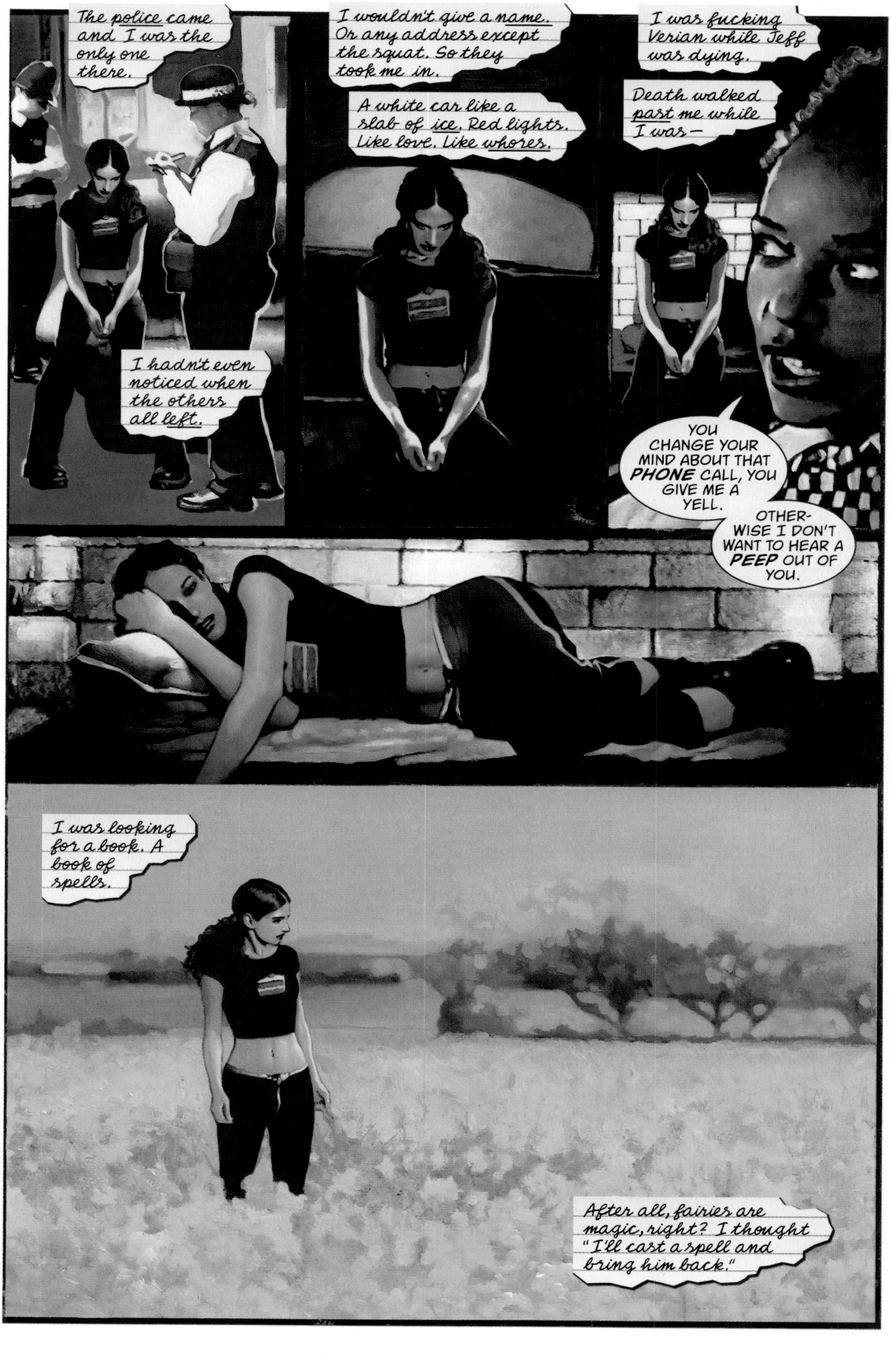
The police came and I was the only one there.
I hadn't even noticed when the others all left.
I wouldn't give a name. Or any address except the squat. So they took me in.
A white car like a slab of ice. Red lights. Like love. Like whores.
I was fucking Verian while Jeff was dying.
Death walked past me while I was—
YOU CHANGE YOUR MIND ABOUT THAT PHONE CALL, YOU GIVE ME A YELL.
OTHER-WISE I DON'T WANT TO HEAR A PEEP OUT OF YOU.
I was looking for a book. A book of spells.
After all, fairies are magic, right? I thought "I'll cast a spell and bring him back."

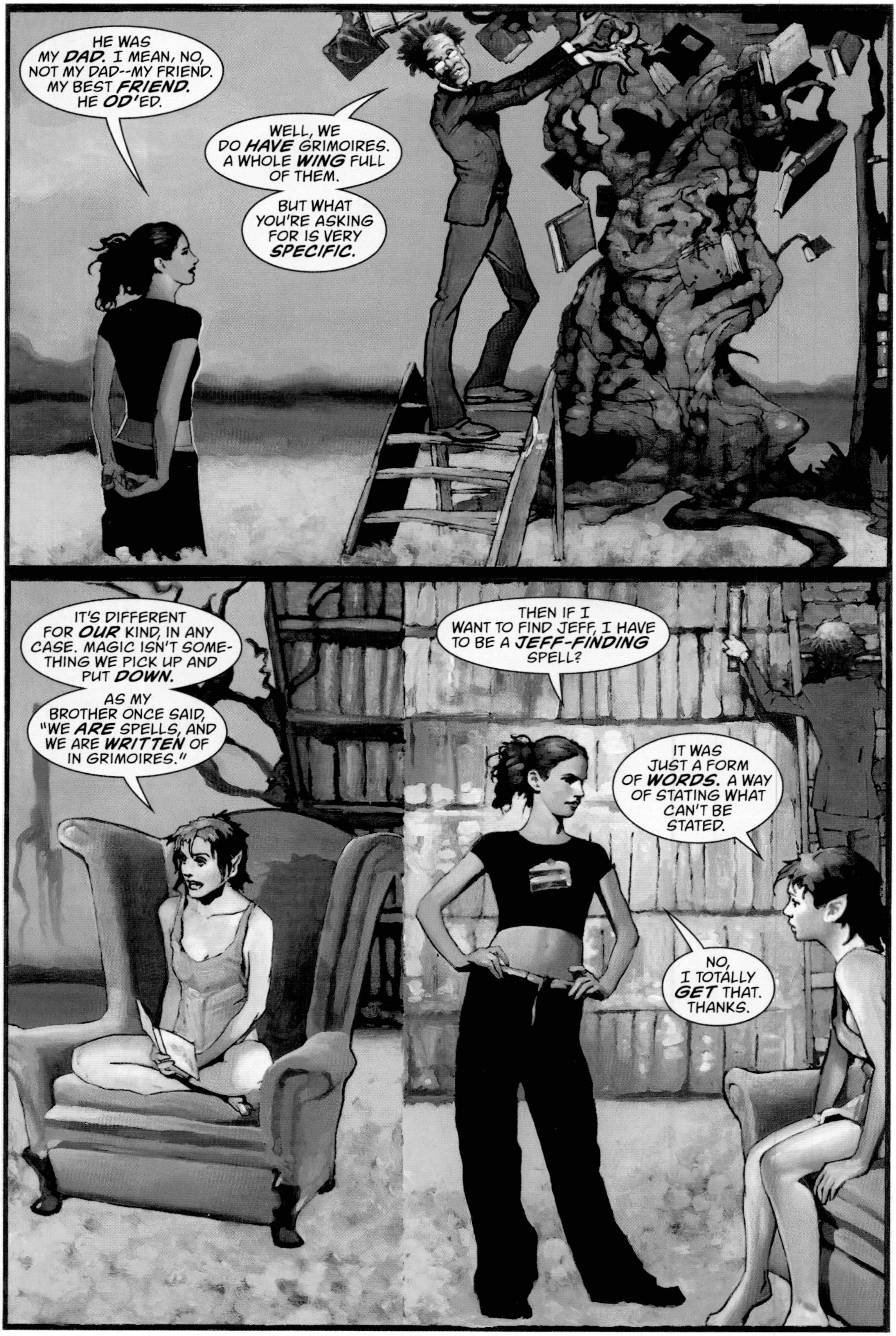
HE WAS MY DAD. I MEAN, NO, NOT MY DAD--MY FRIEND. MY BEST FRIEND. HE OD'ED.
WELL, WE DO HAVE GRIMOIRES. A WHOLE WING FULL OF THEM.
BUT WHAT YOU'RE ASKING FOR IS VERY SPECIFIC.
IT'S DIFFERENT FOR OUR KIND, IN ANY CASE. MAGIC ISN'T SOMETHING WE PICK UP AND PUT DOWN.
AS MY BROTHER ONCE SAID, "WE ARE SPELLS, AND WE ARE WRITTEN OF IN GRIMOIRES."
THEN IF I WANT TO FIND JEFF, I HAVE TO BE A JEFF-FINDING SPELL?
IT WAS JUST A FORM OF WORDS. A WAY OF STATING WHAT CAN'T BE STATED.
NO, I TOTALLY GET THAT. THANKS.

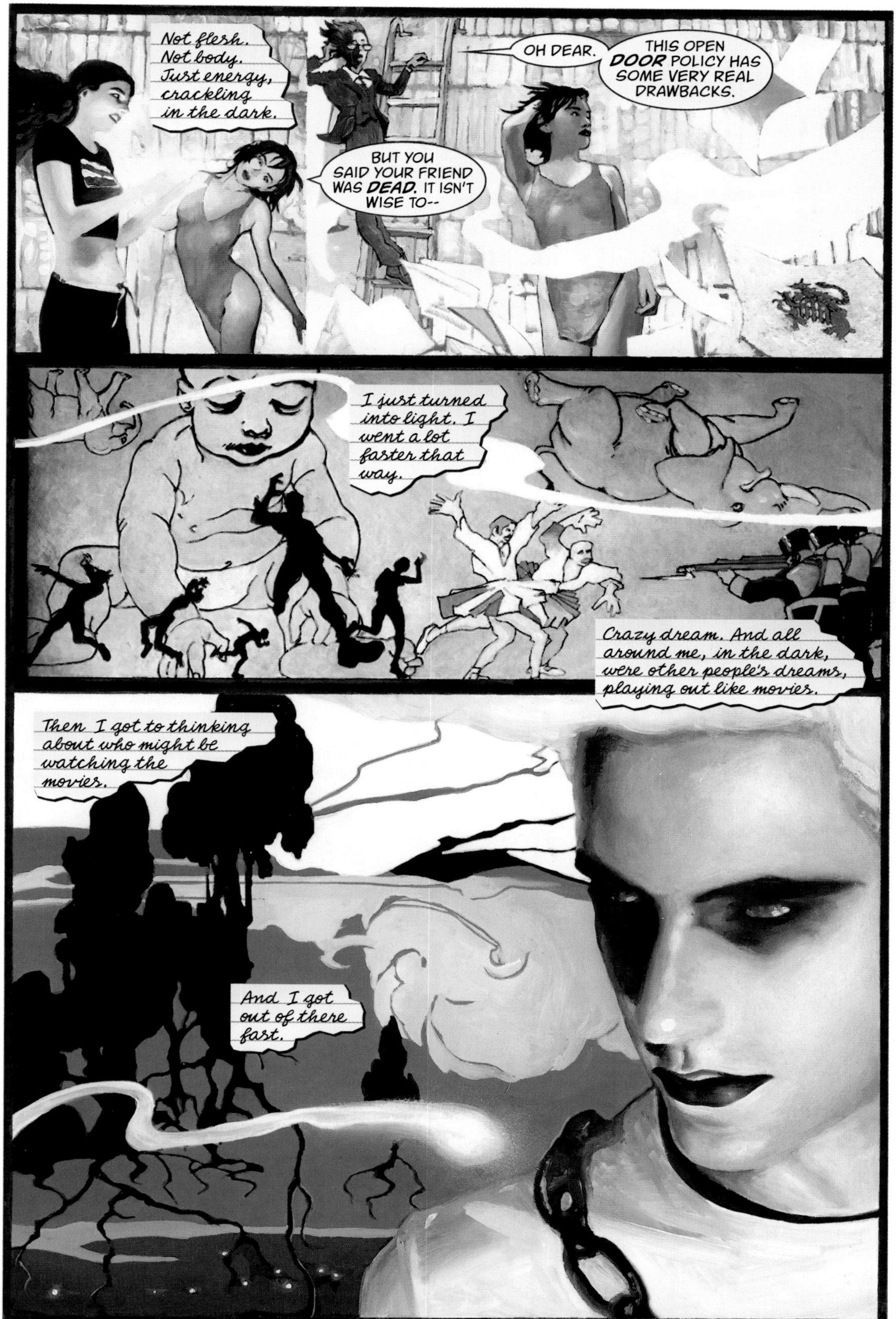

Not flesh. Not body. Just energy, crackling in the dark.
OH DEAR.
THIS OPEN DOOR POLICY HAS SOME VERY REAL DRAWBACKS.
BUT YOU SAID YOUR FRIEND WAS DEAD. IT ISN'T WISE TO--
I just turned into light. I went a lot faster that way.
Crazy dream. And all around me, in the dark, were other people's dreams, playing out like movies.
Then I got to thinking about who might be watching the movies.
And I got out of there fast.

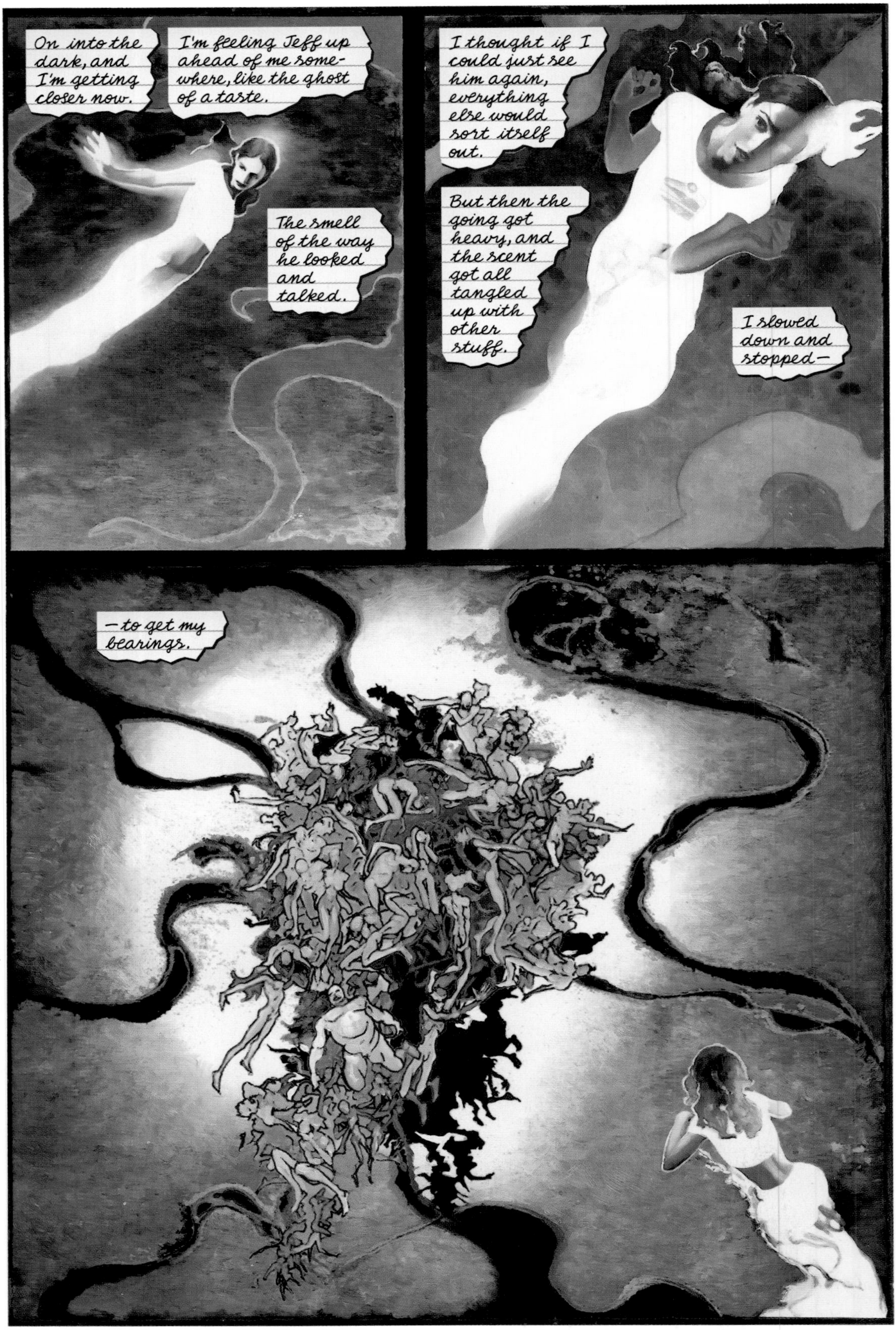
On into the dark, and I'm getting closer now.
I'm feeling Jeff up ahead of me somewhere, like the ghost of a taste.
The smell of the way he looked and talked.
I thought if I could just see him again, everything else would sort itself out.
But then the going got heavy, and the scent got all tangled up with other stuff.
I slowed down and stopped—
—to get my bearings.

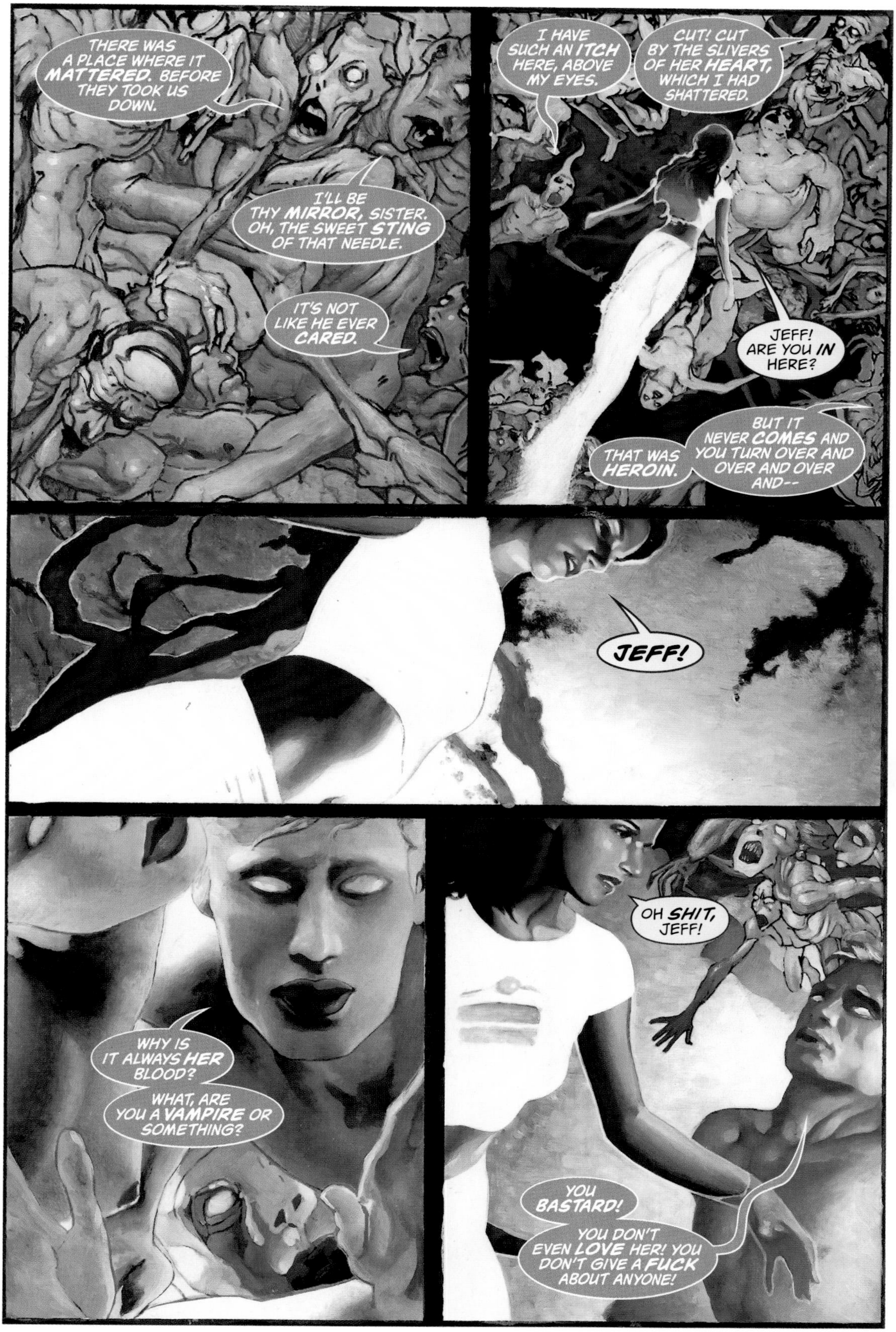

THERE WAS A PLACE WHERE IT MATTERED. BEFORE THEY TOOK US DOWN.
I'LL BE THY MIRROR, SISTER. OH, THE SWEET STING OF THAT NEEDLE.
IT'S NOT LIKE HE EVER CARED.
I HAVE SUCH AN ITCH HERE, ABOVE MY EYES.
CUT! CUT BY THE SLIVERS OF HER HEART, WHICH I HAD SHATTERED.
JEFF! ARE YOU IN HERE?
BUT IT NEVER COMES AND YOU TURN OVER AND OVER AND OVER AND--
THAT WAS HEROIN.
JEFF!
WHY IS IT ALWAYS HER BLOOD?
WHAT, ARE YOU A VAMPIRE OR SOMETHING?
OH SHIT, JEFF!
YOU BASTARD!
YOU DON'T EVEN LOVE HER! YOU DON'T GIVE A FUCK ABOUT ANYONE!

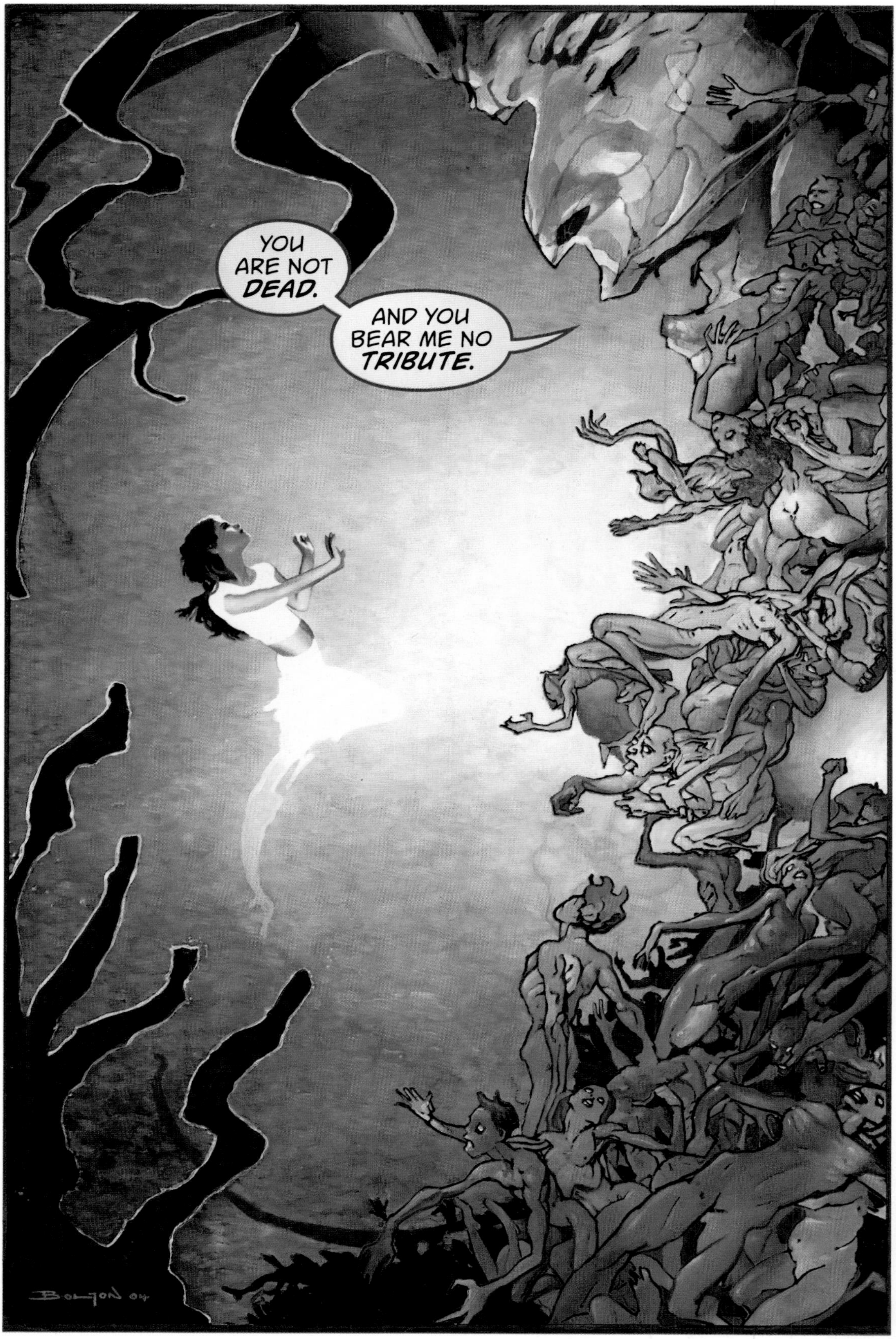
YOU ARE NOT *DEAD.*
AND YOU BEAR ME NO *TRIBUTE.*
BOLTON 04

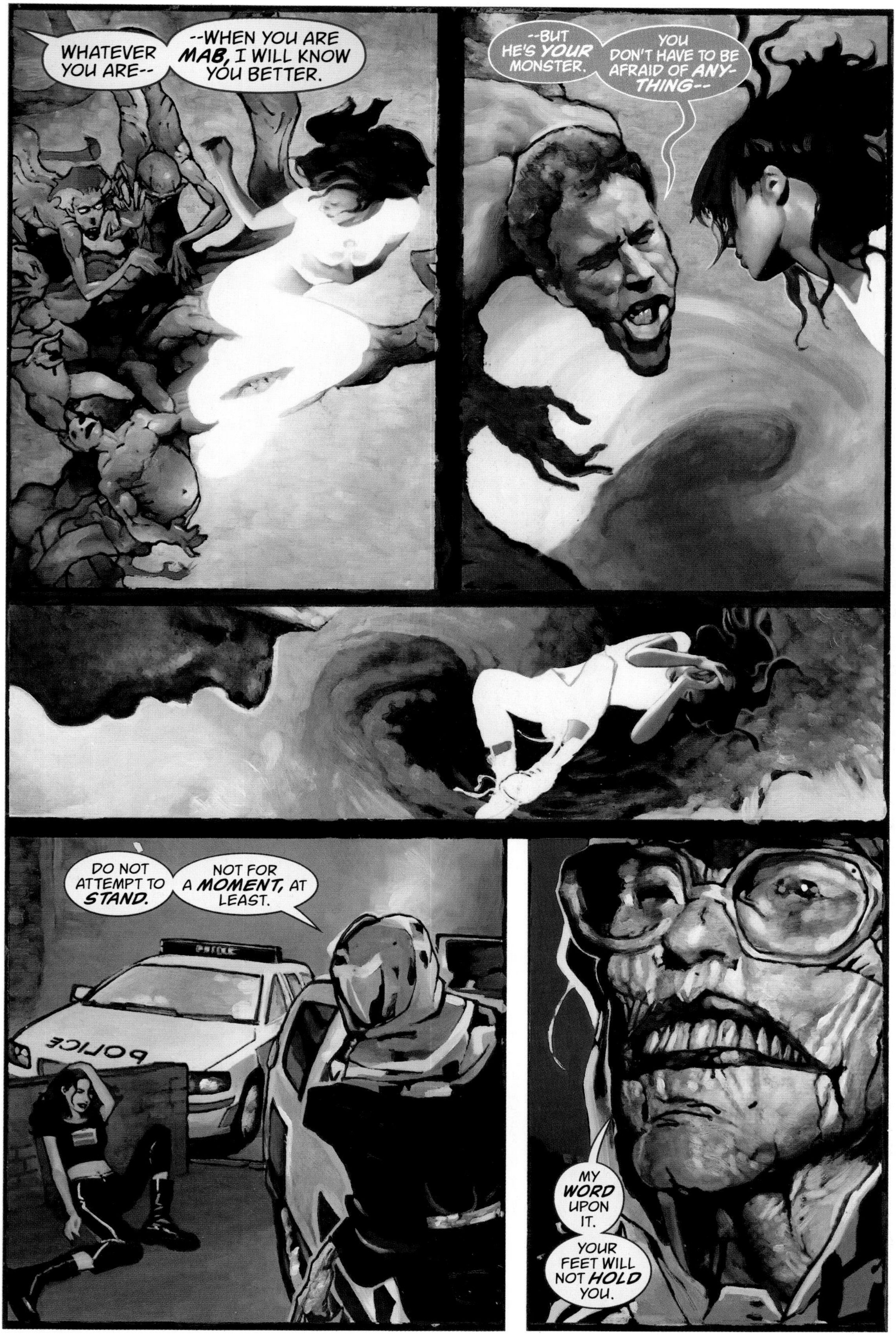
WHATEVER YOU ARE--
--WHEN YOU ARE MAB, I WILL KNOW YOU BETTER.
--BUT HE'S YOUR MONSTER.
YOU DON'T HAVE TO BE AFRAID OF ANY-THING--
DO NOT ATTEMPT TO STAND.
NOT FOR A MOMENT, AT LEAST.
POLICE
MY WORD UPON IT.
YOUR FEET WILL NOT HOLD YOU.

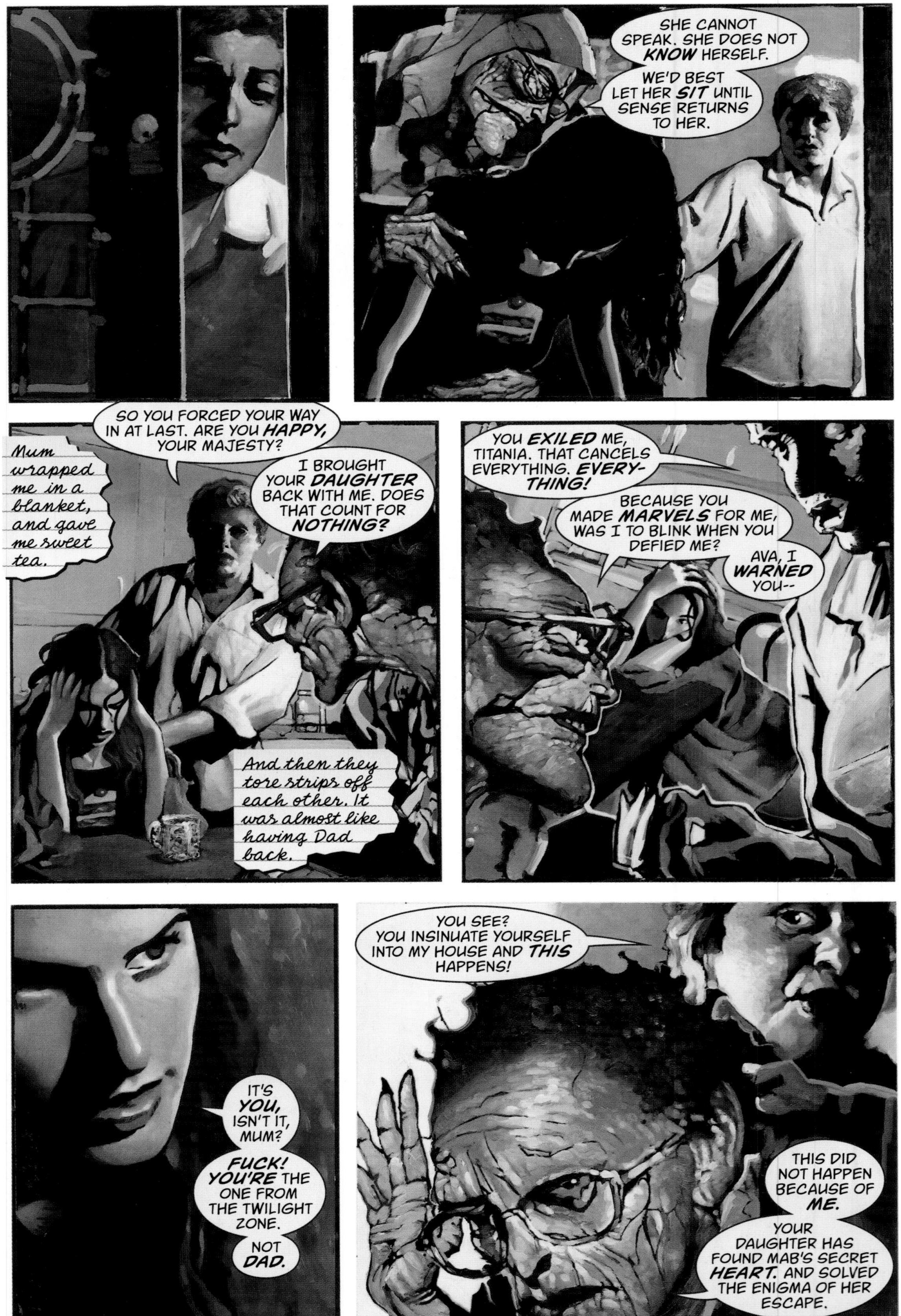
SHE CANNOT SPEAK. SHE DOES NOT KNOW HERSELF.
WE'D BEST LET HER SIT UNTIL SENSE RETURNS TO HER.
Mum wrapped me in a blanket, and gave me sweet tea.
SO YOU FORCED YOUR WAY IN AT LAST. ARE YOU HAPPY, YOUR MAJESTY?
I BROUGHT YOUR DAUGHTER BACK WITH ME. DOES THAT COUNT FOR NOTHING?
And then they tore strips off each other. It was almost like having Dad back.
YOU EXILED ME, TITANIA. THAT CANCELS EVERYTHING. EVERYTHING!
BECAUSE YOU MADE MARVELS FOR ME, WAS I TO BLINK WHEN YOU DEFIED ME?
AVA, I WARNED YOU--
IT'S YOU, ISN'T IT, MUM?
FUCK! YOU'RE THE ONE FROM THE TWILIGHT ZONE.
NOT DAD.
YOU SEE? YOU INSINUATE YOURSELF INTO MY HOUSE AND THIS HAPPENS!
THIS DID NOT HAPPEN BECAUSE OF ME.
YOUR DAUGHTER HAS FOUND MAB'S SECRET HEART. AND SOLVED THE ENIGMA OF HER ESCAPE.

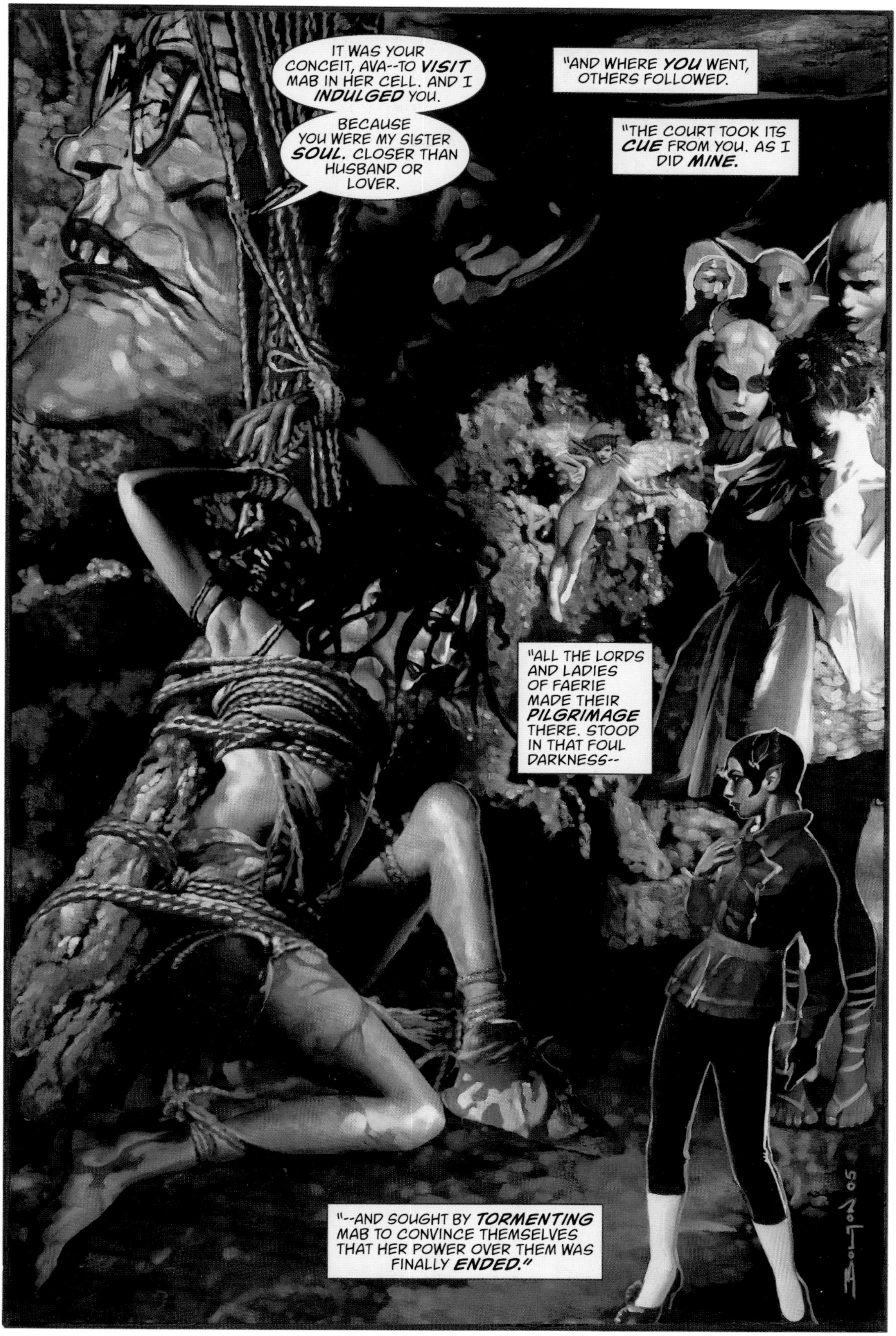
IT WAS YOUR CONCEIT, AVA--TO *VISIT* MAB IN HER CELL. AND I *INDULGED* YOU.
BECAUSE YOU WERE MY SISTER *SOUL.* CLOSER THAN HUSBAND OR LOVER.
"AND WHERE *YOU* WENT, OTHERS FOLLOWED.
"THE COURT TOOK ITS *CUE* FROM YOU. AS I DID *MINE.*
"ALL THE LORDS AND LADIES OF FAERIE MADE THEIR *PILGRIMAGE* THERE. STOOD IN THAT FOUL DARKNESS--
"--AND SOUGHT BY *TORMENTING* MAB TO CONVINCE THEMSELVES THAT HER POWER OVER THEM WAS FINALLY *ENDED.*"

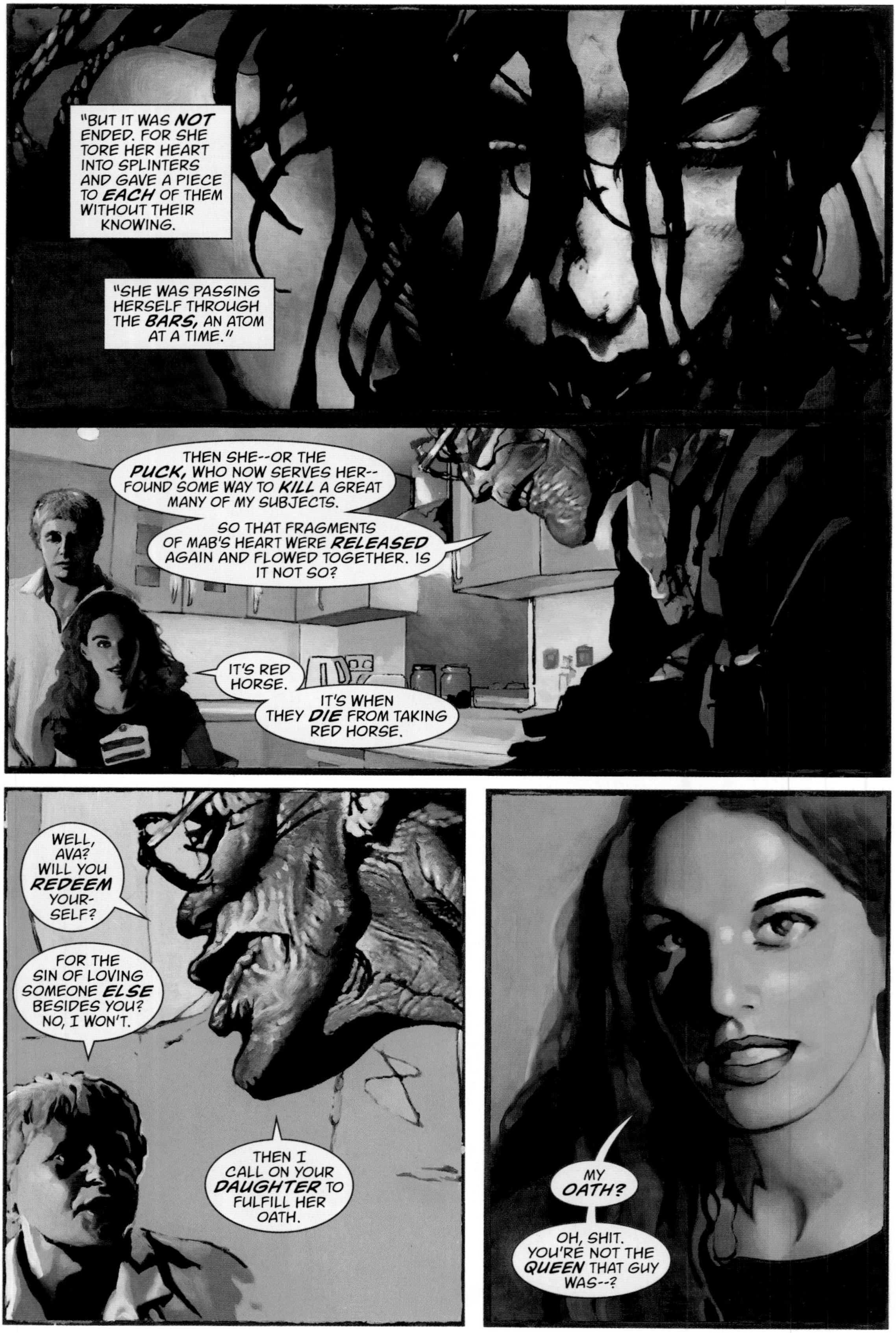

"BUT IT WAS NOT ENDED. FOR SHE TORE HER HEART INTO SPLINTERS AND GAVE A PIECE TO EACH OF THEM WITHOUT THEIR KNOWING.
"SHE WAS PASSING HERSELF THROUGH THE BARS, AN ATOM AT A TIME."
THEN SHE--OR THE PUCK, WHO NOW SERVES HER--FOUND SOME WAY TO KILL A GREAT MANY OF MY SUBJECTS.
SO THAT FRAGMENTS OF MAB'S HEART WERE RELEASED AGAIN AND FLOWED TOGETHER. IS IT NOT SO?
IT'S RED HORSE.
IT'S WHEN THEY DIE FROM TAKING RED HORSE.
WELL, AVA? WILL YOU REDEEM YOUR-SELF?
FOR THE SIN OF LOVING SOMEONE ELSE BESIDES YOU? NO, I WON'T.
THEN I CALL ON YOUR DAUGHTER TO FULFILL HER OATH.
MY OATH?
OH, SHIT. YOU'RE NOT THE QUEEN THAT GUY WAS--?

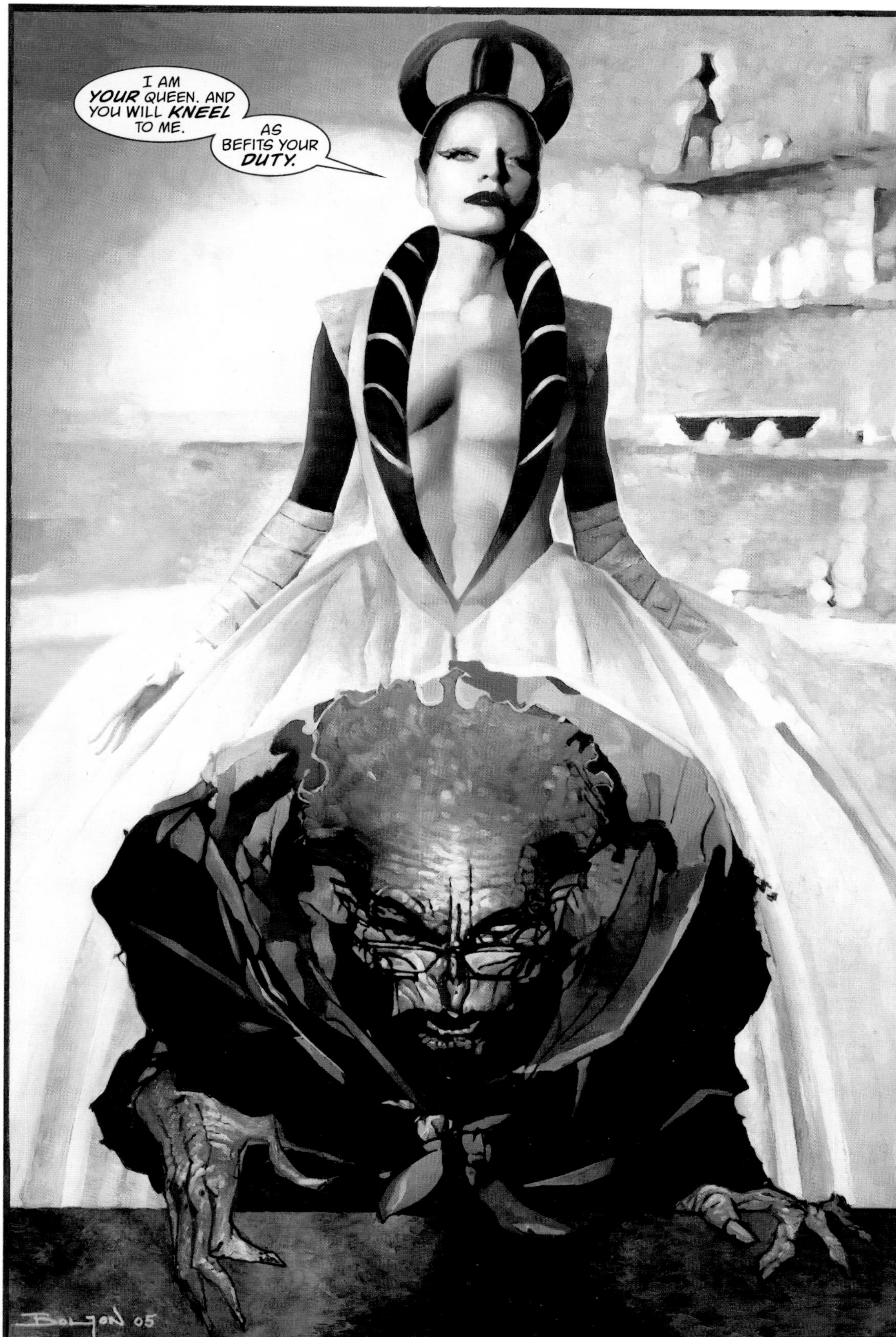
I AM YOUR QUEEN. AND YOU WILL KNEEL TO ME.
AS BEFITS YOUR DUTY.
BOLTON 05

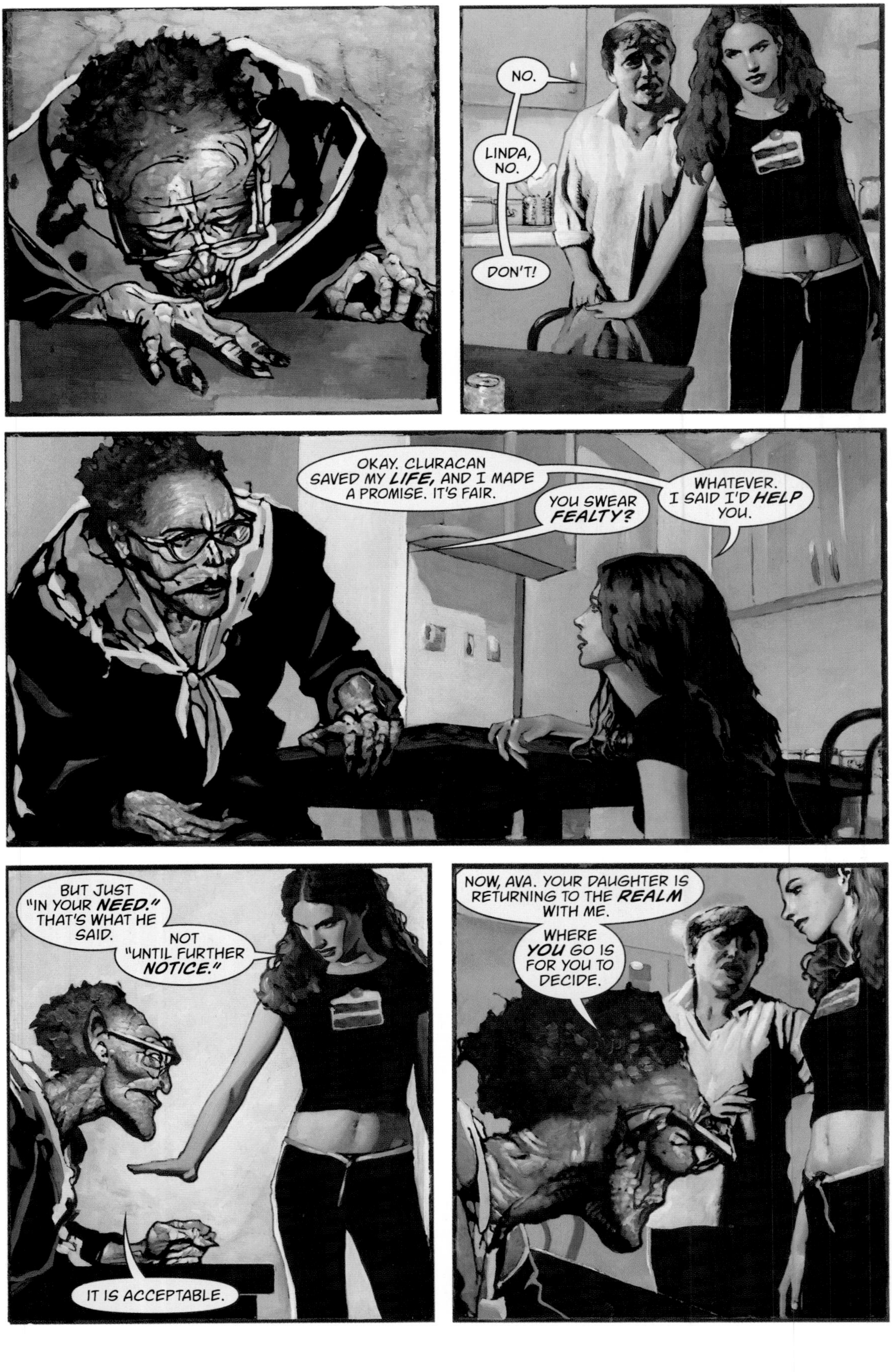
NO.
LINDA, NO.
DON'T!
OKAY. CLURACAN SAVED MY LIFE, AND I MADE A PROMISE. IT'S FAIR.
WHATEVER. I SAID I'D HELP YOU.
YOU SWEAR FEALTY?
BUT JUST "IN YOUR NEED." THAT'S WHAT HE SAID.
NOT "UNTIL FURTHER NOTICE."
IT IS ACCEPTABLE.
NOW, AVA. YOUR DAUGHTER IS RETURNING TO THE REALM WITH ME.
WHERE YOU GO IS FOR YOU TO DECIDE.

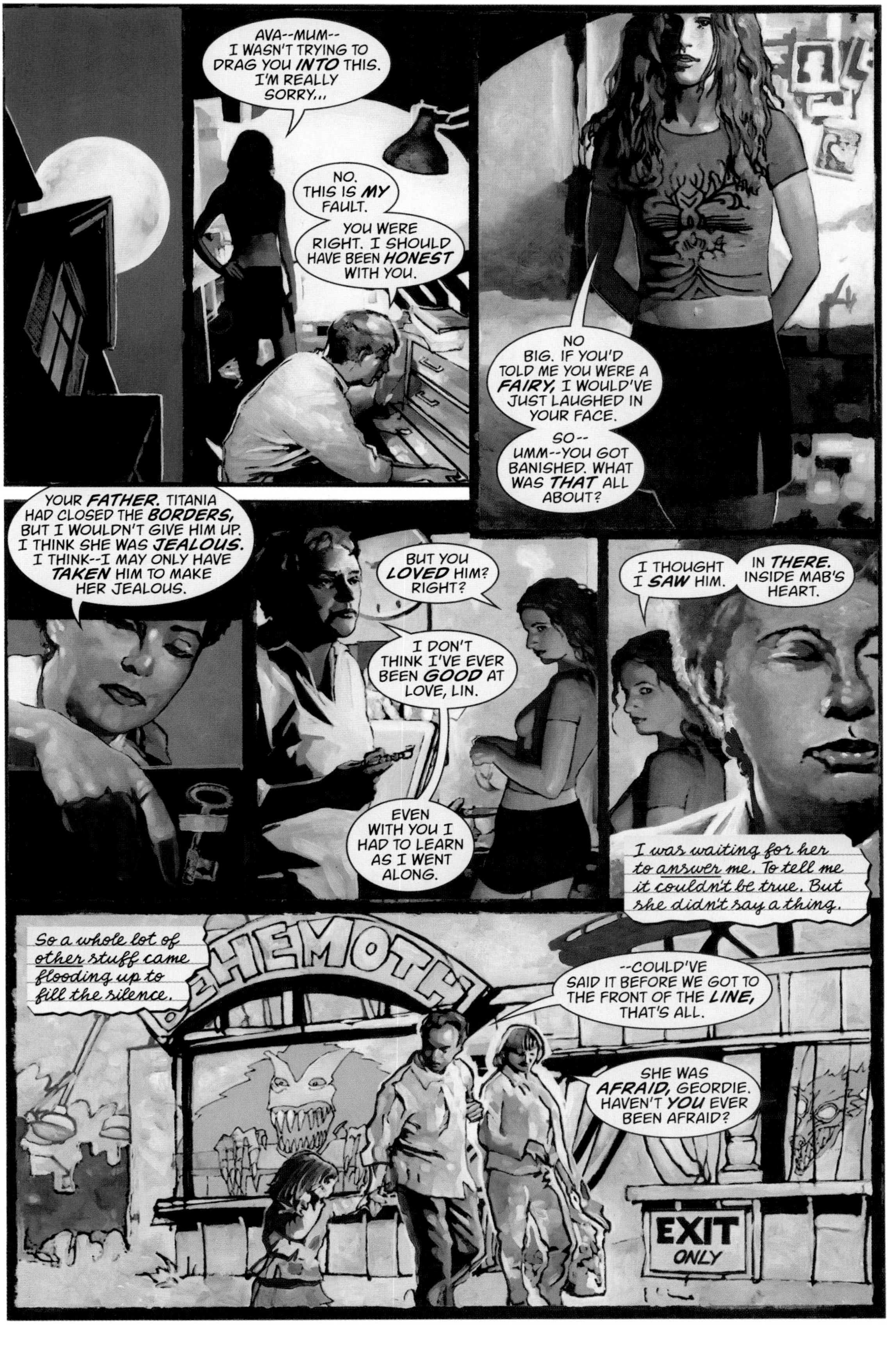
AVA--MUM-- I WASN'T TRYING TO DRAG YOU INTO THIS. I'M REALLY SORRY...
NO. THIS IS MY FAULT.
YOU WERE RIGHT. I SHOULD HAVE BEEN HONEST WITH YOU.
NO BIG. IF YOU'D TOLD ME YOU WERE A FAIRY, I WOULD'VE JUST LAUGHED IN YOUR FACE.
SO-- UMM--YOU GOT BANISHED. WHAT WAS THAT ALL ABOUT?
YOUR FATHER. TITANIA HAD CLOSED THE BORDERS, BUT I WOULDN'T GIVE HIM UP. I THINK SHE WAS JEALOUS. I THINK--I MAY ONLY HAVE TAKEN HIM TO MAKE HER JEALOUS.
BUT YOU LOVED HIM? RIGHT?
I DON'T THINK I'VE EVER BEEN GOOD AT LOVE, LIN.
EVEN WITH YOU I HAD TO LEARN AS I WENT ALONG.
I THOUGHT I SAW HIM.
IN THERE. INSIDE MAB'S HEART.
I was waiting for her to answer me. To tell me it couldn't be true. But she didn't say a thing.
So a whole lot of other stuff came flooding up to fill the silence.
HEMOTH
--COULD'VE SAID IT BEFORE WE GOT TO THE FRONT OF THE LINE, THAT'S ALL.
SHE WAS AFRAID, GEORDIE. HAVEN'T YOU EVER BEEN AFRAID?
EXIT ONLY

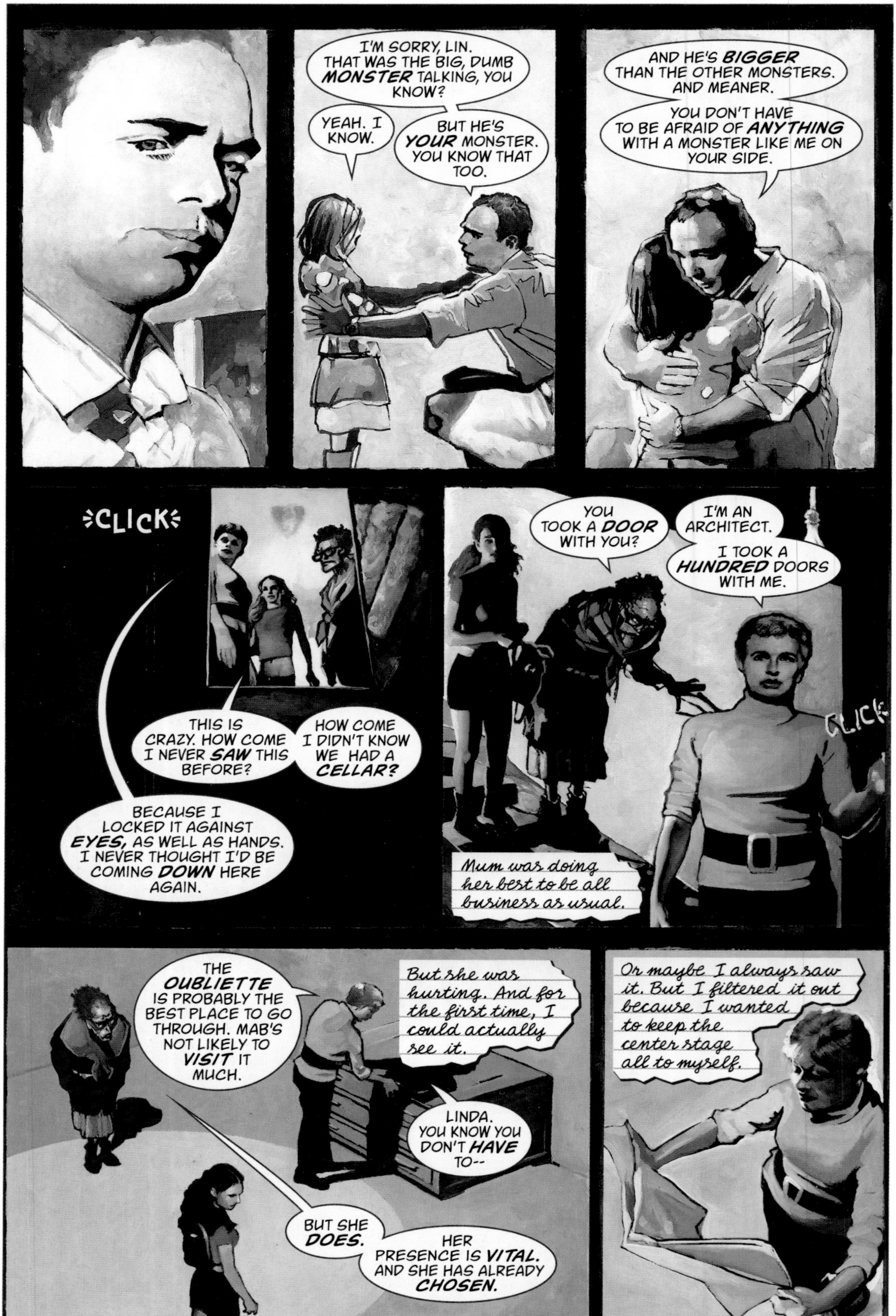
I'M SORRY, LIN. THAT WAS THE BIG, DUMB MONSTER TALKING, YOU KNOW?
YEAH. I KNOW.
BUT HE'S YOUR MONSTER. YOU KNOW THAT TOO.
AND HE'S BIGGER THAN THE OTHER MONSTERS. AND MEANER.
YOU DON'T HAVE TO BE AFRAID OF ANYTHING WITH A MONSTER LIKE ME ON YOUR SIDE.
CLICK
THIS IS CRAZY. HOW COME I NEVER SAW THIS BEFORE?
HOW COME I DIDN'T KNOW WE HAD A CELLAR?
BECAUSE I LOCKED IT AGAINST EYES, AS WELL AS HANDS. I NEVER THOUGHT I'D BE COMING DOWN HERE AGAIN.
YOU TOOK A DOOR WITH YOU?
I'M AN ARCHITECT.
I TOOK A HUNDRED DOORS WITH ME.
Mum was doing her best to be all business as usual.
THE OUBLIETTE IS PROBABLY THE BEST PLACE TO GO THROUGH. MAB'S NOT LIKELY TO VISIT IT MUCH.
But she was hurting. And for the first time, I could actually see it.
LINDA. YOU KNOW YOU DON'T HAVE TO--
BUT SHE DOES.
HER PRESENCE IS VITAL. AND SHE HAS ALREADY CHOSEN.
Or maybe I always saw it. But I filtered it out because I wanted to keep the center stage all to myself.

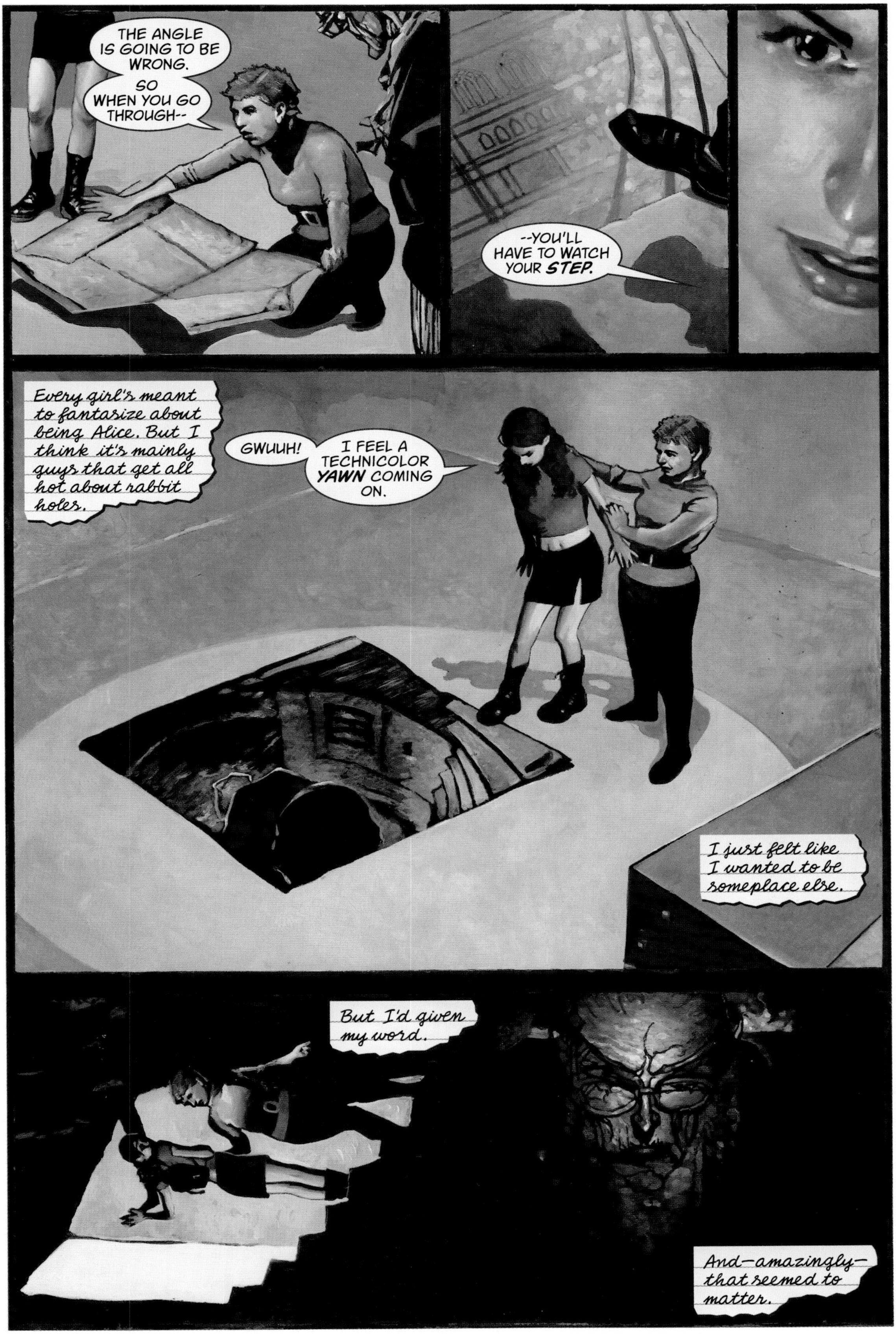
THE ANGLE IS GOING TO BE WRONG.
SO WHEN YOU GO THROUGH--
--YOU'LL HAVE TO WATCH YOUR STEP.
Every girl's meant to fantasize about being Alice. But I think it's mainly guys that get all hot about rabbit holes.
GWUUH!
I FEEL A TECHNICOLOR YAWN COMING ON.
I just felt like I wanted to be someplace else.
But I'd given my word.
And—amazingly—that seemed to matter.

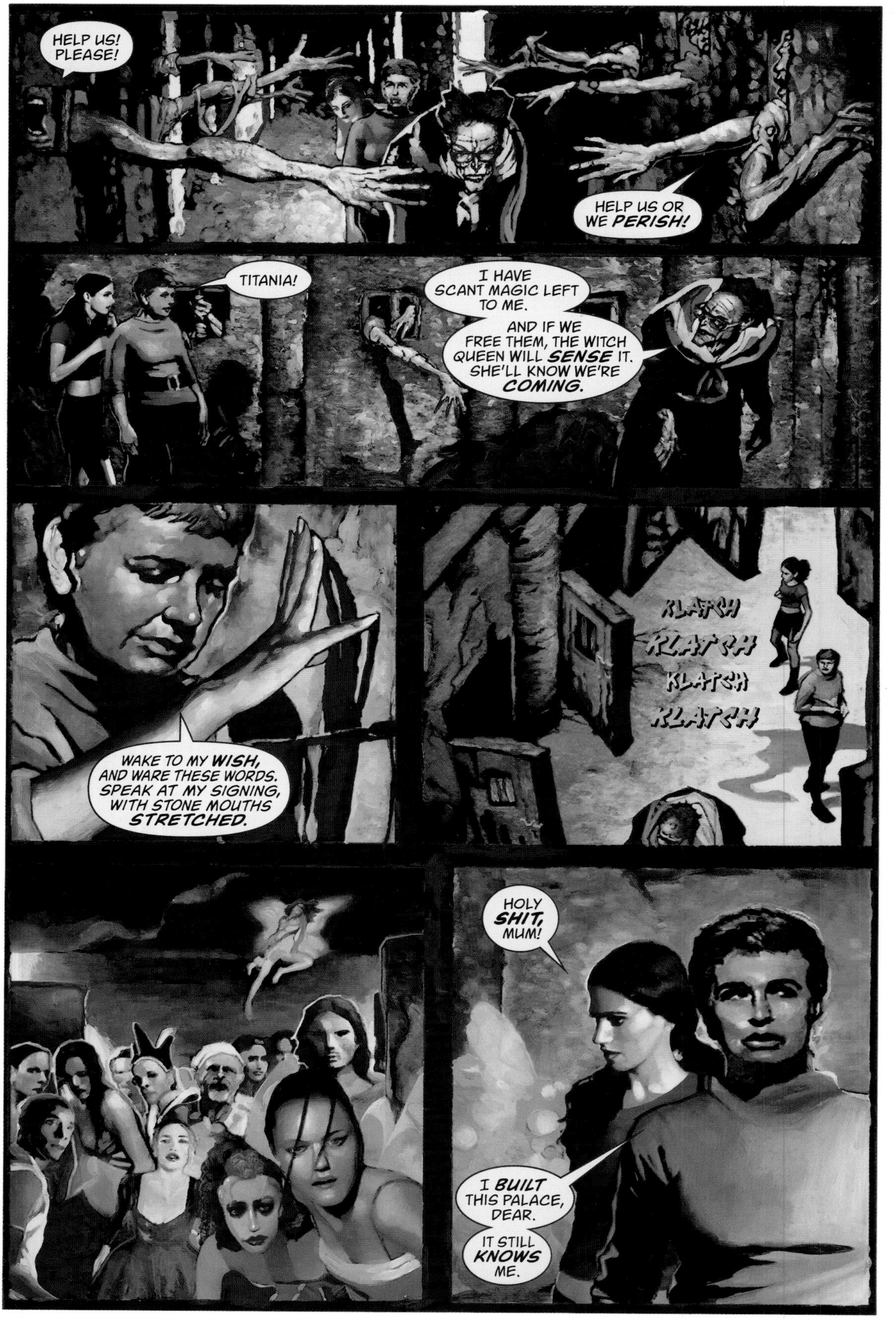
HELP US! PLEASE!
HELP US OR WE PERISH!
TITANIA!
I HAVE SCANT MAGIC LEFT TO ME.
AND IF WE FREE THEM, THE WITCH QUEEN WILL SENSE IT. SHE'LL KNOW WE'RE COMING.
WAKE TO MY WISH, AND WARE THESE WORDS. SPEAK AT MY SIGNING, WITH STONE MOUTHS STRETCHED.
KLATCH
KLATCH
KLATCH
KLATCH
HOLY SHIT, MUM!
I BUILT THIS PALACE, DEAR.
IT STILL KNOWS ME.

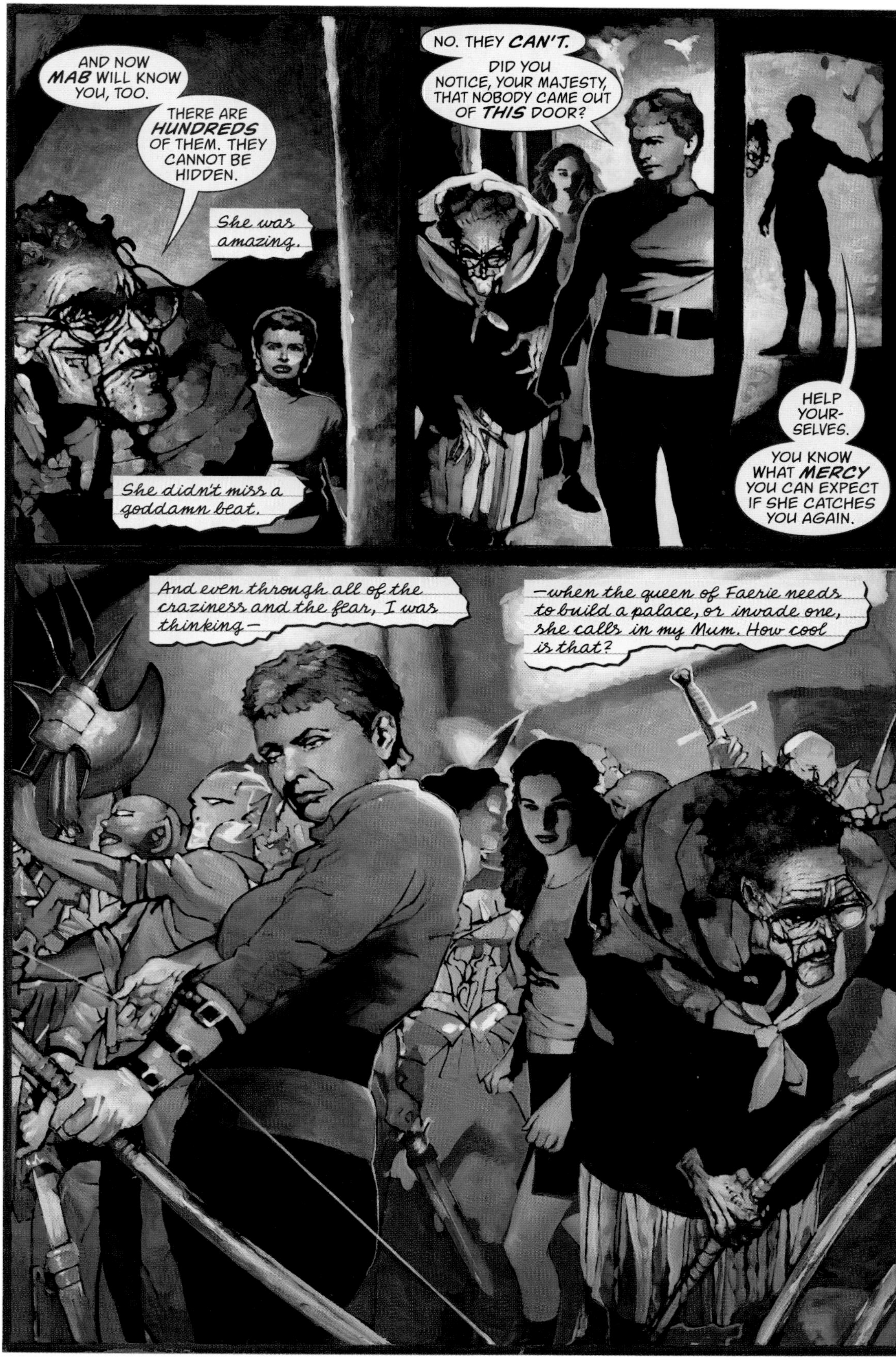
AND NOW MAB WILL KNOW YOU, TOO.
THERE ARE HUNDREDS OF THEM. THEY CANNOT BE HIDDEN.
She was amazing.
She didn't miss a goddamn beat.
NO. THEY CAN'T.
DID YOU NOTICE, YOUR MAJESTY, THAT NOBODY CAME OUT OF THIS DOOR?
HELP YOUR-SELVES.
YOU KNOW WHAT MERCY YOU CAN EXPECT IF SHE CATCHES YOU AGAIN.
And even through all of the craziness and the fear, I was thinking—
—when the queen of Faerie needs to build a palace, or invade one, she calls in my Mum. How cool is that?

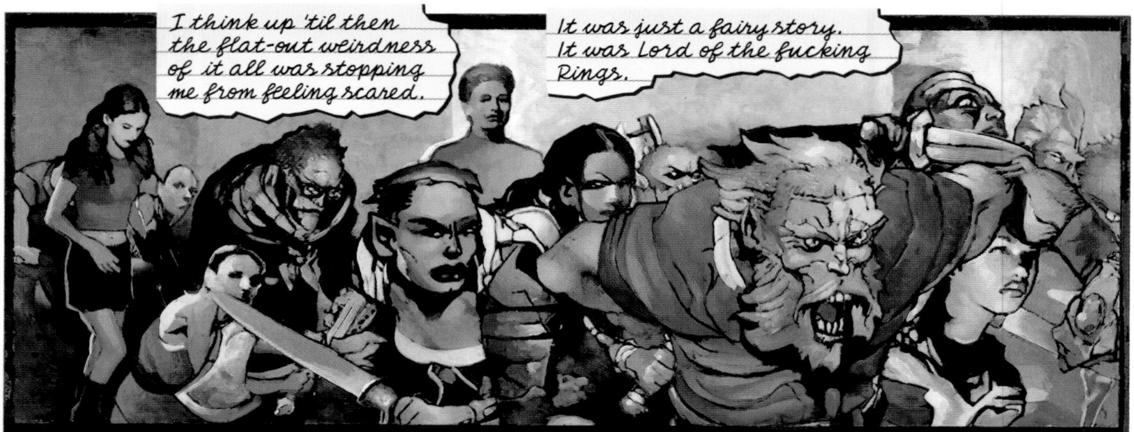
I think up 'til then the flat-out weirdness of it all was stopping me from feeling scared.
It was just a fairy story. It was Lord of the fucking Rings.

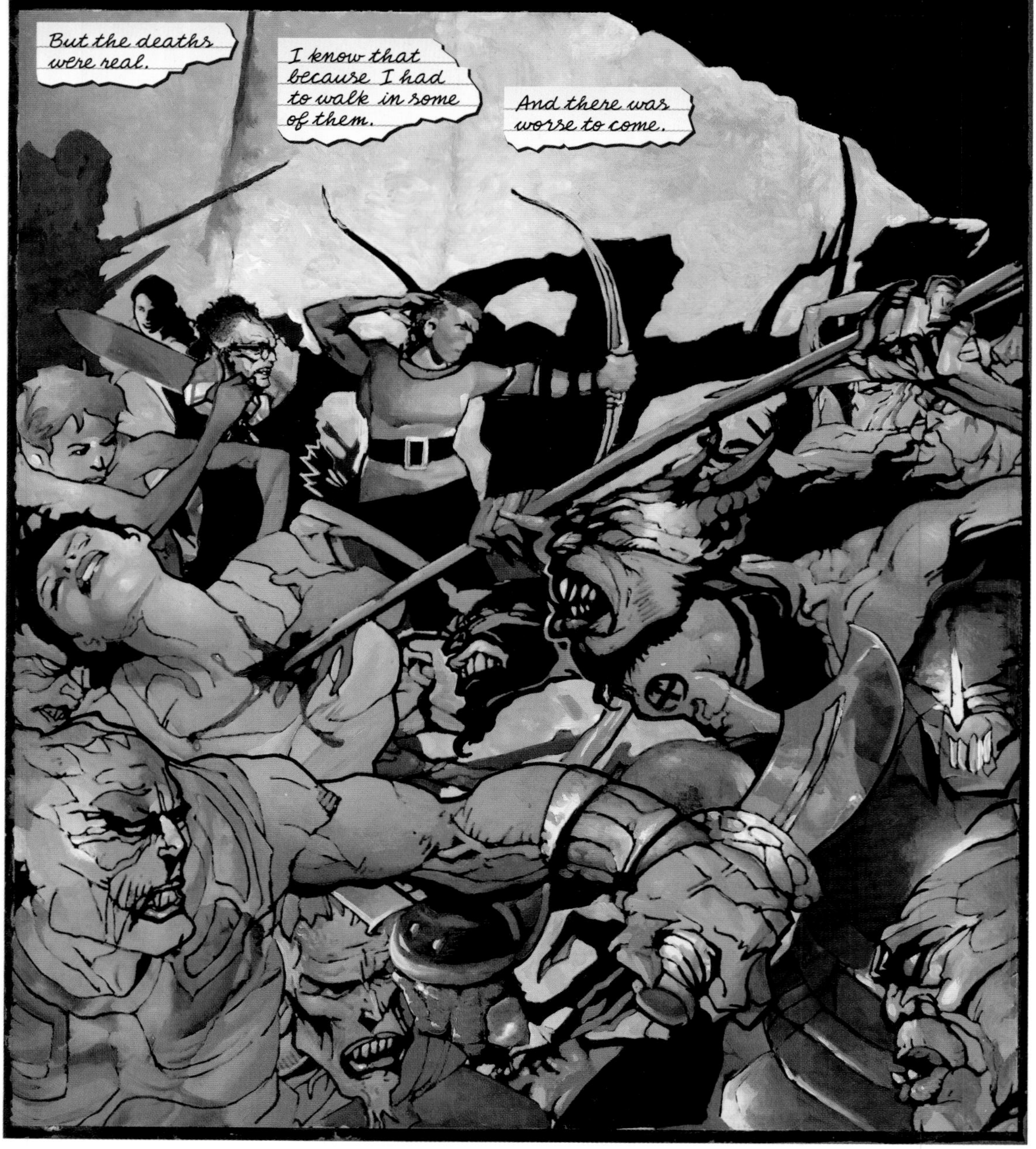
But the deaths were real.
I know that because I had to walk in some of them.
And there was worse to come.

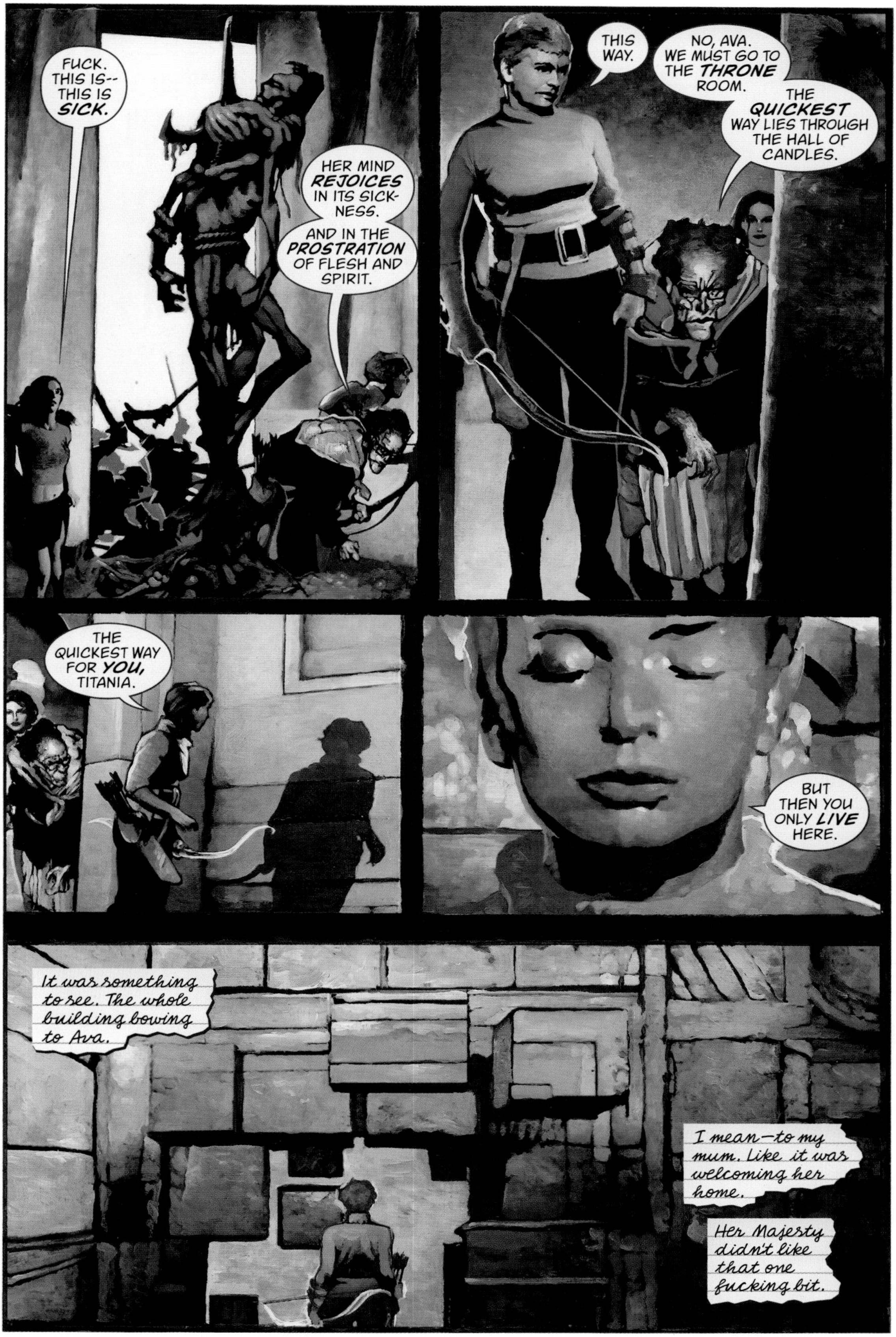
FUCK. THIS IS-- THIS IS SICK.
HER MIND REJOICES IN ITS SICKNESS.
AND IN THE PROSTRATION OF FLESH AND SPIRIT.
THIS WAY.
NO, AVA. WE MUST GO TO THE THRONE ROOM.
THE QUICKEST WAY LIES THROUGH THE HALL OF CANDLES.
THE QUICKEST WAY FOR YOU, TITANIA.
BUT THEN YOU ONLY LIVE HERE.
It was something to see. The whole building bowing to Ava.
I mean—to my mum. Like it was welcoming her home.
Her Majesty didn't like that one fucking bit.

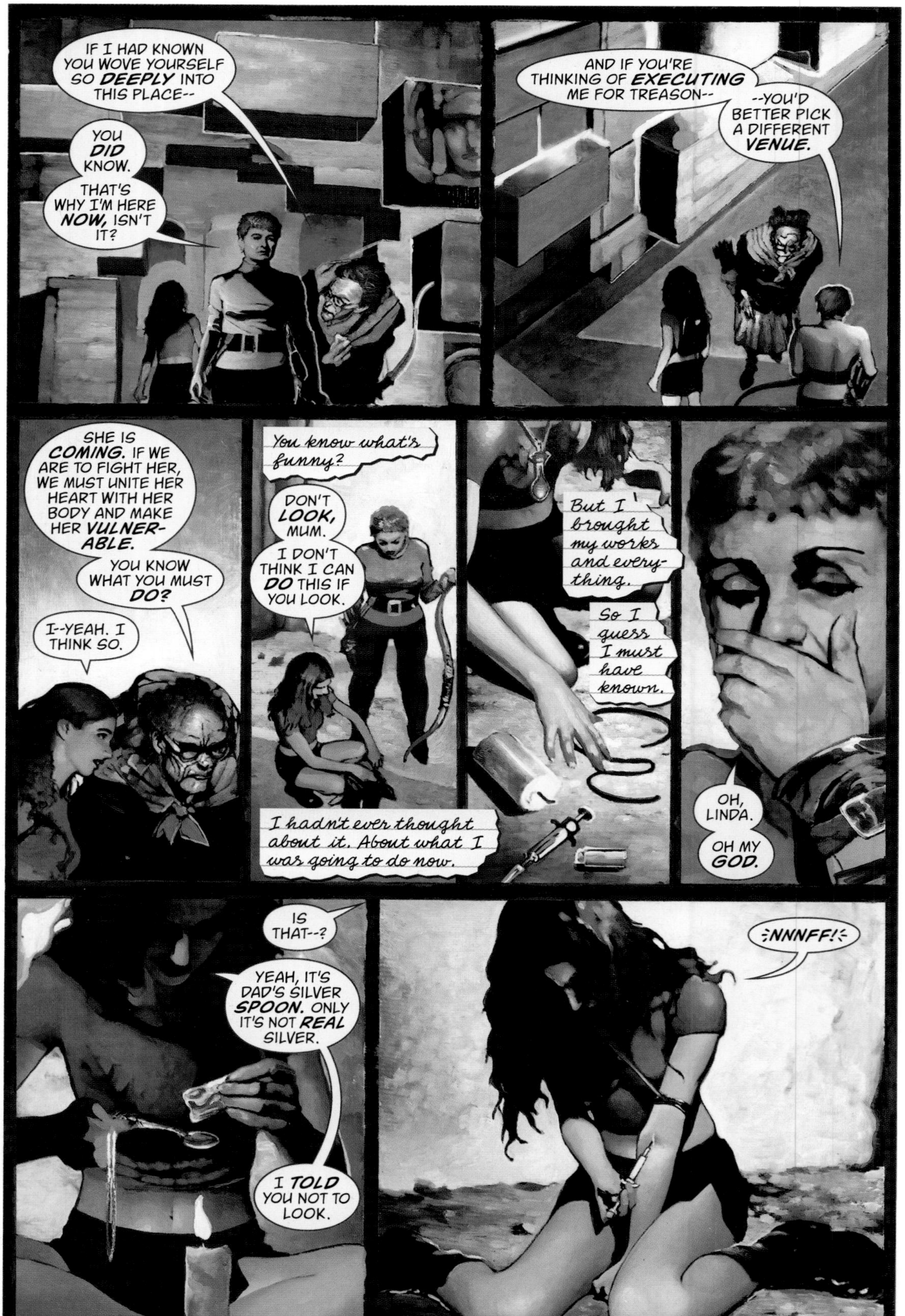
IF I HAD KNOWN YOU WOVE YOURSELF SO DEEPLY INTO THIS PLACE--
YOU DID KNOW.
THAT'S WHY I'M HERE NOW, ISN'T IT?
AND IF YOU'RE THINKING OF EXECUTING ME FOR TREASON--
--YOU'D BETTER PICK A DIFFERENT VENUE.
SHE IS COMING. IF WE ARE TO FIGHT HER, WE MUST UNITE HER HEART WITH HER BODY AND MAKE HER VULNER-ABLE.
YOU KNOW WHAT YOU MUST DO?
I--YEAH. I THINK SO.
You know what's funny?
DON'T LOOK, MUM.
I DON'T THINK I CAN DO THIS IF YOU LOOK.
I hadn't ever thought about it. About what I was going to do now.
But I brought my works and every-thing.
So I guess I must have known.
OH, LINDA.
OH MY GOD.
IS THAT--?
YEAH, IT'S DAD'S SILVER SPOON. ONLY IT'S NOT REAL SILVER.
I TOLD YOU NOT TO LOOK.
NNNFF!

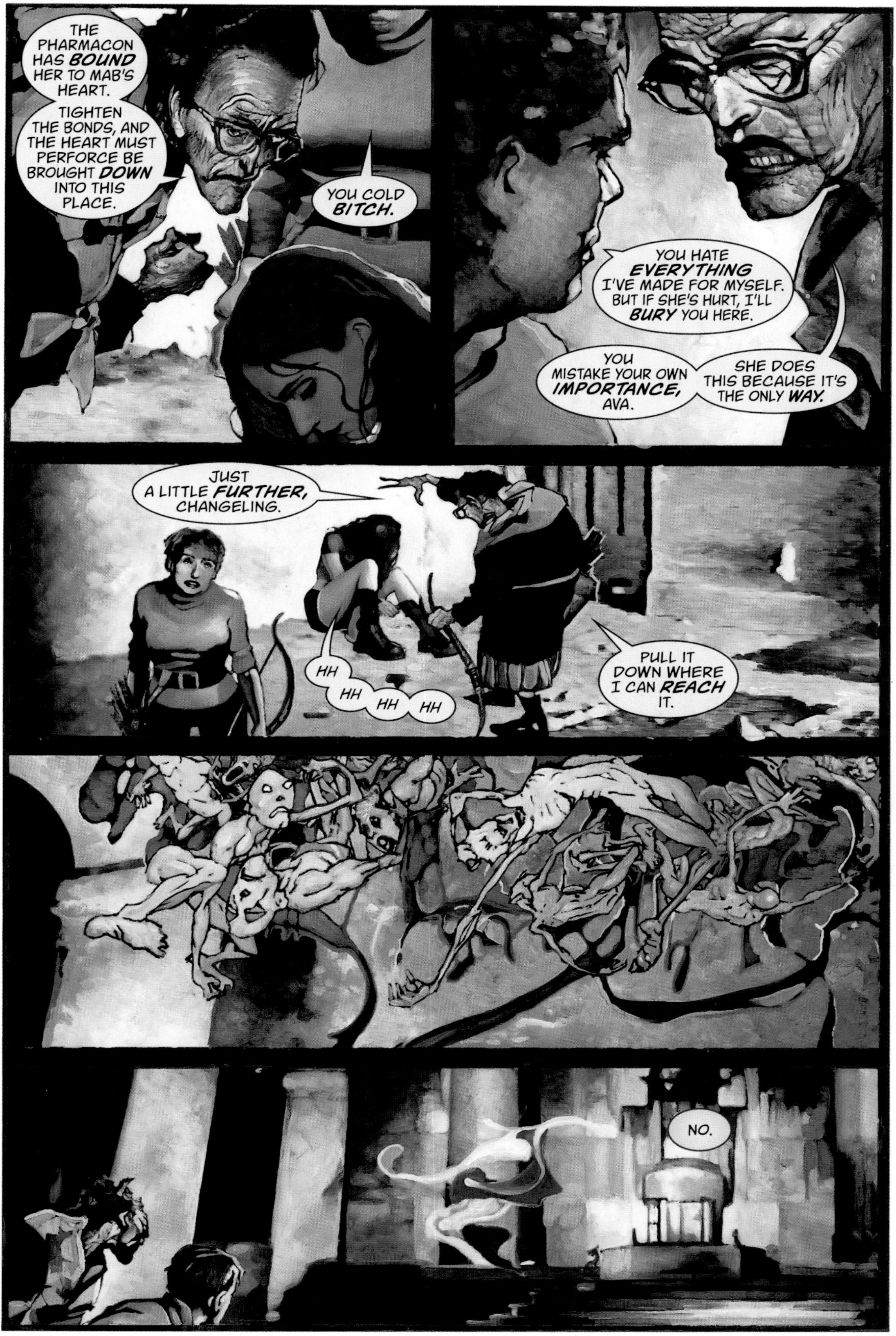
THE PHARMACON HAS BOUND HER TO MAB'S HEART.
TIGHTEN THE BONDS, AND THE HEART MUST PERFORCE BE BROUGHT DOWN INTO THIS PLACE.
YOU COLD BITCH.
YOU HATE EVERYTHING I'VE MADE FOR MYSELF. BUT IF SHE'S HURT, I'LL BURY YOU HERE.
YOU MISTAKE YOUR OWN IMPORTANCE, AVA.
SHE DOES THIS BECAUSE IT'S THE ONLY WAY.
JUST A LITTLE FURTHER, CHANGELING.
HH
HH
HH
HH
PULL IT DOWN WHERE I CAN REACH IT.
NO.

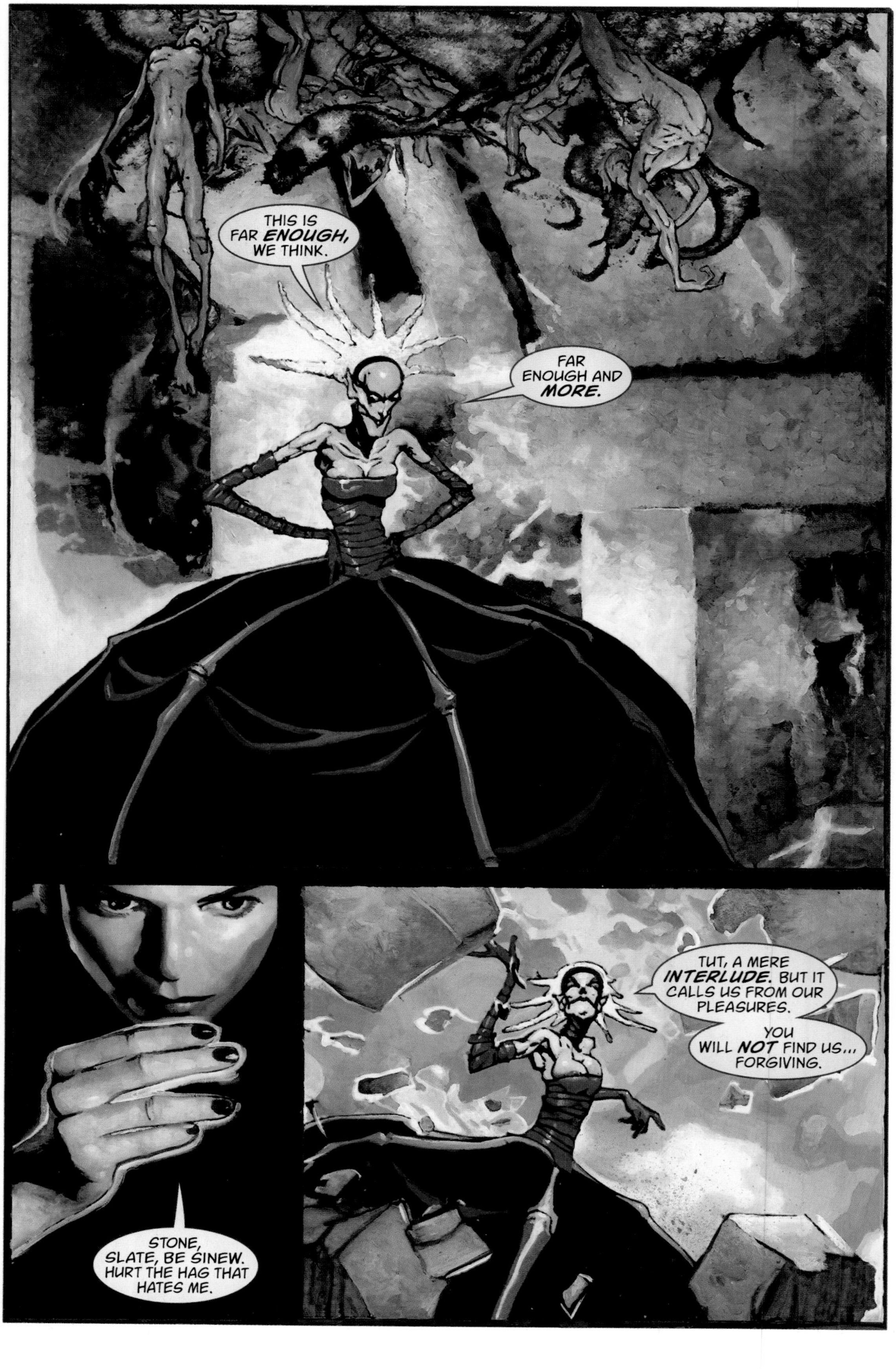
THIS IS FAR ENOUGH, WE THINK.
FAR ENOUGH AND MORE.
STONE, SLATE, BE SINEW. HURT THE HAG THAT HATES ME.
TUT, A MERE INTERLUDE. BUT IT CALLS US FROM OUR PLEASURES.
YOU WILL NOT FIND US... FORGIVING.

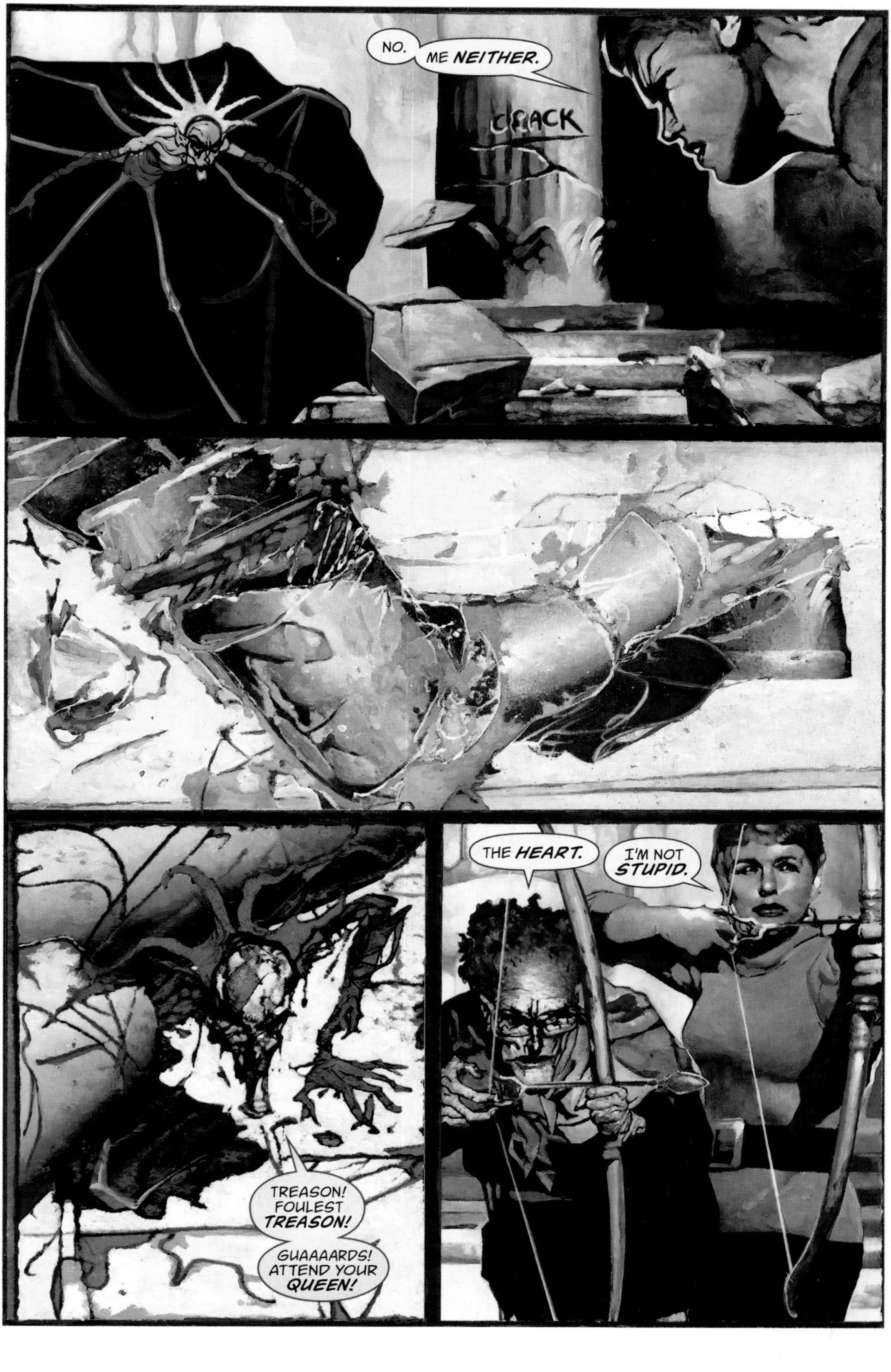
NO.
ME NEITHER.
CRACK
THE HEART.
I'M NOT STUPID.
TREASON! FOULEST TREASON!
GUAAAARDS! ATTEND YOUR QUEEN!

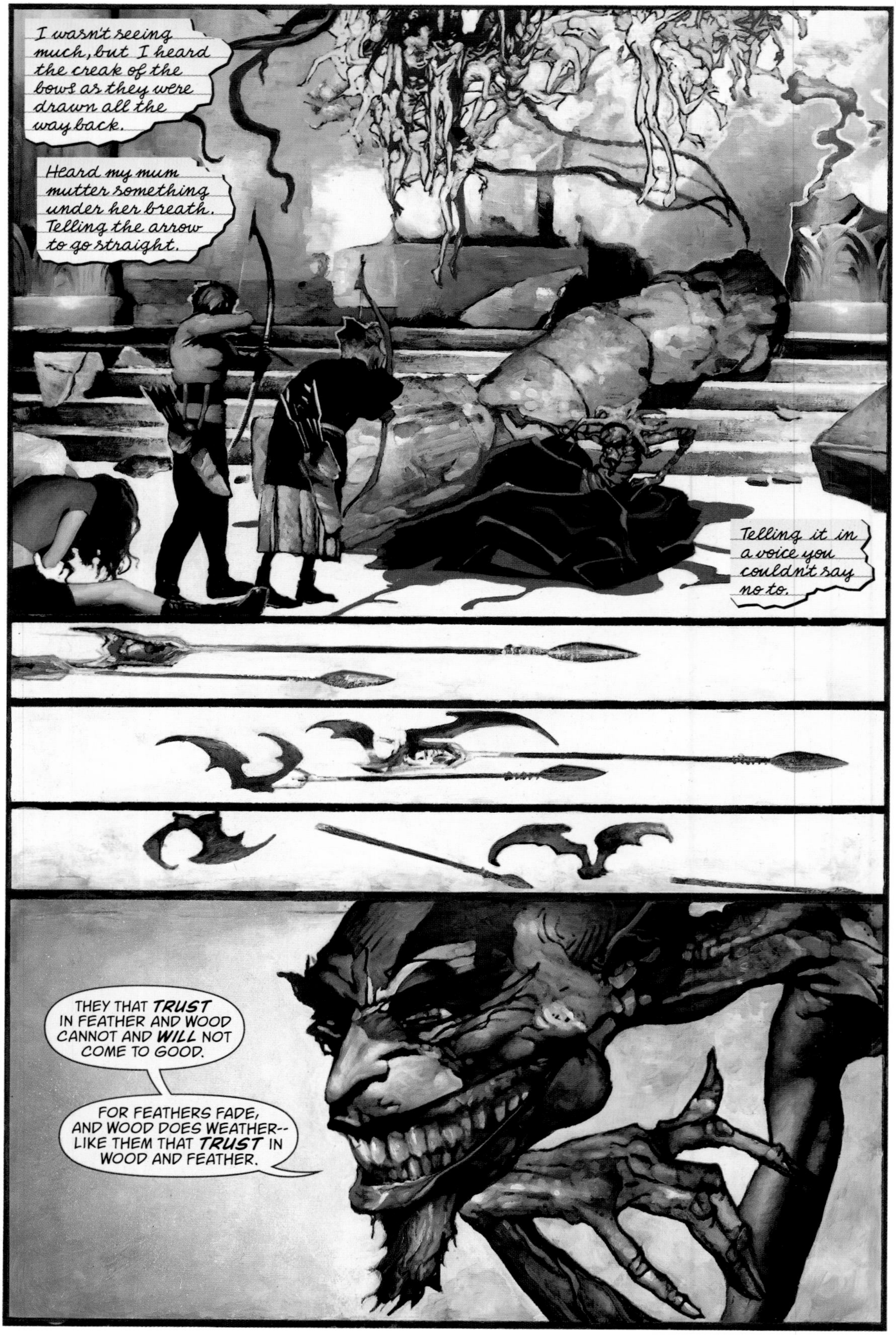
I wasn't seeing much, but I heard the creak of the bows as they were drawn all the way back.
Heard my mum mutter something under her breath. Telling the arrow to go straight.
Telling it in a voice you couldn't say no to.
THEY THAT TRUST IN FEATHER AND WOOD CANNOT AND WILL NOT COME TO GOOD.
FOR FEATHERS FADE, AND WOOD DOES WEATHER-- LIKE THEM THAT TRUST IN WOOD AND FEATHER.

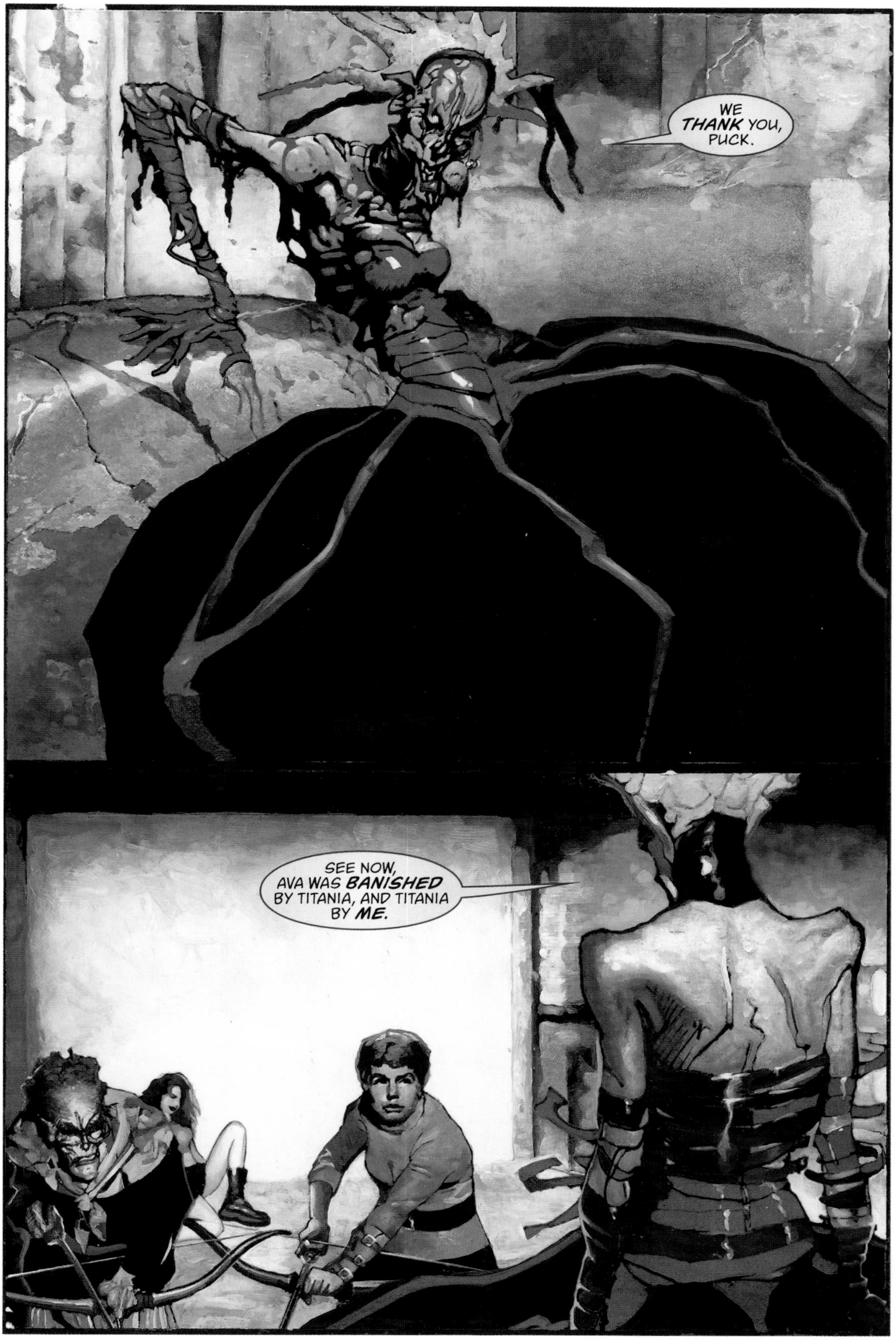
WE **THANK** YOU, PUCK.
SEE NOW, AVA WAS **BANISHED** BY TITANIA, AND TITANIA BY **ME.**

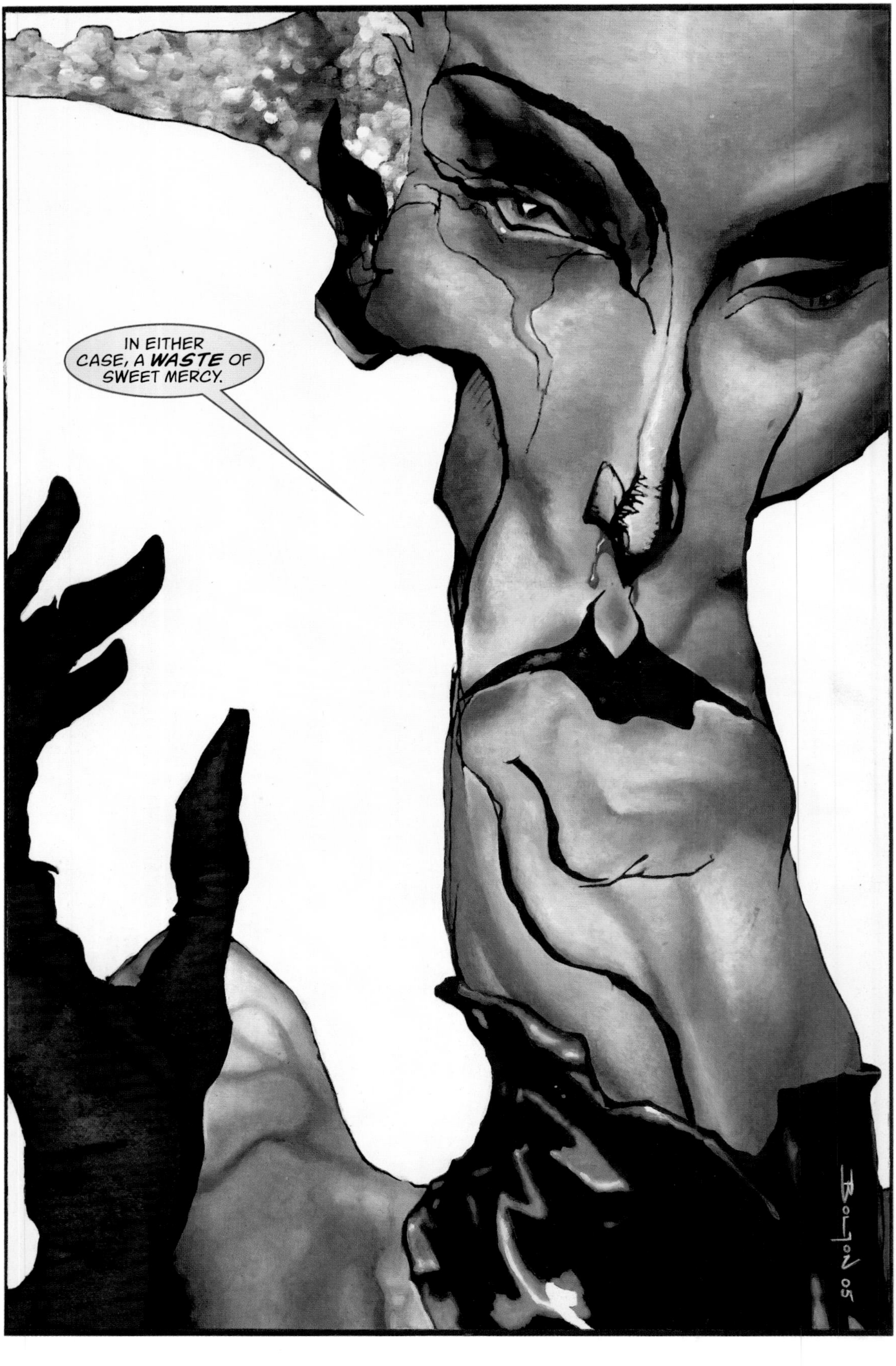
IN EITHER CASE, A *WASTE* OF SWEET MERCY.
BOLTON 05

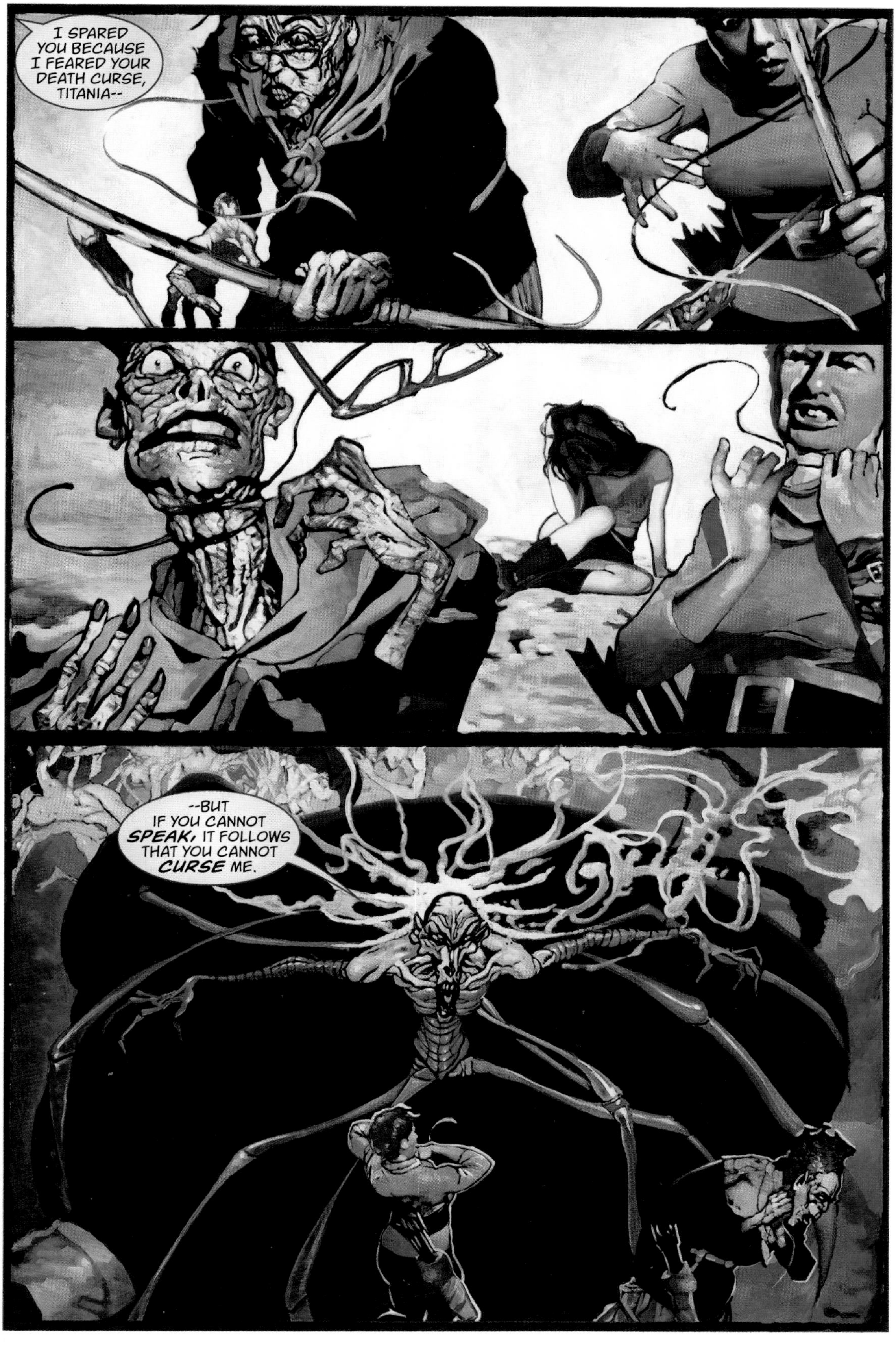
I SPARED YOU BECAUSE I FEARED YOUR DEATH CURSE, TITANIA--
--BUT IF YOU CANNOT SPEAK, IT FOLLOWS THAT YOU CANNOT CURSE ME.

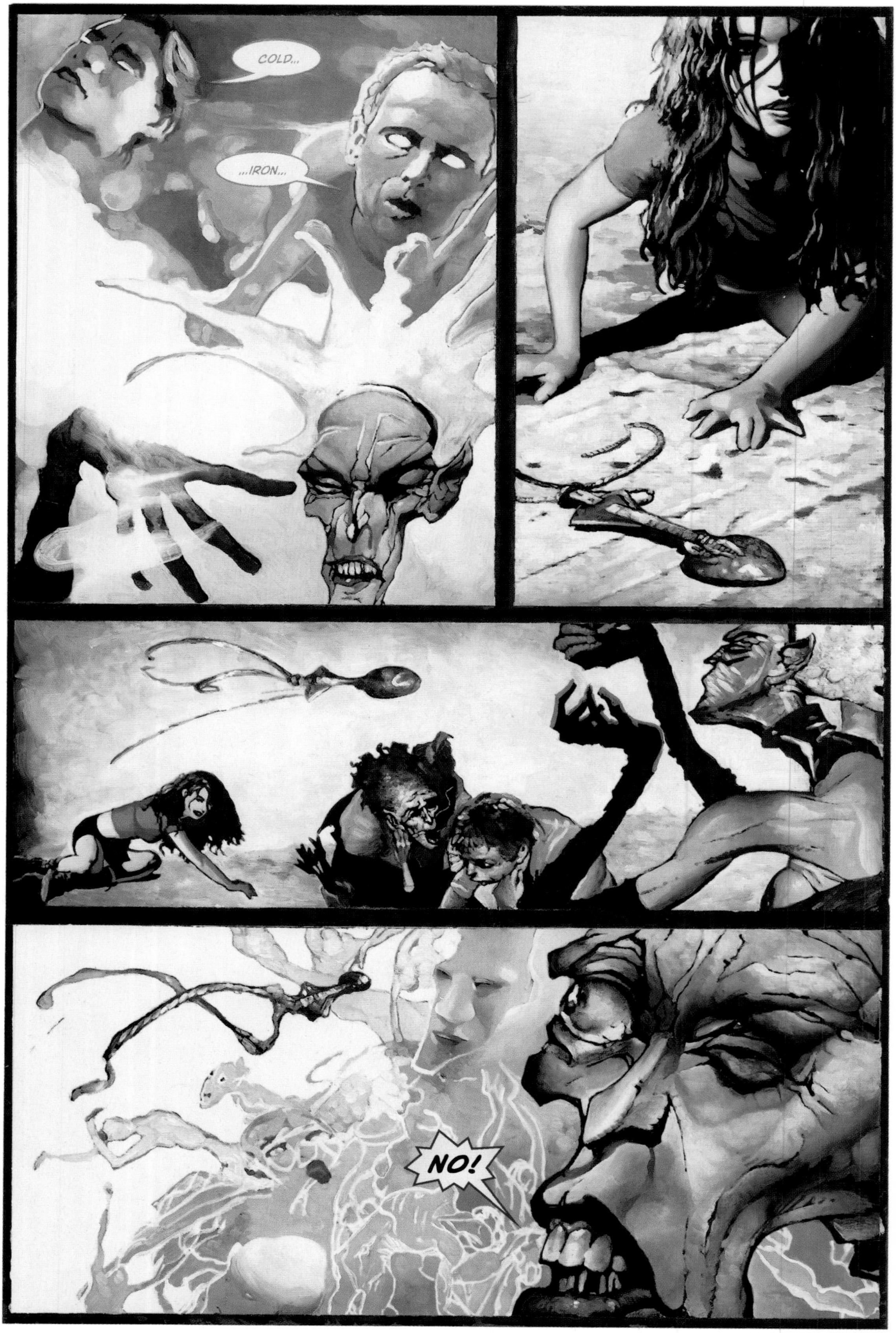
COLD...
...IRON...
NO!

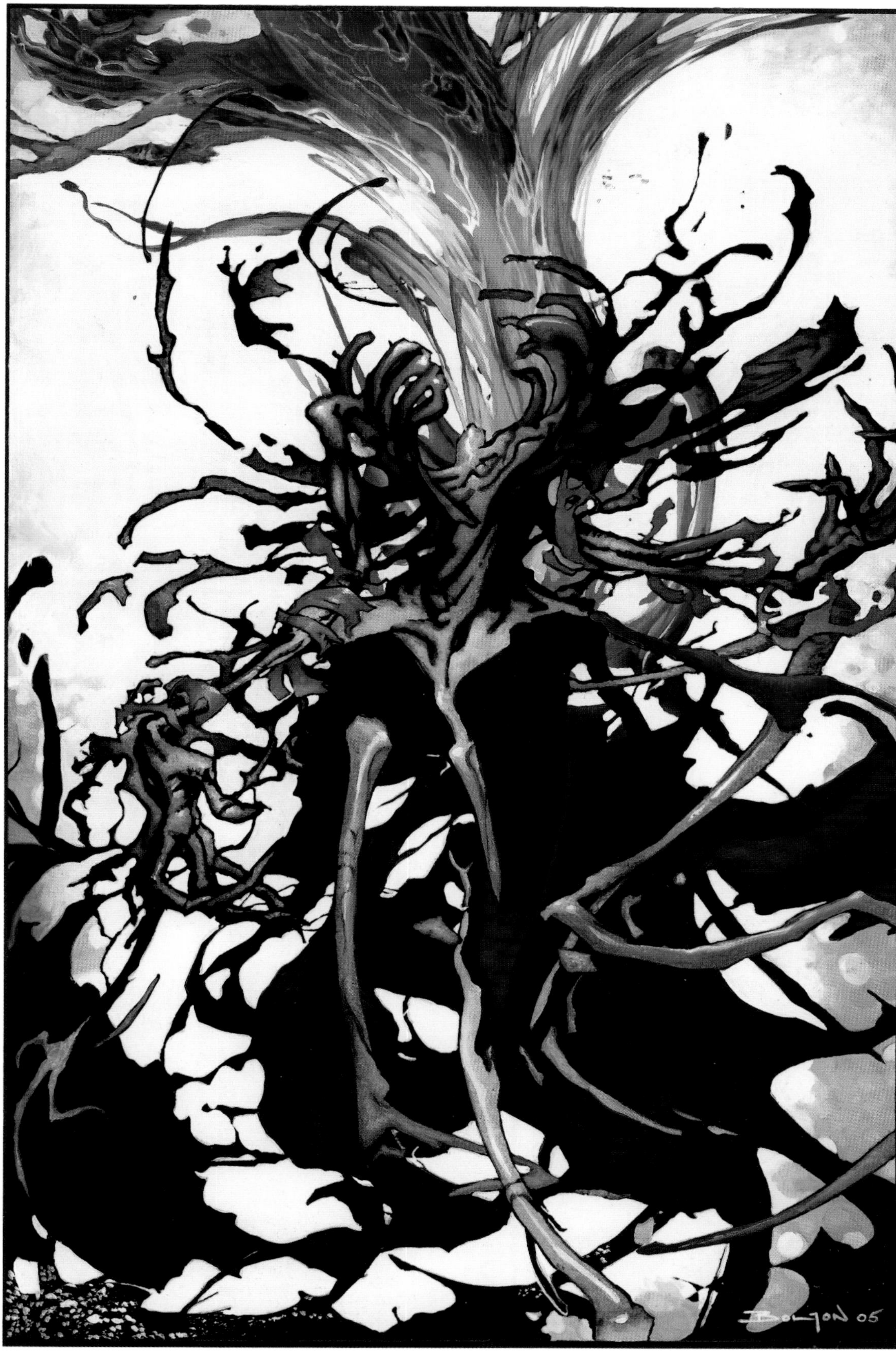
BOLTON 05

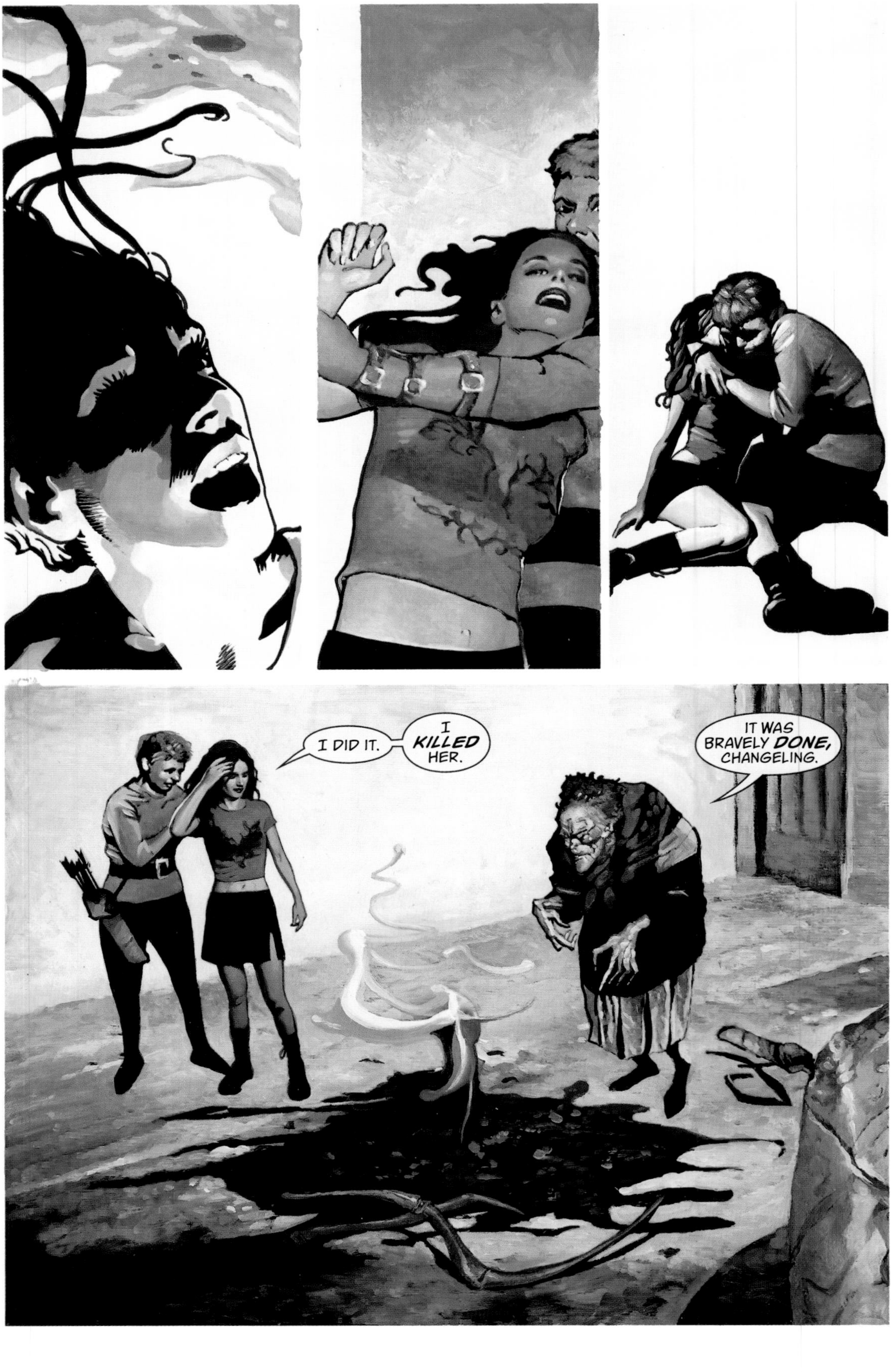
I DID IT.
I KILLED HER.
IT WAS BRAVELY DONE, CHANGELING.

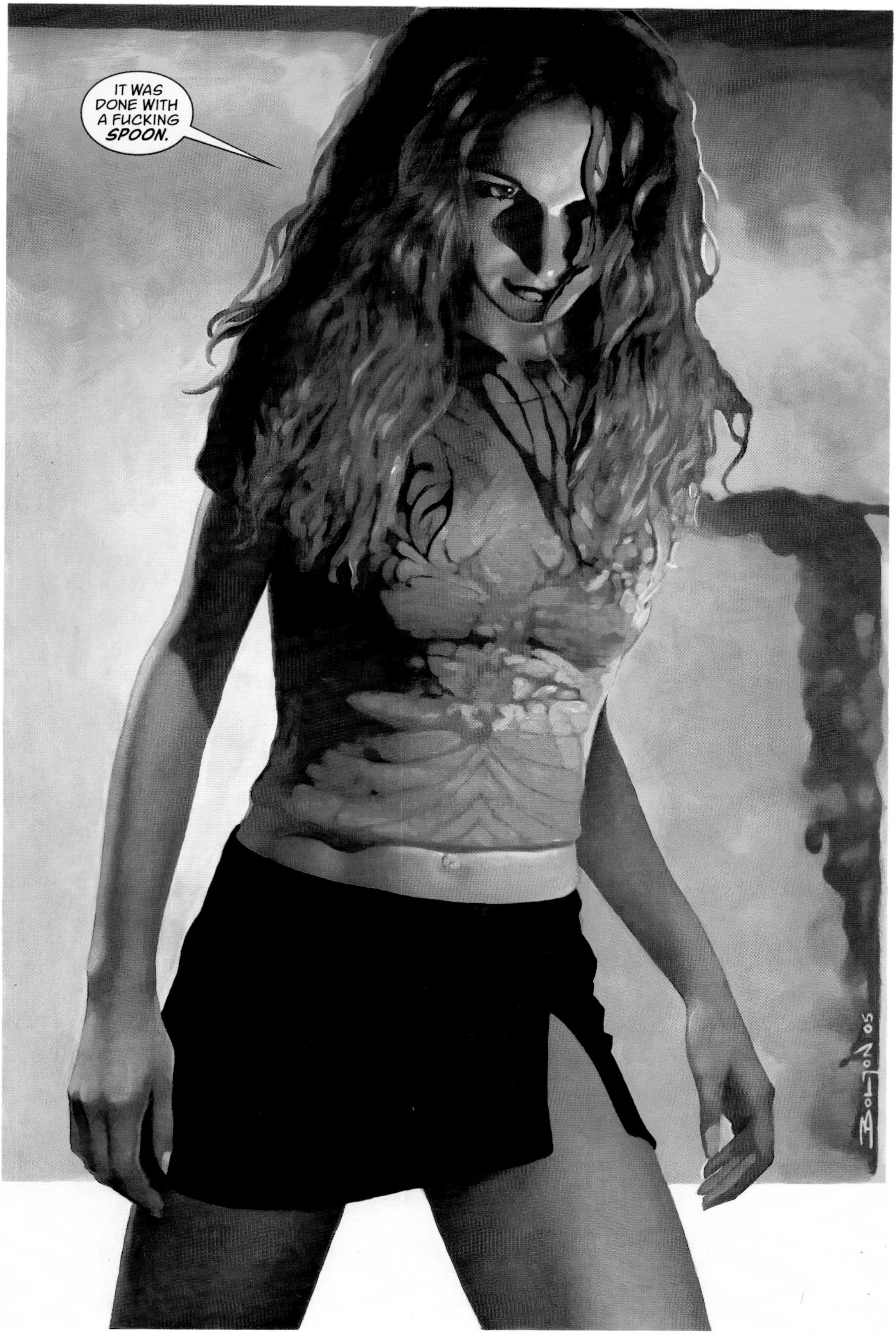
IT WAS DONE WITH A FUCKING SPOON.

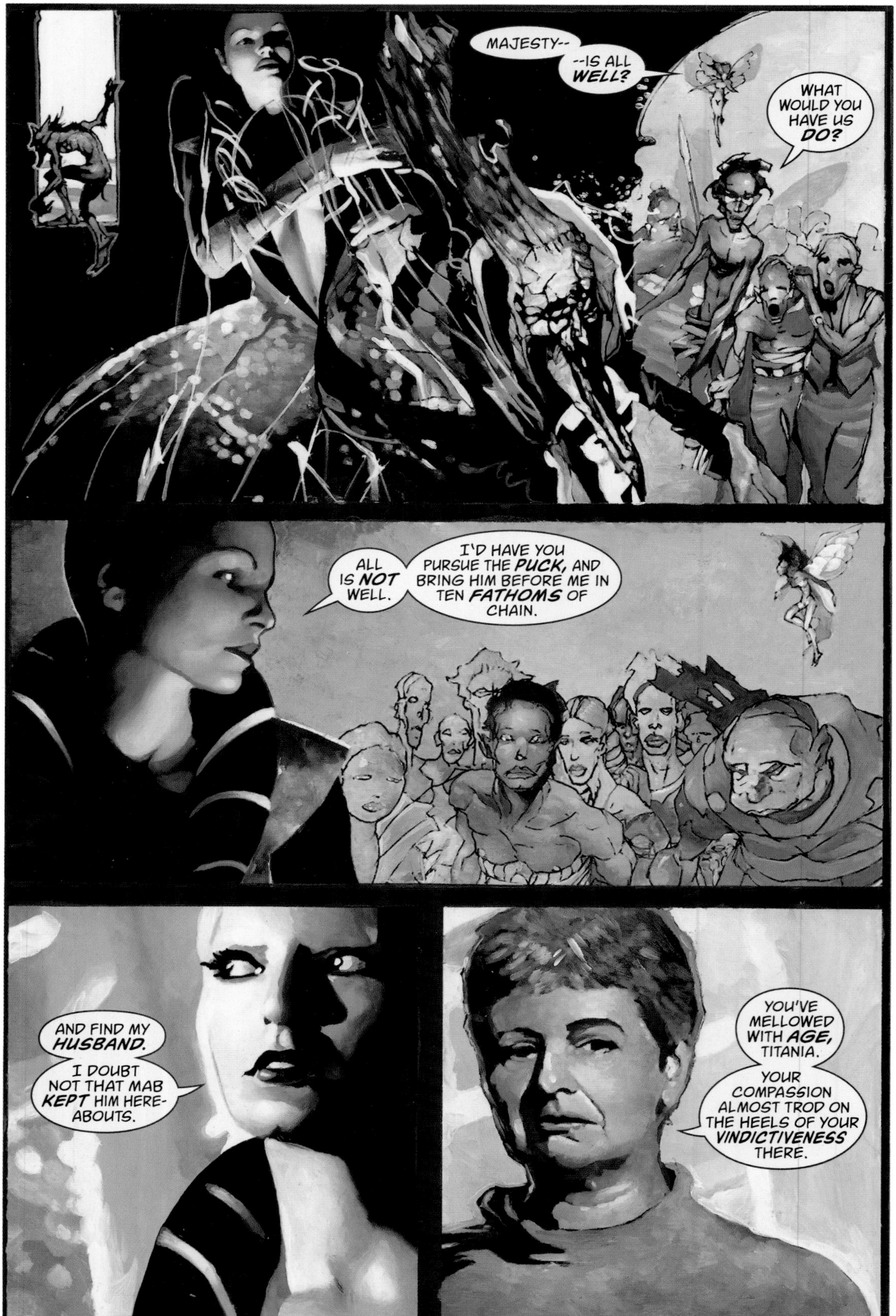
MAJESTY--
--IS ALL WELL?
WHAT WOULD YOU HAVE US DO?
ALL IS NOT WELL.
I'D HAVE YOU PURSUE THE PUCK, AND BRING HIM BEFORE ME IN TEN FATHOMS OF CHAIN.
AND FIND MY HUSBAND.
I DOUBT NOT THAT MAB KEPT HIM HERE-ABOUTS.
YOU'VE MELLOWED WITH AGE, TITANIA.
YOUR COMPASSION ALMOST TROD ON THE HEELS OF YOUR VINDICTIVENESS THERE.

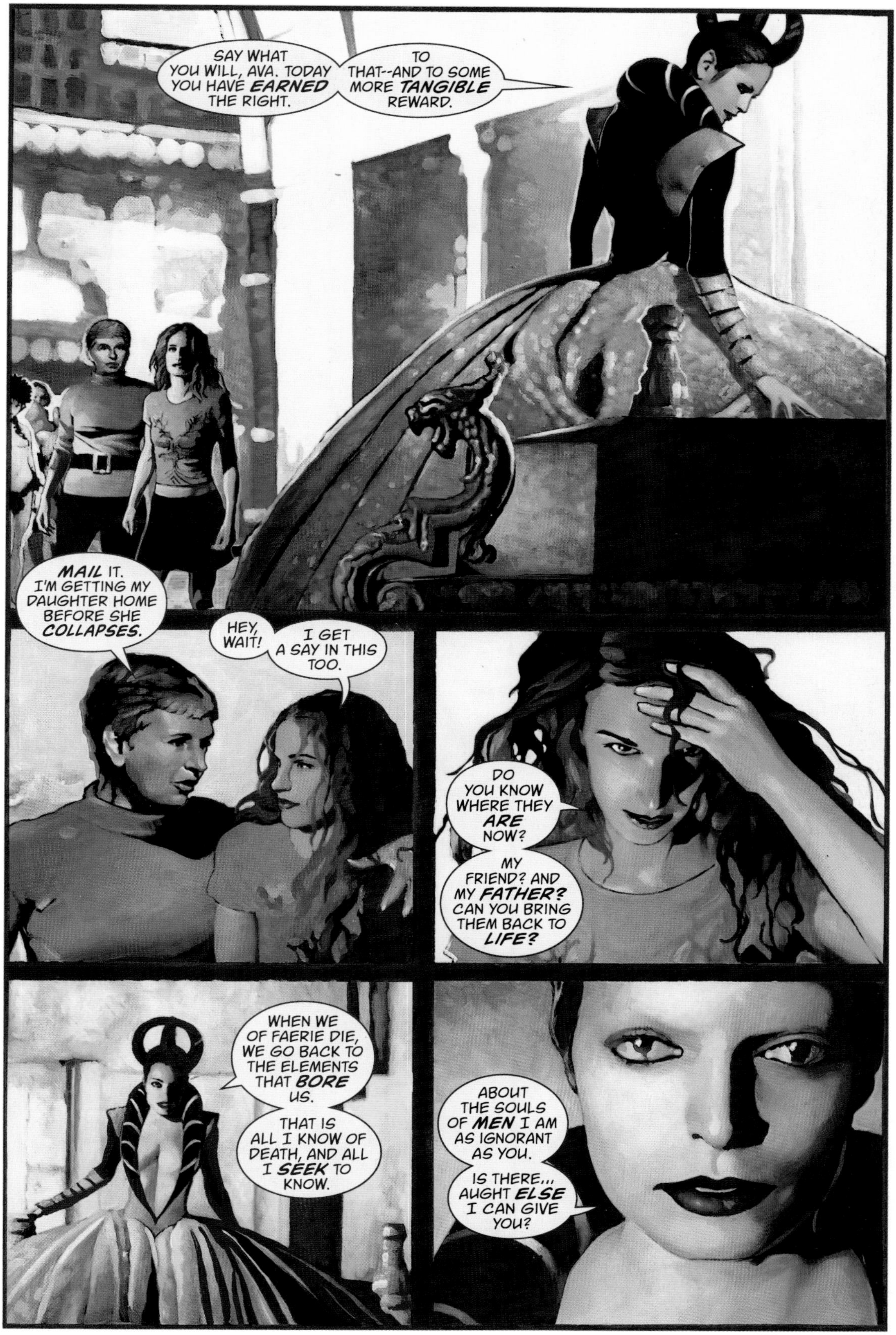
SAY WHAT YOU WILL, AVA. TODAY YOU HAVE EARNED THE RIGHT.
TO THAT--AND TO SOME MORE TANGIBLE REWARD.
MAIL IT. I'M GETTING MY DAUGHTER HOME BEFORE SHE COLLAPSES.
HEY, WAIT!
I GET A SAY IN THIS TOO.
DO YOU KNOW WHERE THEY ARE NOW?
MY FRIEND? AND MY FATHER? CAN YOU BRING THEM BACK TO LIFE?
WHEN WE OF FAERIE DIE, WE GO BACK TO THE ELEMENTS THAT BORE US.
THAT IS ALL I KNOW OF DEATH, AND ALL I SEEK TO KNOW.
ABOUT THE SOULS OF MEN I AM AS IGNORANT AS YOU.
IS THERE... AUGHT ELSE I CAN GIVE YOU?

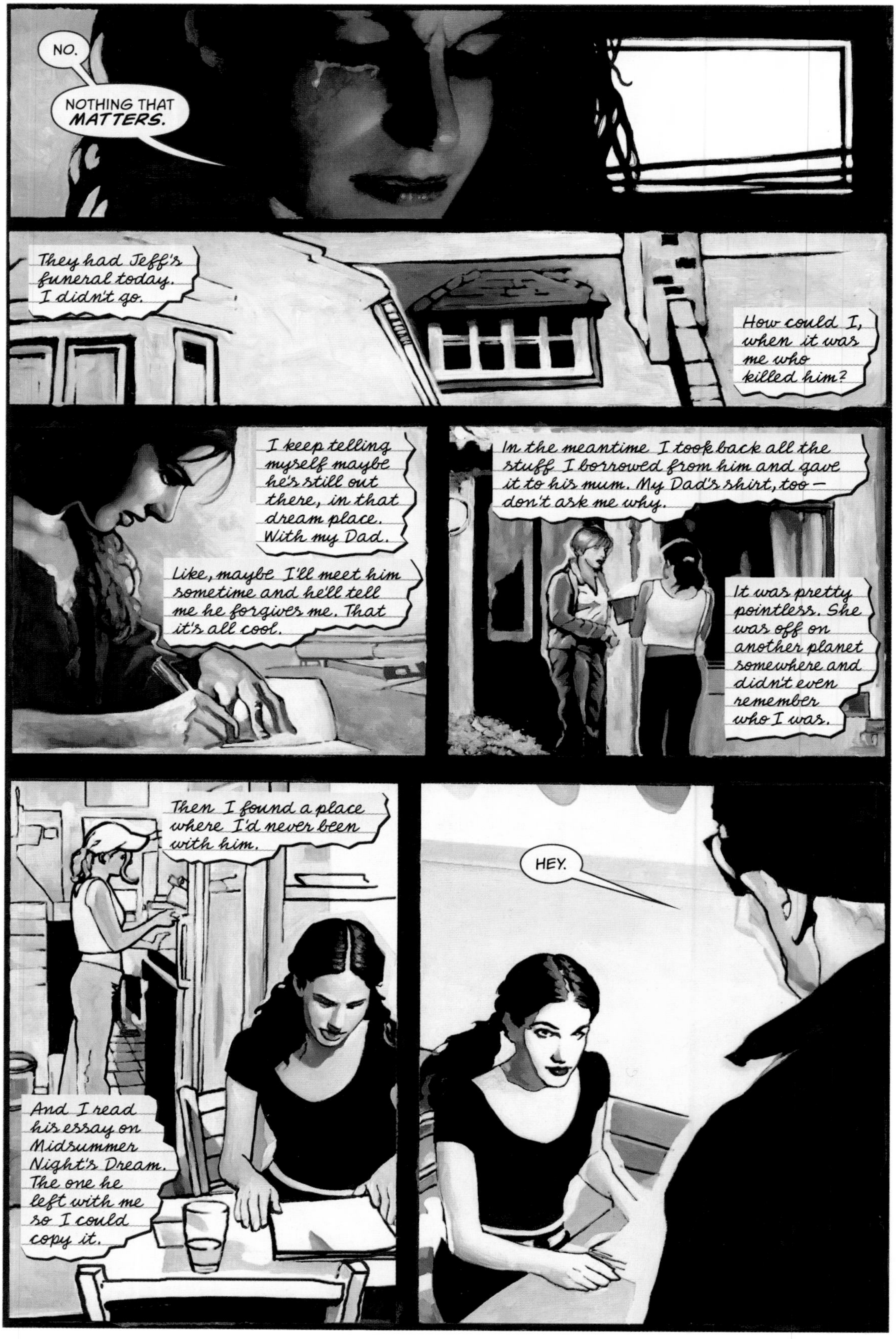
NO.
NOTHING THAT MATTERS.
They had Jeff's funeral today. I didn't go.
How could I, when it was me who killed him?
I keep telling myself maybe he's still out there, in that dream place. With my Dad.
Like, maybe I'll meet him sometime and he'll tell me he forgives me. That it's all cool.
In the meantime I took back all the stuff I borrowed from him and gave it to his mum. My Dad's shirt, too— don't ask me why.
It was pretty pointless. She was off on another planet somewhere and didn't even remember who I was.
Then I found a place where I'd never been with him.
And I read his essay on Midsummer Night's Dream. The one he left with me so I could copy it.
HEY.

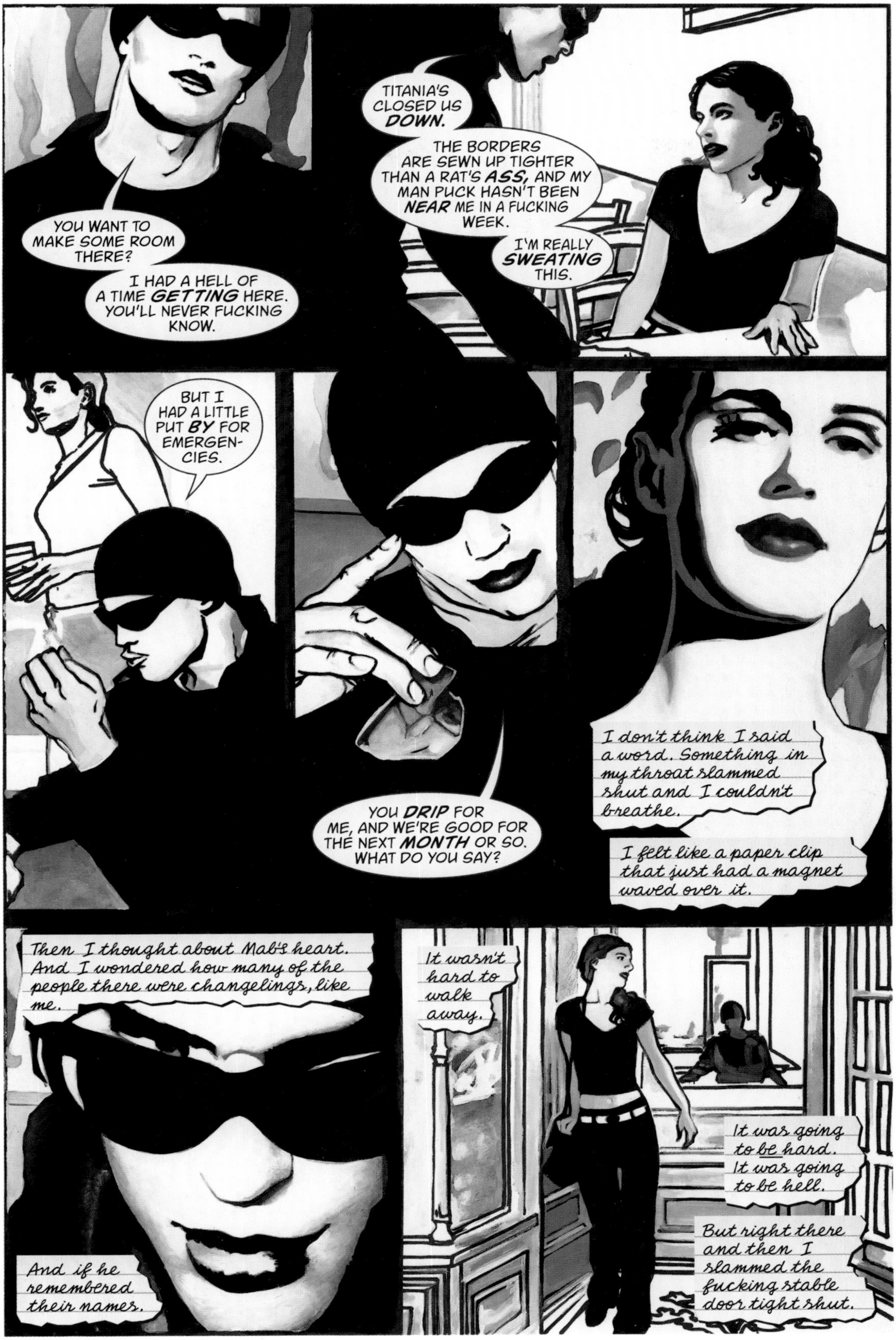

YOU WANT TO MAKE SOME ROOM THERE?
I HAD A HELL OF A TIME GETTING HERE. YOU'LL NEVER FUCKING KNOW.
TITANIA'S CLOSED US DOWN.
THE BORDERS ARE SEWN UP TIGHTER THAN A RAT'S ASS, AND MY MAN PUCK HASN'T BEEN NEAR ME IN A FUCKING WEEK.
I'M REALLY SWEATING THIS.
BUT I HAD A LITTLE PUT BY FOR EMERGEN-CIES.
YOU DRIP FOR ME, AND WE'RE GOOD FOR THE NEXT MONTH OR SO. WHAT DO YOU SAY?
I don't think I said a word. Something in my throat slammed shut and I couldn't breathe.
I felt like a paper clip that just had a magnet waved over it.
Then I thought about Mab's heart. And I wondered how many of the people there were changelings, like me.
And if he remembered their names.
It wasn't hard to walk away.
It was going to be hard. It was going to be hell.
But right there and then I slammed the fucking stable door tight shut.

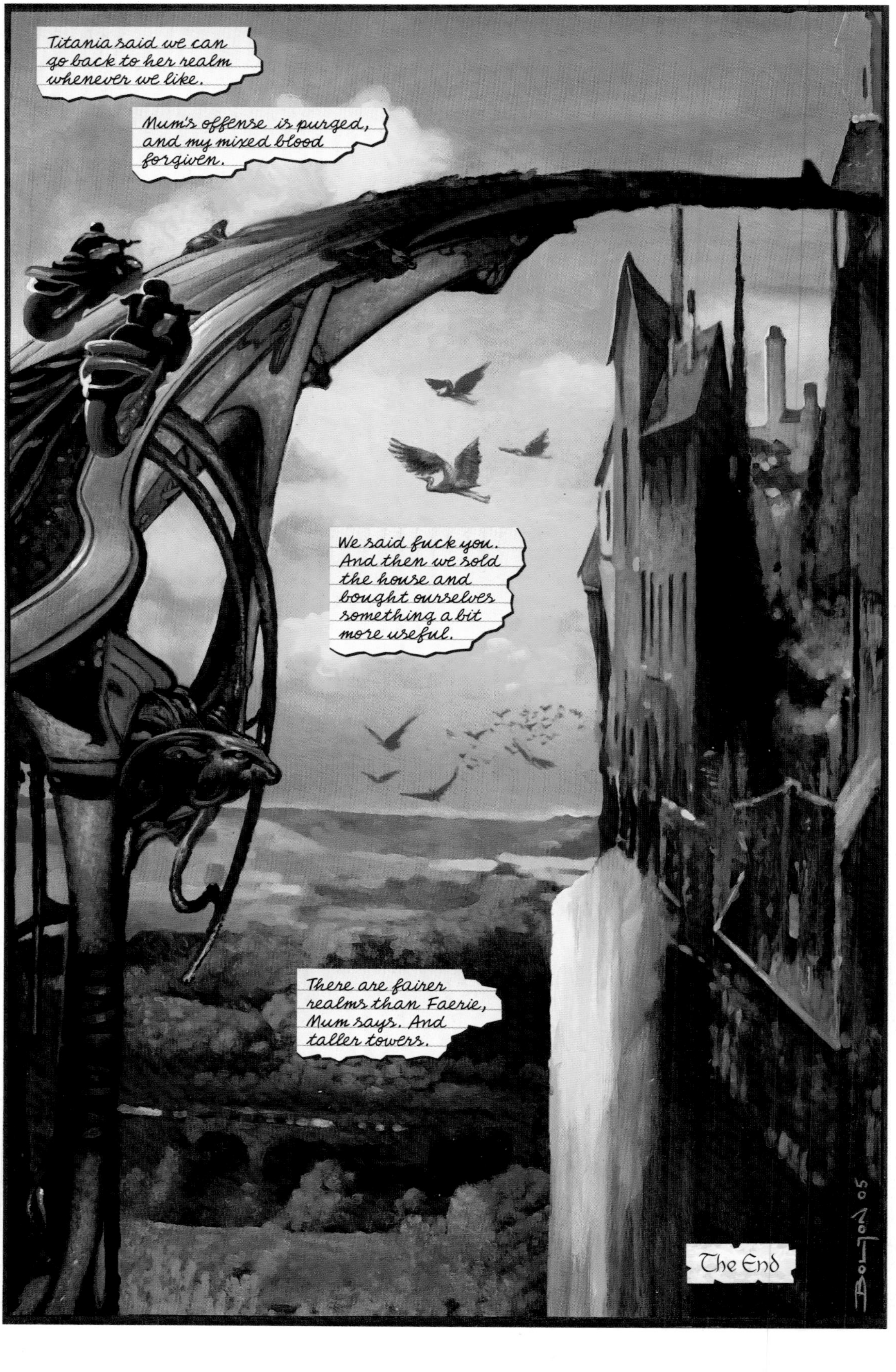
Titania said we can go back to her realm whenever we like.
Mum's offense is purged, and my mixed blood forgiven.
We said fuck you. And then we sold the house and bought ourselves something a bit more useful.
There are fairer realms than Faerie, Mum says. And taller towers.
The End

Look for these other VERTIGO books:

All titles are suggested for mature readers.

100 BULLETS
Brian Azzarello/Eduardo Risso

With one special briefcase, Agent Graves gives you the chance to kill without retribution. But what is the real price for this chance — and who is setting it?

THE BOOKS OF MAGIC
John Ney Rieber/Peter Gross/various

The continuing trials and adventures of Tim Hunter, whose magical talents bring extra trouble and confusion to his adolescence.

FABLES
Winner of seven Eisner Awards
Bill Willingham/Mark Buckingham/
Steve Leialoha/various

The immortal characters of popular fairy tales have been driven from their homelands and now live hidden among us, trying to cope with life in 21st-century Manhattan.

FABLES: 1001 NIGHTS OF SNOWFALL
Bill Willingham/various

This collection of short stories is lavishly painted by comic book luminaries and is the perfect entry point for new readers.

JOHN CONSTANTINE: HELLBLAZER
Jamie Delano/Garth Ennis/Warren Ellis/
Brian Azzarello/Steve Dillon/Marcelo Frusin/
various

Where horror, dark magic, and bad luck meet, John Constantine is never far away.

THE INVISIBLES
Grant Morrison/various

The saga of a terrifying conspiracy and the resistance movement combatting it — a secret underground of ultra-cool guerrilla cells trained in ontological and physical anarchy.

LUCIFER
Mike Carey/Peter Gross/Scott Hampton/
Chris Weston/Dean Ormston/various

Walking out of Hell (and out of the pages of THE SANDMAN), an ambitious Lucifer Morningstar creates a new cosmos modeled after his own image.

PREACHER
Garth Ennis/Steve Dillon/various

A modern American epic of life, death, God, love, and redemption — filled with sex, booze, and blood.

PRIDE OF BAGHDAD
Brian K. Vaughan/Niko Henrichon

Inspired by a true story that examines life during wartime as four lions roam the decimated streets of Baghdad.

THE SANDMAN
Neil Gaiman/various

One of the most acclaimed and celebrated comics titles ever published — a rich blend of modern myth and dark fantasy by the *New York Times* best-selling author.

SWAMP THING
Alan Moore/Stephen Bissette/
John Totleben/Rick Veitch/various

The writer of V FOR VENDETTA and the series that revolutionized comics — a masterpiece of lyrical fantasy.

TRANSMETROPOLITAN
Warren Ellis/Darick Robertson/various

Take an exuberant trip into a frenetic future, where outlaw journalist Spider Jerusalem battles hypocrisy, corruption, and sobriety.

Y: THE LAST MAN
Winner of multiple Eisner Awards
Brian K. Vaughan/Pia Guerra/José Marzán, Jr.

An unexplained plague kills every male mammal on Earth — all except Yorick Brown and his pet monkey. Will he survive this new, emasculated world to discover what killed his fellow men?

IT'S A BIRD...
Steven T. Seagle/Teddy Kristiansen

A stunning semi-autobiographical hardcover that tells one of the most realistic Superman tales ever — without featuring Superman.

THE LOSERS
Andy Diggle/Jock

A hard-hitting crime/espionage series that mixes real-world scenarios with widescreen action.

V FOR VENDETTA
Alan Moore/David Lloyd

One of the accomplishments that cemented Alan Moore's reputation — now a major motion picture. A powerful story about loss of freedom and individuality.

WE3
Grant Morrison/Frank Quitely

The unforgettable story of three innocent pets — a dog, a cat, and a rabbit — who have been converted into deadly cyborgs by a sinister military weapons program.

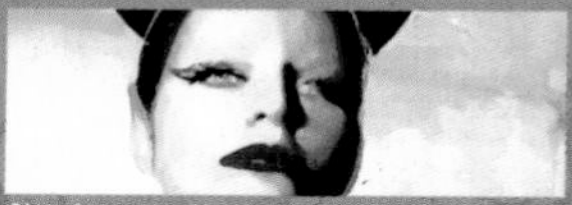

Check out vertigocomics.com for art and info on every one of our hundreds of books.

To purchase any of our titles, call 1-888-COMIC BOOK for the comics shop nearest you or go to your local book store.